P9-API-562

# TIMELESS EARTH

## 400 OF THE WORLD'S MOST IMPORTANT PLACES

$59.95

3 1489 00573 8537

# TIMELESS
# EARTH

## 400 OF THE WORLD'S MOST IMPORTANT PLACES

# HAMMOND

**VP, Publisher** Chuck Lang
**Publishing Director** Karen Prince

Produced for Hammond World Atlas Corporation by
BONNEVILLE CONNECTION
310 Parmenter, Sutton, Quebec, J0E 2K0, Canada

**Writer** Patrick Bonneville
**Designer** Philippe Hémono
**Editorial Supervisor** Lori Baird
**Consultant Writers** Kimberly Murray, Alain Forget
and HYLAS PUBLISHING
129 Main Street, Irvington, NY, 10522, USA

**Cover Design** Marian Purcell, Karen Prince, Jeff Beebe
**Cover Picture Credits** High view from Lake Peyto, Canada
Goncalo Veloso de Figueiredo; Stonehenge at Sunset by Daniel
Gilbey; Hopi Point, Grand Canyon by zschnepf; Eiffel Tower by
Villedieu Christophe; Taj Mahal, Copyright: Galyna Andrushko
**Back cover** Kilimanjaro at Sunrise. View from Amboseli, Kenya
Antonio Jorge Nunes
**Half Title Page** Storm weather in Machu-Picchu city
Galyna Andrushko
**Full Title Page:** Grand Canyon View by zschnepf

Printed and bound in Italy

ISBN-13: 978-084-370993-3

Compilation Copyright © 2008 by Hammond
World Atlas Corporation

Text Copyright © 2008 by Patrick Bonneville
Society

All rights reserved. No part of this book may be
used or reproduced in any form or by any means,
electronic or mechanical, including photocopying,
recording, or by any information storage and
retrieval system, without permission in writing
from the publisher.

Published by HAMMOND WORLD ATLAS
CORPORATION, part of the Langenscheidt
Publishing Group
36-36 33rd Street, Long Island City, NY, 11106

HAMMOND World Atlas
Part of the Langenscheidt Publishing Group

**S**ince the main mission of the World Heritage is to pass on our legacy to future generations, we dedicate this book to our children, Elizabeth, Florence, Juliette, and Olivier.

Patrick Bonneville
Philippe Hémono

# CONTENTS

What history should teach us is that, alongside an infinite diversity of cultures, there does exist one, global civilization based on shared values of tolerance and freedom. It is a civilization defined by its tolerance of dissent, its celebration of cultural diversity, its insistence on fundamental, universal human rights, and its belief in the right of people everywhere to have a say in how they are governed.

It is a civilization based on the belief that the diversity of human cultures is something to be celebrated, not feared. Indeed, many wars stem from people's fear of those who are different from themselves. And only through dialogue can such fears be overcome.

—Kofi Annan
"Dialogue among Civilizations" speech
September 5th, 2000

Former Secretary General of the United Nations
Member of The Global Elders

# INTRODUCTION

In the spring of 1945, 50 allied nations signed the United Nations Charter, creating the organization that would bear the same name. Later that year, UNESCO—the United Nations Educational, Scientific, and Cultural Organization—was created to promote international collaboration through education, science, and culture. Three decades later, the UN would establish a program designed to protect our global natural and cultural heritage.

It was 1960. In southeast Egypt, construction was started on the Aswan High Dam on the Nile River. The dam would control flooding and supply electricity to millions—but it would also create an enormous reservoir that would forever submerge some of the world's most important ancient Egyptian treasures—including the Temple of Rameses II and the Temple of Hathor.

In response to this potential tragedy, UNESCO began a campaign to save those treasures—raising $80 million and mobilizing support from some 50 countries. In the end, the colossal 3,000-year-old stone monuments were dismantled, moved to higher ground, and then painstakingly reassembled.

From this success was born the UNESCO World Heritage Trust, an international organization that spearheads efforts to identify, protect, and preserve historic sites and natural areas of worldwide significance. *Timeless Earth* is a pictoral introduction to 400 of these spectacular places. All of the sites in the UNESCO World Heritage program—and in *Timeless Earth*—fall into two broad categories: natural and cultural.

## PROTECTION OF NATURAL SITES

In 1948, the International Union for the Conservation of Nature (IUCN) was founded to help countries conserve the integrity and diversity of nature and to ensure the equitable and ecologically sustainable use of natural resources. Today, organizations such as the World Wide Fund for Nature (WWF), National Geographic, and the Sierra Club are members of IUCN, as are various states and government and nongovernmental agencies from around the world. They share the same objective: to protect the natural environment, which includes the parks and reserves all over the world.

## PROTECTION OF CULTURAL SITES

World War II destroyed some of the world's greatest monuments and cities. As a result, more than 100 states met at The Hague, Netherlands, in 1954 to agree on the first international treaty focusing exclusively on the protection of cultural heritage. It was there that the Convention for the Protection of Cultural Property in the Event of Armed Conflict was adopted. According to the plan, important buildings and monuments would be marked with an emblem of the Convention. Special units within military forces would be created that would be responsible for protecting these buildings and monuments. The sites would not only be protected during war time, but also in times of peace. This 1954 meeting laid the groundwork for the creation of

a cultural heritage program. Another decade would pass before the official establishment of an international organization dedicated to the conservation and protection of cultural heritage sites around the world. The Venice Charter of 1964 created the International Council on Monuments and Sites (ICOMOS)—a nongovernmental organization of landscape architects, architects, archeologists, urban planners, engineers, administrators of heritage, art historians and archivists that offers guidance and advice to UNESCO.

## THE WORLD HERITAGE CONVENTION

The World Heritage Convention was first discussed at the UN Conference on the Human Environment, held in Stockholm, Sweden, in June 1972. Representatives from 113 countries as well as dozens of intergovernmental and nongovernmental organizations attended. The conference is recognized as the beginning of modern political and public awareness of global environmental issues.

At the convention, the International Union for the Conservation of Nature (IUCN) and UNESCO jointly proposed a program that would protect both natural and cultural heritage sites. UNESCO would manage the program; IUCN would offer advice and evaluate the natural sites; ICOMOS and ICCROM (Center for the Study of the Preservation and Restoration of Cultural Property) would do the same for the cultural sites.

René Maheux, former general director of UNESCO, explained the importance of protecting both heritages at the Stockholm Conference: "Longtime subjects of research and distinct, even rival,

devotion, nature and culture emerge simultaneously threatened, and, with them, humankind itself, which exists within their union."

A few months after the Stockholm conference, a single text was agreed upon by all parties concerned. The Convention Concerning the Protection of World Cultural and Natural Heritage was officially adopted by the General Conference of UNESCO on 16 November 1972.

## THE FIRST SITES

At a meeting of the Intergovernmental Committee for the Protection of World Cultural and Natural Heritage in Washington, D.C, in 1978, 13 sites were inscribed on the World Heritage List:

Aachen Cathedral (Germany)
City of Quito (Ecuador)
Krakow's Historic Center (Poland)
Galapagos Islands (Ecuador)
Island of Gorée (Senegal)
L'Anse aux Meadows (Canada)
Mesa Verde (United States of America)
Nahanni (Canada)
Lalibela (Ethiopia)
Simien (Ethiopia)
Wieliczka Salt Mine (Poland)
Yellowstone (United States of America)

## THE WORLD HERITAGE CONVENTION TODAY

Today, 185 countries have ratified the World Heritage Convention. Every year, countries are invited to submit sites that might meet the criteria for being listed. That there are many sites on the list does not mean that every site submitted is accepted. Potential sites must be of outstanding value and meet one of the ten selection criteria established by the World Heritage Convention. Specialists from the IUCN, ICOMOS, and ICCROM evaluate each submission and then make a recommendation to the World Heritage Committee.

The World Heritage Committee, which meets annually, consists of representatives from 21 of the States Parties (countries) that have ratified the World Heritage Convention. The Committee implements the World Heritage Convention, allocates World Heritage Fund monies, and manages the inscription (addition) or removal of a site from the list. It also decides on the inscription or deletion of properties from the World Heritage in Danger list—a list of sites facing serious and specific dangers, which require prompt action.

Each country is responsible for its World Heritage sites. Neither UNESCO nor the World Heritage Committee can intervene without the official support of that nation. Rather, UNESCO and the World Heritage Committee together play the role of guardian. The goal is to raise awareness about sites that are endangered or facing short or long-term threats. These organizations have influence on authorities within participating countries, and this influence has led to many of the world's collective heritage sites being better managed.

## CHALLENGES AND THE FUTURE

The World Heritage Convention enjoys a positive reputation all over the world because of its proven success. Members of the Convention are proud to have their countries' sites listed. It creates awareness and international support for the preservation of sites that have been judged to have value for the whole world. The label "World Heritage Site" imparts great prestige.

The program works; it has created strong, genuine cooperation among countries in preserving and celebrating our heritage. But many important challenges exist, too, due in part to the program's popularity as well as its limits. Below are comments from relevant experts about the World Heritage Convention.

**CHRISTINA CAMERON,** former chair of the World Heritage Committee, and Canada Research Chair on Built Heritage at the University of Montreal:

"The World Heritage Convention is perhaps the most widely recognized and effective conservation instrument in the world, mobilizing a global movement for the protection of our shared heritage. Since its adoption in 1972, the Convention has encouraged intercultural dialogue and unprecedented levels of international cooperation. When we take our places during Committee sessions as representatives from different regions of the world, we celebrate our diverse cultures and work towards the collective good, the protection of the world's cultural and natural heritage.

"World Heritage Sites that are protected and shared with others can promote an understanding of the diversity of the world's cultures and ecosystems. They can also be a vital force in contributing to the sustainability and well-being of our communities.

The long-term conservation of our World Heritage Sites depends on the will of future generations to take over stewardship responsibilities. Engaging today's youth will shape the decision-makers of tomorrow. Our indigenous peoples remind us that we do not inherit the earth from our ancestors, we borrow it from our children."

**DENIS RICARD,** Secretary General of the World Heritage Cities Organization:

"The Organization of World Heritage Cities is composed of the over 230 cities inscribed on the UNESCO World Heritage List as possessing outstanding universal value for mankind. The OWHC was created to help those cities, which have a combined population of over 122 million, to adapt and improve their conservation and management methods in keeping with the specific requirements of having a city inscribed on UNESCO's list.

"The objective of the organization is to make a constructive contribution to the holistic sustainable development of its member cities. It aims to provide pathways, strategies and proposals for the resolution of existing problems and thus encourages, on both regional and international levels, cooperation and the exchange of information and expertise among the managers of historic cities throughout the world.

"The Organization of World Heritage Cities has long promoted the cooperation of the various actors involved in cultural heritage conservation and management, particularly the interaction between mayors and the cities' Heritage Management Specialists. It has been said that the OWHC is the only international platform where mayors, decision-makers and experts meet together to discuss issues

of mutual concern for World Heritage Cities. This synergy of authority and expertise has thus far yielded many positive and significant results.

"The job of a mayor of a World Heritage City is not easy. Most mayors are not heritage experts, but the responsibility of preserving or managing historic monuments becomes partly theirs once they are elected. To assist the local authorities in this difficult task, the OWHC organizes, at its World Congresses, held every two years, special workshops for mayors on issues of heritage.

"In the effort to preserve and manage a city's heritage, conflicts often arise between the local authorities and the community. It is therefore essential that the public understand the importance of its cultural heritage in order to be convinced of the need to preserve it and, where possible, to participate in the development process. Our public awareness programs have focused on youth, as an investment in the future, and recently, through journalists' workshops, on engaging the media.

"The OWHC strives to promote unity, solidarity, cooperation, exchange and dialogue among its members, to ensure that the heritage of humanity will remain a heritage with humanity, to achieve an improved level of conservation and management, while at the same time providing a better quality of life for the citizens of World Heritage Cities."

**DINU BUMBARU,** Secretary General of the International Council on Monuments and Sites (ICOMOS):

"For many people, the sole expression of the World Heritage Convention of 1972 is the list of cultural and natural sites whose 'outstanding universal value' had been acknowledged by the World Heritage Committee. The vast and diverse panorama these sites offer, whether of natural processes or human endeavor, is a sample of the rich heritage of planet Earth. As an advisory body specifically identified in the text of the World Heritage Convention, ICOMOS is the nongovernmental organization contributing to its implementation.

"Our participation takes many forms: as an advisor to the World Heritage Committee itself, as a partner of UNESCO's World Heritage Center and of other organizations, and as an international network of professionals, institutions, and national and international committees. ICOMOS advises the Committee on all cultural sites, including cultural landscapes, that have been proposed by States Parties for inscription on the list, based on our evaluation and scholarly review of each proposal's outstanding universal value, authenticity and integrity and the effectiveness of the management system in place to ensure adequate long-term protection and conservation, a fundamental condition since each state remains sovereign. ICOMOS also carries out broader thematic studies on subjects such as African rock art, antique theaters, railways, cultural landscapes in the Pacific or Latin American historic towns.

"In 2005, ICOMOS published a review of the list to identify historical, cultural and geographical gaps, considering the ever enriching nature of cultural heritage which, compared to scientifically defined natural heritage, results from ongoing cultural processes and each generation's sense of discovery. ICOMOS is currently reflecting on the fundamental theme of outstanding universal value in a culturally diverse world, and on new threats to heritage, such as urban development pressures dramatically affecting the skyline and landscapes of cities and the meaningful presence of their landmarks, or the impact of global climate change on cultural heritage, from archeological sites to buildings, cities and sacred or traditional landscapes. (Many of these risks are identified through the Heritage at Risk Reports published by ICOMOS with contributions from its worldwide network.)

"Yet our work with the World Heritage Convention is not limited to the list's yearly additions and management. Increasingly, ICOMOS is paying attention to the visionary and inspiring nature of the convention, in particular its Article 5, which encourages states to adopt general policies that give heritage a function in the life of the community and integrate its conservation into planning programs.

"Written in 1972, and with the participation today of 185 states parties, the convention remains an outstanding and still remarkably relevant tool for promoting cooperation and dedicated action to achieve the ever more necessary goals of conserving and protecting heritage monuments and sites in a changing world. As an advisory body to the World Heritage Committee, ICOMOS is proud to participate in its implementation for the benefit of the greater human family, today for tomorrow."

**DAVID SHEPPARD,** Head of the International Union for the Conservation of Nature's Protected Areas Program:

"Natural World Heritage sites are the 'crown jewels of nature' and include such treasures as the Galapagos Islands in Ecuador, the Grand Canyon in the United States and the Great Barrier Reef in Australia. Together these areas represent a priceless asset that must be handed down intact to future generations.

"These unique natural World Heritage sites face major threats and challenges—from overarching issues such as climate change, which will have a major impact on glaciers in sites such as Mount Kilimanjaro, and on coral reefs, such as those in Belize. Other threats and challenges include armed conflict and the movement of refugees in the World Heritage sites in the Democratic Republic of the Congo, and also inappropriate developments within the sites themselves. World Heritage has also proved to be a useful tool for addressing threats. President Putin of Russia personally intervened, for example, to protect the Lake Baikal World Heritage site in Russia by insisting that a proposed oil pipeline be relocated outside the boundaries of the area.

"The future challenges facing natural World Heritage sites require a concerted effort from the world community. It is important that efforts to protect these sites be undertaken jointly between different countries, and that people at all levels—from those living close to or within these sites, to the highest political decision-makers—are fully engaged and supportive of World Heritage. It is also important to support the rangers and other staff, who work in difficult, and occasionally very dangerous, conditions in these areas."

## A SHARED HERITAGE

Our ancestors left a spectacular legacy; Mother Nature has given us sites of indescribable beauty. World heritage belongs to all of us, Egyptians, Greeks, Asians, Arabs, Americans, Africans, people from the North, South, East and West. We share the same past and we will share the same future. In this century, the world seems to be getting smaller, with fewer boundaries and greater tensions arising from our differences. Now more than ever, we must open our arms to the world, to our siblings from different cultures and origins. Their heritage is our heritage, and our heritage is theirs. World Heritage has power to bring us all together, fighting for the same cause.

*Timeless Earth* is a celebration of all that World Heritage represents.

Thank you UNESCO and all the other organizations involved in making the Convention of the World Heritage work. Most of all, thanks to the local people working hard every day in the field to preserve these sites and protect our heritage.

*—Patrick Bonneville,*
*with Christina Cameron,*
*Denis Ricard, Dinu Bumbaru*
*and David Sheppard*

The Earth is home to a great diversity of flora and fauna. The International Union for the Conservation of Nature (IUCN) monitors the natural World Heritage sites for UNESCO. Based in Gland, Switzerland, the IUCN brings together 83 states, 108 government agencies, 766 non-governmental agencies, 81 international organizations and about 10,000 experts and scientists from countries around the world.

According to the IUCN (data 2007), 16,119 species around the world are currently threatened with extinction; 99 percent of these species are at risk due to human actions. Examples of such harmful activities are: destruction of natural habitats, introduction of alien species that disturb ecosystems, extraction of natural resources, pollution, and excessive hunting and poaching. With our natural heritage in such a fragile state, we must take responsibility for the damage we have caused and work to save the species we have put in danger.

*"We are in serious ecological overshoot, consuming resources faster than the Earth can replace them. The consequences of this are predictable and dire. It is time to make some vital choices. Change that improves living standards while reducing our impact on the natural world will not be easy."*

—World Wide Fund International's Director General James Leape

The Horseshoe Bend and Colorado River, near Grand Canyon National Park, United States.

# CENTRAL AMAZON

## Brazil

**Total protected area:**

15,063,756 acres

**Significance:**

Home to a wide range of threatened species, including the giant arapaima fish, the Amazonian manatee, the black caiman and two species of river dolphin.

*Jaguars are found only in the rain forests of Central and South America, though they once ranged much more widely. Their prey includes fish, iguanas, anacondas, turtles, birds and small mammals.*

Brazil's Central Amazon Conservation Complex is the largest protected area of rain forest in the Amazon Basin, one of the most biodiverse regions on the planet. The Amazon rain forest, sometimes called the planet's "lungs," produces about 20 percent of the earth's oxygen. The site contains a wide range of ecosystems, including the igapó forests and varzea watercourses, with their constantly moving mats of vegetation, which support the largest array of electric fish in the world.

Today, the rain forest in the Amazon Basin is under threat from logging, water pollution and the clearing of land for farming and ranches. The World Wide Fund for Nature (WWF) reports that 10 to 12 percent of the Amazon rain forest is now gone forever because of deforestation. Only 3.5 percent of the Brazilian Amazon's total area of 865 million acres (350 million ha) is officially protected.

*"Today the world has come to realize the Amazon rainforest problem and, everywhere, people are concerned about what they should do to help avoid its destruction."*

—The Amazon Rainforest organization

*Mining is a major factor in the deforestation of the rain forest. Roads built to access the mines inevitably bring more settlers to the area.*

Greenpeace has been a leader in the campaign against deforestation in the Amazon. Here the ship Arctic Sunrise protests the destructive effect of industrial soya farms on the rain forest.

# GALÁPAGOS ISLANDS

*The marine iguana is one of the most famous examples of the Galápagos Islands' distinctive wildlife, the inspiration for Charles Darwin's theory of evolution by natural selection.*

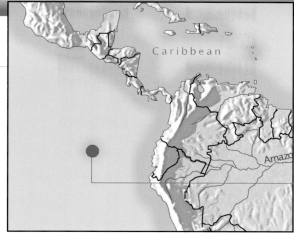

## WORLD HERITAGE IN DANGER

### Ecuador

**Threat:**

The 5,000 species found in the Galápagos Islands are under threat from an explosion of tourism to the region.

Located at the confluence of three ocean currents in the Pacific Ocean, 620 miles (1,000 km) west of Ecuador, the 19 islands that constitute the Galápagos archipelago have been called "a living museum and showcase of evolution." This isolated ecological region has one of the highest concentrations of unique species in the world, including marine and land iguanas, giant tortoises, Galápagos penguins and a "singular group of finches," as Charles Darwin observed when he visited the islands in 1835. In June 2007 the International Union for Conservation of Nature (IUCN) and UNESCO declared that the Galápagos Islands are threatened by a huge increase in tourism: the archipelago's number of annual visitors increased from 40,000 in 1996 to 120,000 in 2007. The government of Ecuador wants to take steps to rectify the situation, but it is our collective responsibility to avoid visiting the islands to preserve their unique and fragile ecosystem.

During his courtship display, the male frigate bird inflates his gular sac and quivers his wings to attract females that fly overhead.

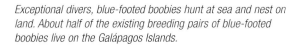

Exceptional divers, blue-footed boobies hunt at sea and nest on land. About half of the existing breeding pairs of blue-footed boobies live on the Galápagos Islands.

*"The natural history of this archipelago is very remarkable: it seems to be a little world within itself; the greater number of its inhabitants, both vegetable and animal, being found nowhere else."*

—Charles Robert Darwin, *Voyage of the Beagle*, 1831

# LAKE TURKANA NATIONAL PARKS

*Lake Turkana is an important habitat for a diverse population of breeding and migrant birds, including the greater flamingo Phoenicopterus rubra.*

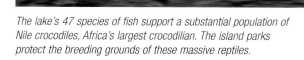

Formerly known as Lake Rudolf, Lake Turkana, in Kenya's Great Rift Valley, is a large, saline lake with three volcanic islands, in a desert wilderness. An important stopover for migrant birds, particularly waterfowl, it is considered a valuable laboratory for studying plant and animal communities. The three national parks protect major breeding grounds of the Nile crocodile, hippopotamus, puff adder and cobra. It is also an outstanding paleontological site because of the hominid and ancestral human fossils that have been found there by Richard Leakey and many others.

*The lake's 47 species of fish support a substantial population of Nile crocodiles, Africa's largest crocodilian. The island parks protect the breeding grounds of these massive reptiles.*

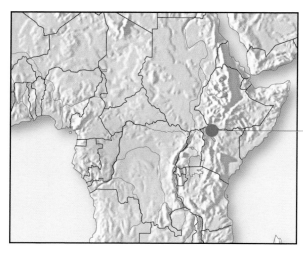

## Kenya

**Total protected area:**

399,038 acres

**Significance:**

The park protects the breeding habitats of the Nile crocodile, hippopotamus, puff adder, cobra and carpet viper.

*Beisa oryx are specially adapted to their arid desert environment in East Africa. They are able to sense rainstorms from far away and to tolerate periods of extreme heat.*

# SELOUS GAME RESERVE

Impalas are found in the Miombo woodlands, a region that has both grassland and woodland habitat. They are able to feed by either grazing or browsing.

## Tanzania

**Total protected area:**

11,070,321 acres

**Significance:**

The reserve, located in an area mostly untouched by humans, is home to large numbers of black rhinoceroses, cheetahs, crocodiles, giraffes and hippopotamuses.

The largest game reserve in Africa, Selous is an enormous sanctuary for Tanzanian wildlife, with large populations of Burchell's zebras, elephants, giraffes, buffaloes, hippopotamuses and crocodiles. There are several small populations of black rhinoceros. The site's wide range of habitats varies from dense forests to grasslands to riverine swamps. The reserve, which has remained relatively undisturbed by humans, is remote. Access is difficult except by air, though it is now possible to reach it by the Tazara railway on the northwest edge. Several factors make travel in the park difficult; tsetse flies, which transmit sleeping sickness, are common in the region; and from March to May, flooding makes crossing the reserve difficult. Since the government undertook an anti-poaching program in 1989, the animal populations of Selous have generally increased. The elephant population in particular had seriously declined from ivory poaching.

*"Mr. Selous is the last of the big game hunters of Southern Africa; the last of the mighty hunters whose experience lay in the greatest hunting ground which this world has seen since civilized man has appeared herein."*

—President Theodore Roosevelt, speaking of his 1909 African expedition guide and good friend. The park was named after Frederick Courteney Selous, British explorer, hunter and conservationist.

Known for their speed and agility, cheetahs are daytime hunters. They prey on the herd animals that graze on the savanna, another name for the open grasslands of the East African plains.

Hippos are common in the reserve, where they gather in large groups along the Rufiji River during the dry season, from June to October.

# ALDABRA ATOLL

## Seychelles

**Total protected area:**
86,487 acres

**Significance:**
This remote atoll is home to the world's largest population of giant tortoises.

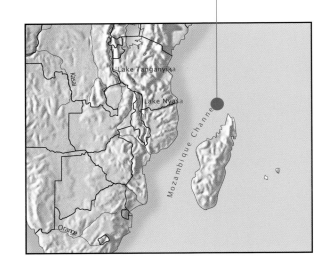

Aremote coral atoll in the Indian Ocean, surrounded by a coral reef, Aldabra is made up of four islands and the lagoon that they enclose. Most of the land surface is ancient coral reef (about 125,000 years old and now above sea level) and limestone. The inaccessible atoll has the largest population of giant tortoises in the world, estimated at 152,000. Weighing as much as 600 pounds (275 kg), they grow to lengths of up to 4 feet (1.2 m) and are one of the world's longest-living animals, with an average lifespan of 100 years. The smaller green turtle and hawksbill turtle also breed on the islands. The atoll is also home to the only remaining species of the flightless birds of the Indian Ocean: the endemic Aldabran white-throated rail.

*Tortoises graze primarily on grasses, herbs and shrub leaves but will supplement their diet with small invertebrates and carrion (including dead tortoises) when vegetation becomes scarce.*

*The giant tortoise has a high, domed shell; thick, heavily scaled legs; and powerful claws. On the tip of its tail is a clawlike spur.*

*Four islands of eroded coral limestone make up the Aldabra atoll, one of the few places in the world where reptiles dominate.*

# GARAMBA NATIONAL PARK

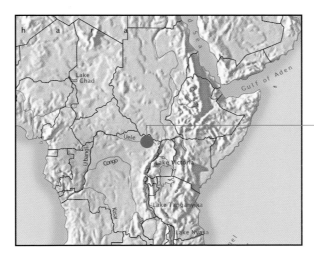

## WORLD HERITAGE IN DANGER

### Democratic Republic of the Congo

**Threat:**

This park, one of Africa's oldest, and home to the last remaining northern white rhinoceroses, is under threat from poaching and an influx of refugees.

Garamba National Park, a huge expanse of savanna and woodlands fed by the Garamba and Dungu rivers, is home to four of the large African mammals: the elephant, giraffe, hippopotamus and the white rhinoceros. The rare white rhino, for which the park is known, is much larger than the black rhino. There are reported to be fewer than 30 remaining in the park.

*Garamba National Park is the only habitat where the endangered white rhino is still found. It has been exterminated throughout central Africa.*

Human conflict has placed all five of the Democratic Republic of the Congo's natural World Heritage sites on the World Heritage in Danger list. The region's protracted civil war, ethnic conflict and political unrest, resulting in a major inflow of refugees, has increased pressure on the parks and their wildlife. These parks—Garamba, Virunga, Kahuzi-Biega, Salonga and Okapi—are priceless treasures that must be protected.

*"It is ironic that now as peace is supposed to be coming to the region, the exploitation of large mammals has escalated."*

—Kes Hillman Smith, Garamba National Park Project, August 2004

*The rhinoceros is poached for its horns, which are used for medicinal purposes and sell for thousands of dollars on the black market.*

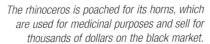

# EVERGLADES NATIONAL PARK

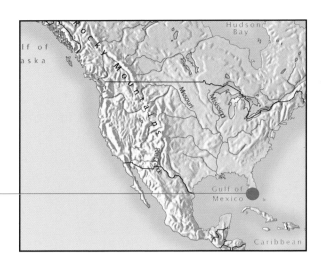

## SUCCESS STORY

### United States of America

**The Challenge:**

To protect the park's fragile ecosystem from encroaching development.

**The Solution:**

The state and federal government worked together to create a plan to save and restore the everglades.

One of the goals of the restoration of the Everglades is to increase the abundance and diversity of native plants and animals. A key measure of its success is the growth of the alligator population.

K nown as "the river of grass" to Native Americans, the Everglades are formed by a shallow, slow-moving sheet of water that flows over Florida's southern tip to the ocean. Well known for the alligators that thrive there, the park's marshland is also a refuge for the threatened manatee and home to more than 400 bird species. Restoration of the Everglades' fragile ecosystem, which has been threatened by urban and agricultural development, is underway. Since the U.S. government's approval of a plan in 2000, changes in the water management system are beginning to restore water levels in the area, and steps have been taken to reduce fertilizer pollution. In 2007, the World Heritage Committee decided that sufficient progress had been made in restoring the site to remove it from the World Heritage in Danger list.

*"Here are no lofty peaks seeking the sky, no mighty glaciers or rushing streams wearing away the uplifted land. Here is land, tranquil in its quiet beauty, serving not as the source of water, but as the receiver of it. To its natural abundance we owe the spectacular plant and animal life that distinguishes this place from all others in our country."*

—U.S. president Harry S Truman, 1947

*Many wading birds call the Everglades home, though their populations are still recovering from overhunting during the last century.*

*The Everglades is a fragile floodplain ecosystem with subtropical vegetation that is unique in the United States. Many of its species migrated from tropical regions.*

*The American alligator is a top predator in the Everglades eco-system. Its prey changes over its lifetime, since its body undergoes such tremendous growth from birth to adulthood.*

# SIAN KA'AN

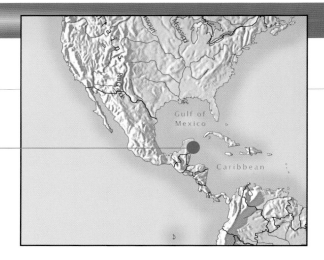

## Mexico

**Total protected area:**

1,304,716 acres

**Significance:**

This area is home to more than 300 species of birds as well as more than 100 mammal species, including pumas, Central American tapirs, Caribbean manatees, spider monkeys and howler monkeys.

The reserve has an abundance of species of marine and wading birds because of the unusual diversity of its aquatic habitats.

The Sian Ka'an biosphere reserve—whose name comes from the Mayan phrase "where the sky is born"—contains the diverse habitats of the Yucatan peninsula's east coast, including tropical forests, coastal dunes, mangroves and marshes. A large marine area, with a barrier reef running through it, makes up roughly a fifth of the reserve. The site's rich flora and fauna include more than 300 species of birds and most of the vertebrate species characteristic of the Yucatan, such as the jaguar, tapir, howler monkey and anteater.

The development of tourist facilities in the northern part of the reserve, which is close to Cancun, is cause for concern. Urban growth along the coast, with inadequate sewage systems that discharge directly into the ocean, seriously threatens the surrounding reef life. Fortunately, some of the more remote parts of the reserve are inaccessible and therefore enjoy a degree of protection.

The brown pelican catches fish by "plunge-diving," plummeting head-first into the water once it has spied its prey from the air, then trapping the fish in its pouch.

Nonaggressive herbivores, manatees slowly propel themselves through the water with their large foreflippers and paddlelike tail, feeding on vegetation. They have no hind limbs.

# MANÚ NATIONAL PARK

Located in the Amazon River basin, Manú is among the world's most biologically diverse protected areas. The park rises from the floodplains of the Manú River to the eastern slopes of the Andes, featuring successive tiers of vegetation as the altitude climbs from 490 to 13,780 feet (150 to 4,200 m) above sea level.

## Peru

**Total protected area:**
4,648,546 acres

### Significance:
Manú is home to 850 bird species and 200 species of mammals, including six species of macaw and 13 species of monkey.

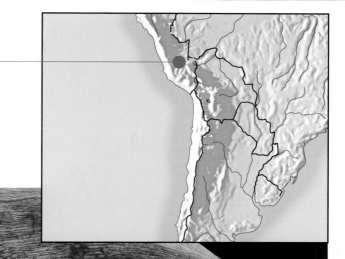

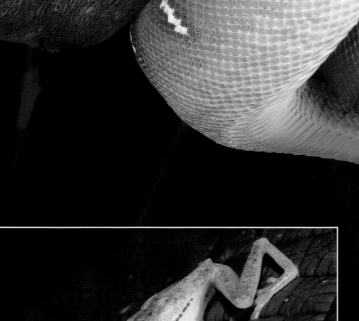

*Emerald tree boas hunt by suspending themselves from a branch and striking at any prey unlucky enough to pass beneath.*

*All in all, some 140 species of amphibians live in Manú National Park.*

The abundant variety of animal and plant life in the tropical forest of the lower tiers is extraordinary. Home to 850 species of birds, the forest also protects rare and endangered species such as the giant otter and giant armadillo. Some botanists claim that more plant species are found in the park than in any other protected area on earth.

> *"Manú protects a greater number of plant and animal species than any other such South American park, with the exception of remote Madidi in Bolivia."*
>
> —Charles A. Munn,
> founder of the Board of Tropical Nature

*Motionless and silent much of the time, sloths spend almost their entire lives in the trees, sleeping, mating and even giving birth while hanging from the branches.*

*The tamarin's family of small, tree-dwelling primates occurs only in Central and South America's tropical rain forests. They forage for insects with their long fingers and sharp claws.*

# PANTANAL CONSERVATION AREA

*Much of the remaining wild population of the hyacinth macaw, estimated at about 3,000 birds, lives in the Pantanal. The parrot has been hunted to near extinction for the pet trade.*

*The Pantanal is one of the most important breeding grounds for the Jabiru stork, as well as other wetland birds such as herons, ibis and ducks.*

## Brazil

**Total protected area:**

464,108 acres

**Significance:**

The Pantanal is a refuge for threatened species such as the jaguar, as well as 80 species of mammals, 650 birds, 50 reptiles and 400 fish.

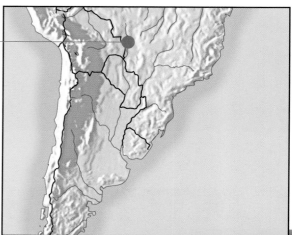

The Pantanal region, 80 percent of which lies in western Brazil, is one of the world's largest freshwater wetland ecosystems. It is a vast alluvial plain bordered by the Amolar Mountains. Within the Pantanal Conservation site are the headwaters of the region's two major rivers, the Cuiabá and the Paraguay, and the palm-tree groves for which the region is known. A refuge for many of the Pantanal's threatened species, such as the jaguar, the site is also a major sanctuary for birds. Yet poaching is a serious problem in the region. The hyacinth macaw, the world's largest parrot, continues to be hunted for the international pet trade, despite being critically endangered.

*"The Pantanal has the greatest concentration of fauna in the Americas. People outside Brazil know only the Amazon … It's a shame, because the Pantanal is a very important ecological place."*

—Dr. Maria Tereza Jorge Pádua,
former Director, Brazil's National Parks

*The Pantanal's many landscapes and ecological regions include river corridors, perennial wetlands and lakes, seasonally inundated grasslands and semideciduous forest.*

# CENTRAL SURINAME NATURE RESERVE

## Suriname

**Total protected area:**

3.954,686 acres

**Significance:**

The reserve's animals are typical of the region and include the jaguar, giant armadillo, giant river otter, tapir, sloths, 8 species of primates and some 400 bird species such as harpy eagle, Guiana cock-of-the-rock and scarlet macaw.

*"This area may contain answers to questions we have not yet learned to ask."*

—James Thorsell,
senior World Conservation Union advisor
to UNESCO's World Heritage Committee

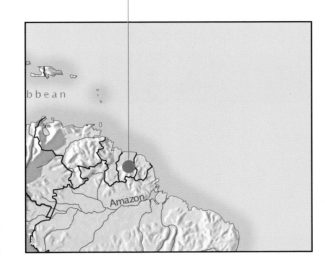

*Sakis have the distinctive broad nose of New World monkeys. They do not have opposable thumbs, as Old World monkeys do, but instead grasp objects between their second and third fingers.*

The Central Suriname reserve protects 3,953,686 acres (1.6 million ha) of unusually pristine primary tropical forest. Its undisturbed mountain and lowland-forest ecosystems contain many of the region's threatened species, such as the jaguar, giant armadillo, and giant river otter, as well as 8 species of primates and 400 bird species. One of the most forested countries in the world, Suriname has a remarkable diversity of plant life. The site, encompassing the watershed of the Coppename River, was established in 1998. It linked together three important reserves in central Suriname to form one of the largest regions of uninhabited, undisturbed tropical primary forest in the world. Due to its large size and inaccessibility, threats to the region are insignificant.

*Though these two are enjoying a daytime nap, squirrel monkeys are diurnal, meaning that they are active by day and sleep at night.*

*The blue poison dart frog is found only in southern Suriname. Its deadly poison, which few predators can survive, is secreted through the skin.*

# TAÏ NATIONAL PARK

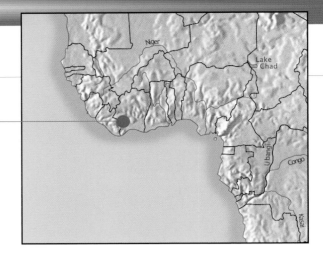

Declared a Forest and Wildlife Refuge in 1926, Taï National Park today protects the pygmy hippopotamus, 11 species of monkey, and other threatened mammal species. Its population of chimpanzees, which has been observed and studied, is well known. As one of the last major tracts of primary tropical forest remaining in West Africa, Taï National Park is remarkable for its biodiversity and rich flora. The park's forest ecosystem depends upon the recovering elephant population. Since 1972, when the Ivorian government proclaimed Tai a national park and prohibited commercial lumber harvesting, the forest has recovered well, but the threats of poaching, farming and illegal gold mining remain. Some 60 poachers are arrested every year by park guards.

## Côte d'Ivoire

### Total protected area:

815,448 acres

### Significance:

The park contains 47 of the 54 species of large mammal known to occur in Guinean rain forest, including the mona monkey, the chimpanzee, the pygmy hippopotamus and the royal antelope.

*Although extremely solitary, male pygmy hippos seek out receptive females during the breeding season. They will mate over a period of two days, both on land and in the water.*

*Jane Goodall was the first to observe a chimp in the wild carefully choosing a twig and stripping off its leaves to use it as a tool.*

*The bond between a chimpanzee mother and child persists for life. Children share their mothers' nests for five years, then stick close by for another two or three years.*

# W NATIONAL PARK OF NIGER

The loss of its migration corridors and the disappearance of some 90 percent of its West African habitat have devastated the population of the mighty African elephant.

## Niger

**Total protected area:**

543,632 acres

**Significance:**

W National Park protects Niger's only remaining populations of elephant and buffalo.

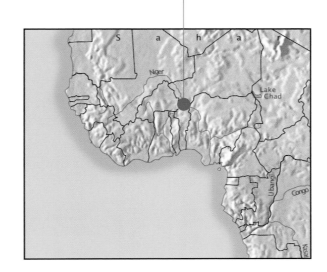

The portion of W National Park that lies in Niger is situated in a transition zone between savanna and forest lands. The park represents important ecosystem characteristics of the West African Woodlands/ Savannah Biogeographical Province.

Established as a national park in 1954, W is named for the shape of the River Niger. It is contiguous to other protected areas in Burkina Faso and Niger, which increases the value of all the sites for the survival of species that require large areas for seasonal migrations. In 1996 the government of Niger officially launched a project to create a Biosphere Reserve in the park that lies in that country.

Cheetahs learn to hunt from their mothers, who catch and bring back small live antelopes from a hunt for their cubs to chase and catch.

The African buffalo, also known as the savanna or cape buffalo, can weigh up to 2,000 pounds (900 kg) and stands as tall as 5 feet (1.5 m) at the shoulder. Powerful animals, African buffaloes mob to fight off predators and can be dangerous to humans.

# VIRUNGA NATIONAL PARK

*From the age of 4 months to 2 or 3 years, gorilla babies ride on their mothers' backs, clinging to their mothers' fur.*

The Virungas—where Dian Fossey studied the mountain gorilla—are known for their spectacular scenery and chain of active volcanoes. The most biodiverse of all of Africa's national parks, Virunga National Park is home to a third of the world's endangered mountain gorilla population and the highest concentration of hippopotamus in Africa. Its remarkably diverse habitats include steppes, lava plains, swamps, lowland and Afromontane forests, savannas on the volcanoes' slopes and the snowfields of Rwenzori. The park is severely threatened by poachers, and there is grave concern that some of the park has been deforested, which led the World Heritage Committee to add the site to the World Heritage in Danger list. In fact, all five World Heritage sites in the DRC are on that list.

*The undisputed leader of the gorillas' social group is the silverback (below), a dominant adult male. In response to a threat or challenge, a male gorilla's display may include hooting and roaring (right), as well as chest-pounding and aggressive charging.*

*"When you realize the value of all life, you dwell less on what is past and concentrate on the preservation of the future."*

—The final entry in Dian Fossey's diary before her murder. Dr. Fossey dedicated her life to the study of mountain gorillas.

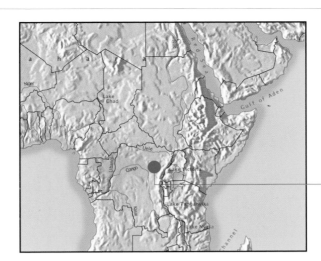

## WORLD HERITAGE IN DANGER

### Democratic Republic of the Congo

**Threat:**

Poachers and deforestation endanger the animals of this World Heritage site.

In July 2007 four gorillas in a group that had been habituated to humans and visited by tourists were shot and killed in Virunga National Park.

# OKAPI WILDLIFE RESERVE

**WORLD HERITAGE IN DANGER**

**Democratic Republic of the Congo**

**Threat:**
Armed conflict in the DRC as well as the poaching of animals at the site led to its placement on the World Heritage in Danger list.

*"The Okapi Wildlife Reserve is a model example of what great things can be achieved when local people and local government, in collaboration with a non-governmental organization, come together in a common cause."*

—Gilman International Conservation

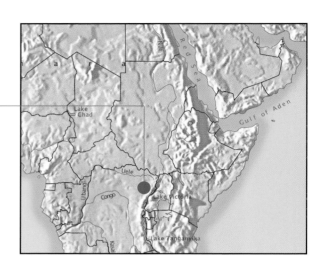

The Okapi Wildlife Reserve lies in the Congo basin's Ituri Forest, a vast rain forest wilderness in northeastern Democratic Republic of the Congo. The Efe and Mbuti pygmies, nomadic hunter-gatherers, live in the forest, about a fifth of which is now reserve. It contains 13 primate species, the most of any African forest, and is one of Africa's most important forest preserves for birds.

The site is also home to about 5,000 of the estimated 30,000 okapis—a rare relative of the giraffe—in the world. Beyond the Ituri Forest, okapis were not known to exist until 1900, when Sir Henry Morton Stanley, who had heard from the Mbuti pygmies of an animal they called "o'api," glimpsed one running through the forest. He reported it to the governor of Uganda, Sir Harry Johnston, who was intrigued and decided to search for the animal. At the time it was considered impossible that an undiscovered big mammal might exist in Africa. Threats to the site in the past decade have included incursions by armed militias, refugees, coltran miners and poachers.

The okapi is the giraffe's only living relative. Both have large, upright ears; highly sensitive hearing; and long prehensile tongues that they use to strip buds and leaves from branches.

The okapi's zebra-like stripes, which are eye-catching in the open, help camouflage the animal in the rain forest's mix of light and shade.

Okapis are not only well hidden in their habitat, they are extremely wary by nature. Therefore they are elusive and hard to observe in the wild.

# BWINDI IMPENETRABLE NATIONAL PARK

*Gorillas live in groups of up to 40, though the average is about 11 members, who move together through their home range, foraging for food, resting and sleeping in nests of leaves.*

### Uganda

**Total protected area:**

79,301 acres

**Significance:**

Bwindi Impenetrable Forest is home to half of the world's population of mountain gorillas.

*"The Bwindi Impenetrable Forest is the Place of Darkness."*

—Aliette Frank, *National Geographic*

*The mountain gorilla eats a vegetarian diet of roots, shoots, fruit, wild celery and tree bark and pulp.*

Bwindi Impenetrable Forest, in the highlands of southwestern Uganda, is an important "ecological island forest" known for its exceptional biodiversity. Situated where the lowland and mountain forests meet, it has the richest wildlife in East Africa. Eighty-four percent of Africa's butterfly species are found there, as well as some 350 species of birds. The extremely rugged terrain of steep hills and narrow valleys hosts more than 200 species of trees and over 100 species of ferns. The Impenetrable

Forest is also home to almost half of the world's remaining mountain gorillas.

In a 2007 census, some 340 gorillas within the Bwindi Impenetrable Park were identified, representing a 12 percent growth in population over the past decade—an encouraging sign. Nevertheless, with fewer than 750 individuals surviving in the wild throughout the world, vigilance is imperative. Many of these animals live in the Democratic Republic of the Congo, a fragile and troubled region.

*As the leader and protector of the group, the silverback not only has absolute authority, but he will also defend its members with his life if the group is attacked.*

# WRANGEL ISLAND RESERVE

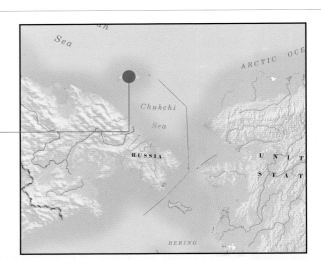

A self-contained ecosystem far above the Arctic Circle, the Wrangel Island Reserve includes Wrangel Island, Herald Island and the surrounding waters. Large and mountainous, Wrangel Island has an unusually rich natural history for the Arctic, due in part to the fact that it did not undergo glaciation during the Ice Age. Its biodiversity is exceptional for the region. The reserve is a breeding ground for Asia's snow goose and a feeding ground for the gray whale migrating from Mexico, as well as the northernmost nesting ground for 100 migratory bird species. Established as a wildlife refuge in 1960, Wrangel Island has the largest population of Pacific walrus in the world. The site of ancestral polar bear dens, the island also was a prehistoric home to mammoths. Mammoth tusks and skulls found on the island attest to their relatively recent presence.

## Russia

**Total protected area:**

1,803,869 acres

**Significance:**

Wrangel is a breeding ground for polar bears, seals and lemmings.

*The reserve's islands have the largest populations of polar bears in the Arctic. An estimated 350 to 600 females den on the two islands annually. Polar bears hunt their prey from ice floes around the islands.*

*The thick coat of insulating fur that protects polar bears from the cold even partially covers the bottom of their paws.*

*"I have named this northern land Wrangel Land as an appropriate tribute to the memory of a man who spent three consecutive years north of latitude 68°, and demonstrated the problem of this open polar sea forty-five years ago."*

—Captain Thomas Long, 1867

*A seal pup weighs about 70 pounds (32 kg) at birth. After nursing for a period of 12 to 18 days, it will have almost tripled its weight.*

# GOLDEN MOUNTAINS OF ALTAI

*Altai's system of mountain ridges is the highest point of the head-waters of the Ob' River, Western Siberia's principal waterway and one of the longest rivers in the world.*

The major mountain range in Western Siberia, the Altai contains the head-waters of Siberia's longest river, the Ob', and the habitat of the globally endangered snow leopard. It is a high, mountainous region of glaciers, alpine meadows, moss- and lichen-covered tundra and the steppes of Western Siberia. Reindeer are found in the higher areas, as well as golden eagle, imperial eagle and Mongolian gazelle.

The Altai highland's many lakes include the exceptionally clear and deep Lake Teletskoe, one of the most pristine and biologically diverse lakes in Central Asia. The region also contains the complete sequence of central Siberia's altitudinal vegetation zones: steppe, forest-steppe, mixed forest, subalpine and alpine, as well as extensive glaciation.

*The site protects the highest, most pristine parts of the Altai Mountains and includes about 1,500 glaciers; high peaks as well as lower slopes and foothills; and deep mountain valleys.*

## Russia

### Total protected area:

3,982,000 acres

### Significance :

This site is home to 13 threatened species of birds and 4 threatened species of mammals, including the golden and imperial eagles, the snow leopard and the Mongolian gazelle.

*Largely uninhabited, the territory of the Golden Mountains of Altai site has a few small settlements within it and is used by herders for seasonal settlements.*

# KOMODO NATIONAL PARK

## Indonesia

**Total protected area:**

541,956 acres

**Significance:**

The park is home to more than 4,000 Komodo dragons (*Komodo monitor*), the world's largest living lizard.

The Indonesian archipelago is the only place on Earth that the giant, aggressive lizards known as Komodo dragons are found. The largest lizards in the world, Komodo dragons grow to be 10 feet (3 m) long. They have lived for millions of years on these volcanic islands, where they hunt large and small fauna in a hilly landscape of dry savanna and sandy island beaches.

With their sharp claws, powerful legs, serrated teeth, and venomous bite, Komodo dragons have flourished as the dominant predators on Indonesia's volcanic islands for millions of years.

Founded in 1980 as a preserve to protect the Komodo dragon and its habitat, the park is also known for the biodiversity of its marine life, which includes whales, dolphins, sharks and manta rays. The park is devoted to protecting all of the species within its borders.

*"Now listening to the short hissing that came like a gust of evil wind, and observing the action of that darting, snake-like tongue, that seemed to sense the very fear that held me, I was affected in a manner not easy to relate."*

—William Douglas Burden, director of the Zoological Museum and Botanical Gardens at Bogor, Java (1927)

Komodo dragons feed on carrion, deer, pigs, smaller dragons and other lizards and even large water buffalo. Their long, forked tongues help them to pick up smells over long distances.

Komodo National Park includes three major islands of the Indonesian archipelago—Komodo, Rinca and Padar—and many smaller islands. More than 3,000 people live within the park.

# TROPICAL RAINFOREST HERITAGE OF SUMATRA

## Indonesia

**Total protected area:**

6,412,691 acres

**Significance:**

This site, consisting of three parks, is home to 180 mammal species, including the Sumatran tiger, the Sumatran rhino, the Sumatran elephant, the orangutan and the Malayan sun bear.

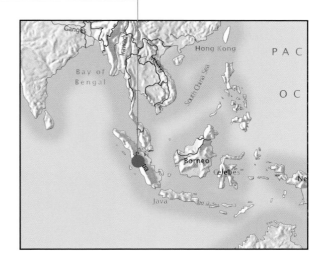

This mountainous site of lush rain forest straddles the equator along the spine of the Bukit Barisan Mountains, known as "the Andes of Sumatra." Only pockets are left of what was once a vast tropical rain forest, with lakes, waterfalls and caves on the island of Sumatra. The three national parks that make up the Rain Forest Heritage site—Gunung Leuser, Kerinci Seblat and Bukit Barisan Selatan—are remnants of the island's lowland and mountain forests. Dedicated to conserving Sumatra's biodiversity, the parks are considered critically important to the island's threatened species and the preservation of its natural heritage.

The site protects a range of habitats of exceptional biodiversity, from marine to subalpine. An estimated 10,000 species of plants, including the world's largest flower (*Rafflesia arnoldi*) and the world's tallest flower (*Amorphophallus titanium*), grow in Sumatra's forested mountains. The parks are a refuge for the island's mammals, including the Sumatran tiger, Sumatran rhino, Sumatran elephant, orangutan and Malayan sun bear.

*"Indonesia's island of Sumatra has seen a dramatic acceleration of forest loss in the past few decades. Predictions forecast an almost complete clearing of forests by 2010, with only the steepest slopes and deepest peat swamps surviving."*

—World Wide Fund for Nature

*The orangutan, whose name derives from a Malay phrase meaning "person of the forest," is the most solitary of the great apes. It is found only in the lush rain forests of Sumatra and Borneo.*

*Long-tailed macaques, widespread throughout the tropical rain forests of Southeast Asia, store their meals of meat, fruit and seeds in cheek pouches.*

*Orangutans stay with their mothers for the first eight years of their lives, learning to forage for fruit and to build nests in the trees.*

# MANAS WILDLIFE SANCTUARY

The Manas Wildlife Sanctuary, established in 1985 in the foothills of the Himalayas, is a refuge for many of India's endangered species, such as the tiger, golden langur, pygmy hog, Indian rhinoceros and Indian elephant. The Manas River flows through the park, accompanied by five smaller

### India

**Total protected area:**

128,500 acres

**Significance:**

Fifty-five species of mammals—31 of which are threatened—live in the Manas Sanctuary.

*About half of the tigers remaining in the wild are the Bengal tigers of India. A tiger's roar can be heard from 2 miles (3 km) away.*

rivers. The region protected by the Manas Sanctuary remains wilderness and has the highest concentration of wildlife in India. Alluvial grasslands blanket more than 45 percent of the park, alongside a mixture of evergreen and deciduous forests. This range of flora is the ideal habitat for tigers, buffalos and elephants. Part of an important Bengal tiger reserve, the Manas Sanctuary also protects a migratory corridor for elephants and other animals along the Bhutan border. Among its varied habitats are wetlands that provide a home to threatened pelican and stork species.

*"India, being home to about 60 percent of the world's wild tiger population, is now the best hope for tiger survival."*

—The Sierra Club

*Powerful and stealthy nocturnal hunters, tigers will travel long distances to find their prey and can eat as much as 60 pounds (27 kg) in a night.*

# THUNGYAI–HUAI KHA KHAENG WILDLIFE SANCTUARIES

The Thungyai–Huai Kha Khaeng Sanctuaries are among Southeast Asia's most outstanding sites due, in part, to the beauty and scarcity of the forests they protect. The region, which includes evergreen, deciduous and bamboo forests, has, for the most part, been undisturbed by logging or agriculture. Asiatic wild dogs, tigers, leopards, Asian elephants and Asian tapirs are among the threatened mammals found in the forests. All five of Thailand's macaque species are found there as well. Together, the sanctuaries make up the only territory in Thailand vast enough for such large mammals to survive.

The site's other important habitats are its small lakes, ponds and swampy areas. The sanctuaries' wetlands are a refuge for many of the country's rare birds, including the green peafowl, red-headed vulture and crested kingfisher, as well as rare reptiles and amphibians, such as the Indian monitor, the giant Asiatic toad and the giant frog.

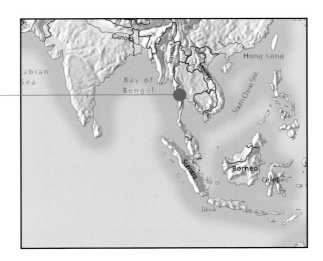

## Thailand

### Total protected area:
2,985,775 acres

### Significance:
The sanctuaries are home to 153 species of mammals, 490 species of birds, 41 species of reptiles and 108 species of fish.

*Clouded leopards are remarkably good climbers, with large paws, sharp claws and rotating rear ankles that enable them to climb down trees headfirst like a squirrel.*

*Elephants use their trunks to smell, breathe, trumpet, drink and spray themselves with water. Asian elephants' trunks have a fingerlike feature with which they can grab small items.*

# NOEL KEMPFF MERCADO NATIONAL PARK

Male howler monkeys, whose long beards cover their large throats, can be heard from up to 3 miles (5 km) away when announcing their presence in a territory.

## Bolivia

**Total protected area:**

3,764,517 acres

**Significance:**

The park is home to a rare black jaguar population and 9 species of macaw, possibly the highest number of the rare birds in any one protected area.

One of the largest and most intact parks in the Amazon Basin, Bolivia's Noel Kempff Mercado National Park hosts many habitat types, from evergreen Amazonian forests to biodiverse Cerrado savanna. Scattered pockets of dry forests, one of the continent's most endangered ecosystems, also dot the landscape. The alluvial plains of the Paraguá and Itenéz rivers, which are characterized by flooded savannas and swamps, also contain termite plains—flat stretches of land covered by thousands of termite mounds. These termite plains are the major habitat for both the giant anteater and the giant armadillo. Another striking natural phenomenon in the park is the unusual forest of lianas, which form a low, very thick canopy. The evolutionary history of the park dates back to the Precambrian period.

In 1988, the park's name was changed to honor Noel Kempff Mercado, the distinguished Bolivian biologist who negotiated with the Bolivian government to create the national park. Today it protects numerous threatened large vertebrate populations, contains an estimated 4,000 species of flora and provides a home to more than 600 species of birds.

Extremely sought after as pet birds for their vibrant blue feathers, the hyacinth macaw is one of the most expensive birds in the world, and one of the endangered species the park now protects.

Like many arboreal New World monkeys, the long-haired spider monkey has a prehensile tail, which it uses to grip branches and forage for food.

# DARIEN NATIONAL PARK

Occupying the Pacific coast of Panama, and bordering Colombia, Darien National Park bridges the habitats of Central and South America. The park contains extensive lowland tropical forest, as well as varied types of montane forest, including cloud forest and elfin forest.

Home to giant anteaters, jaguars, ocelots, capybaras, howler monkeys, brown-headed spider monkeys, agoutis and the Harpy eagle, these Panamanian forests are considered to be the most diverse eco-systems in tropical America. The region's variety of habitats—sandy beaches, rocky coasts, mangrove and palm forest swamps and tropical forests—is truly exceptional to behold. In addition, three Amerindian ethnic groups—the Embera, Waunana and Kuna—live within the park.

*Tailless, with webbed feet, capybaras are the world's largest rodent. These highly social, semiaquatic animals graze in herds on aquatic plants; they also bark and purr.*

*Panama's rain forest is one of the few remaining refuges for the harpy eagle, an impressive predator with powerful 5-inch (13-cm) talons and a 7-foot (2-m) wingspan. It is the largest raptor living in the Americas.*

*The American crocodile, one of the largest crocodilian species, reaches lengths of 20 feet (6 m). It was heavily hunted for its skin in the mid-20th century and remains endangered today. A strict carnivore, the crocodile's diet ranges from cattle to frogs.*

## Panama

**Total protected area:**
1,475,219 acres

**Significance:**
The park contains a remarkable variety of habitats and wildlife, including the giant anteater, jaguar, howler monkey, brown-headed spider monkey, Baird's tapir, harpy eagle, Cayman croc-odile and the American crocodile.

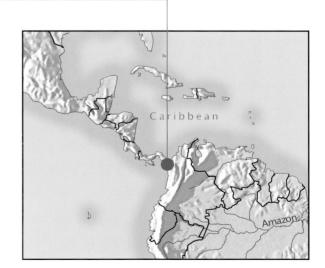

# SICHUAN GIANT PANDA SANCTUARIES

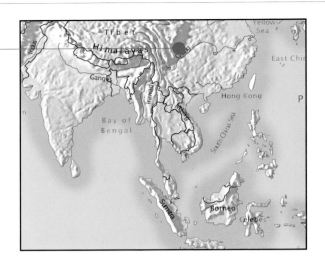

## China

**Total protected area:**
2,284,489 acres

**Significance:**
More than a third of all the world's pandas live in this protected area.

*Pandas have two features that are unique to the species: broad, flat molars and a large wrist bone that functions as an opposable thumb while they hold and eat bamboo.*

More than 30 percent of the world's pandas, classified as a "national treasure" by the Chinese government, live in the sanctuaries' seven nature reserves and nine parks in the Qionglai and Jiajin Mountains. The site protects the largest remaining contiguous habitat of the highly endangered giant panda and is a center for the captive breeding of the species. Other globally endangered animals, including the red panda, the snow leopard and the clouded leopard, also live in the sanctuaries. The mountainous site is one of the richest botanical regions in the world, other than tropical rain forests, with an estimated 6,000 species of flora. Tourism, a fast-growing source of income, is fairly new to the area. Only 1 percent of the reserve is open to tourists and the number of visitors is limited.

In May 2008, a devastating earthquake in China also affected the panda sanctuaries. According to UNESCO, six staff members were killed, more than half of the sanctuaries' buildings collapsed, and the area's infrastructure severely damaged. At the time of this writing, plans were being approved to send emergency assistance to the sanctuaries.

*"We wanted an animal that is beautiful, endangered, and loved by many people in the world for its appealing qualities."*

—Sir Peter Scott, one of the founders of the World Wide Fund for Nature, about the organization's logo

The contiguous habitat the sanctuary provides is invaluable. Many panda populations have become isolated in narrow belts of bamboo no more than 3,200 to 3,900 feet (1,000 to 1,200 m) wide.

*"To protect an animal is not just putting it living in the zoo, but keeping it alive in its home."*

—Lu Zhi, panda specialist at Peking University

Classified as bears, giant pandas have a carnivore's digestive system but eat bamboo almost exclusively. Though they are able to climb trees, they live mainly on the ground.

The panda's survival is endangered by rapid habitat loss as huge areas of forest have been cleared for farming, timber and fuel. Approximately 1,600 pandas remain in the wild.

# GOUGH AND INACCESSIBLE ISLANDS

*Almost half of the world's population of the endangered northern rockhopper penguin breeds on Gough Island.*

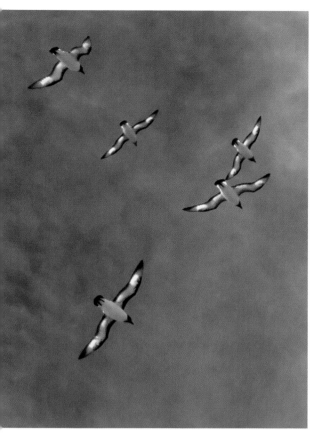

*Two species of petrel are endemic to the islands, the spectacled petrel on Inaccessible Island and the Atlantic petrel on Gough.*

M ountainous, beautiful and undisturbed, with spectacular steep cliffs and boulder beaches, Gough and Inaccessible islands are havens for nesting birds. Two of the most important seabird colonies in the world, the southern Atlantic islands are major breeding sites for the northern rockhopper penguin, petrel, puffin and albatross.

The fur seal and elephant seal are native breeding marine mammals, but no reptiles, amphibians, or native terrestrial mammals are found on the two islands. The only introduced mammal is the house mouse, which has increased in average size and thrives on the islands. Gough Island has 2 endemic species of land birds; there are at least 10 endemic invertebrate species on Inaccessible Island.

Sealers and whalers visited in the late 18th and early 19th centuries while hunting the native fur seal and southern right whale. Despite these visitations, the islands have never been inhabited.

### United Kingdom

**Total protected area:**

983,232 acres

**Significance:**

Gough and Inaccessible Islands are among the most important seabird colonies in the world.

*Near the islands' coastal cliffs, where salt spray from the sea is constant, the landscape is dominated by high tussock grassland.*

*Biological research and weather monitoring are the only activities permitted on the island, which remains an undisturbed ecosystem.*

*"House mice, introduced accidentally on Gough by sealers during the 19th century, have become extremely abundant in all the habitats of the island. They have evolved to a large body size and are thought to have a significant impact on the island's invertebrates and plants. But even more frightening, it has recently been shown that they predate on chicks of winter breeding sea birds."*

—Marie-Helene Burle, research biologist

# SERENGETI NATIONAL PARK

*Although male lions are larger than females—and more visible, with their manes—females often do the majority of the pride's hunting.*

*"We walked for miles over burnt out country ... Then I saw the green trees of the river, walked two miles more and found myself in paradise."*

—Stewart Edward White, American hunter, 1913

## Tanzania

**Total protected area:**

3,648,016 acres

**Significance:**

Serengeti National Park is home to 70 larger mammals, including blue wildebeests, gazelles, zebras and buffalos.

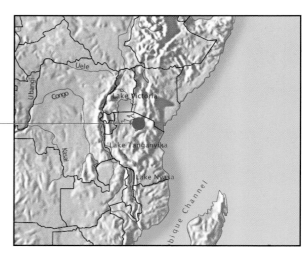

*A group of zebras finds extra protection in a herd of wildebeests.*

The savanna of the Serengeti is an extraordinary ecosystem where a spectacular massive migration of wildlife occurs each year across vast plains. Immense herds of herbivores—wildebeest, gazelles and zebras—pursued by their predators—lions, hyenas and jackals—migrate between grazing grounds in one of the most impressive natural events in the world, a phenomenon sometimes also called the Circular Migration.

Famous as the site of the greatest concentration of large mammals in the world, an ecosystem essentially unchanged since the Pleistocene, the Serengeti is an important center of scientific research. In the late 1950s, Dr. Bernhard Grzimek, president of the Frankfurt Zoological Society, and his son Michael, with filmmaker Alan Root, conducted pioneering work in aerial surveys of wildlife, resulting in the best-selling book and film *Serengeti Shall Not Die*.

*One and a half million wildebeests migrate every year in one the of largest mass movements on earth, traveling up to 1,000 miles in all.*

# RAIN FORESTS OF THE ATSINANANA

## Madagascar

**Total protected area:**

Not available

**Significance:**

80% to 90% of the island's species are found only in Madagascar.

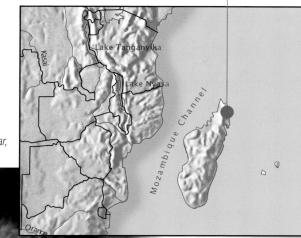

At least 25 species of lemur, all of which are endemic to Madagascar, are found in the lush rain forests of Atsinanana.

During mating season, male ring-tailed lemurs coat their tails with strong-smelling secretions and brandish them to assert their dominance; tails are also carried upright to keep troops together.

As many as 90 percent of the species found in Madagascar's rain forest, including its lemurs, are unique to the island, having evolved in isolation. These six national parks are representative of the most important habitats of the island's plant and animal life, which includes many rare and threatened species. Rapid deforestation as land has been cleared for farming has resulted in a drastic loss of habitat for the lemur, among others. Only 8.5 percent of eastern Madagascar's original rain forest remains. The remnants of the forest that the Atsinanana site protects are crucial to the preservation of the unique ecosystems and biodiversity of Madagascar, the fourth-largest island in the world. The site is a refuge for all types of lemurs, which today are illegal to hunt or capture for trade.

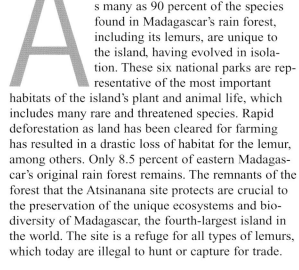

Red ruffed lemurs have a repertoire of sounds that they use to alert or warn each other, including grunting, gurgling and cackling.

# KEOLADEO NATIONAL PARK

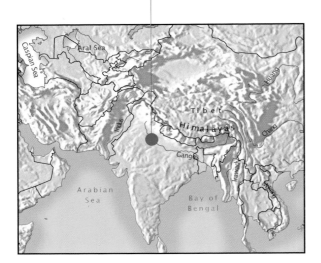

## India

**Total protected area:**

7,100 acres

**Significance:**

Keoladeo is considered to be one of the world's finest areas for birds, with a unique collection of some 364 species.

*Keoladeo is one of the only wintering grounds of the western population of Siberian crane. There is a thriving eastern population in Jiangxi, China.*

*White-throated kingfishers subsist on crabs, frogs, lizards and insects, as well as fish. They make precision dives for their prey, whether in water or grass, and can hover before plunging.*

*"With so many demands on water, maintenance of inflow during drought is often a major problem, even at Keoladeo National Park, one of the most actively protected wetlands in Asia."*

—BirdLife International

This park, once a private duck-hunting reserve for maharajas, is a major wintering ground for aquatic birds from Afghanistan, Turkmenistan, China and Siberia. It is an artificially created marsh, built in the 1850s for the maharaja and fed by a system of canals, sluices and dykes.

Designated a bird sanctuary in 1956, Keoladeo is now well known as the nesting place for thousands of rare and highly endangered birds during the winter. A breeding site for herons, storks and cormorants, the park, with its rich aquatic vegetation, is also a winter home for large numbers of migrant ducks. The critically endangered Siberian crane is one of the 364 species of birds that have been recorded in the park, which is also home to macaques and langurs.

*Every year during the monsoon season, river flooding washes millions of fish-fry into the park's canal system and marshes, providing the major source of food for many of the wading birds.*

# WET TROPICS OF QUEENSLAND

## Australia

**Total protected area:**
2,210,160 acres

**Significance:**
Australia's richest fauna is found in the Wet Tropics, home to both tree-kangaroo species.

*Of the nine species that are endemic to the rain forests of the Wet Tropics region, four are species of ringtail possum.*

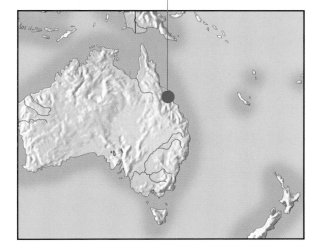

*Kookaburras' beaks, which make them such effective predators, grow up to 4 inches (10 cm) long, more than a fifth of their body length.*

*Rainbow lorikeets typically congregate in large groups, but separate into pairs for nesting, for which they often find a tree hollow.*

The Wet Tropics site protects Australia's remaining rain forest, which stretches along the continent's northeast coast. It is considered the most important ecosystem in the world for primitive flowering plants, with some 90 species of orchids, as well as the largest and smallest cycad in the world. The site is now the only habitat for some rare and endangered species. The various types of rain forest found in the region include multi-storied vine forests and, at the higher, wetter altitudes, forests of ferns. The Wet Tropics also contain Wallaman Falls, the highest waterfall in Australia.

The flightless Australian cassowary, one of the largest birds in the world, is among the 370 species of bird found in the Australian rain forest. The site is also home to about a third of the continent's mammal species, including green possums, fierce marsupial cats, tree-climbing kangaroos and rare bats. Various reptiles—the taipan, the estuarine crocodile and the death adder—are also found there. Today, the region is considered vulnerable to the threat of invasive pest species and deforestation.

# TASMANIAN WILDERNESS

## Australia

**Total protected area:**

3,419,050 acres

**Significance:**

This site is home to the Tasmanian devil, orange-bellied parrot, Pedra Branca skink and swamp galaxias.

*"In the afternoon, about 4 o'clock, we saw land, which we had east by north from us by our estimate ten miles distant. It was very high land."*

—Dutch explorer Abel Tasman, who discovered the island on November 24, 1642

*There is evidence that Aborigines used the Cradle Mountain region as summer hunting grounds during the ice age 10,000 years ago.*

*Tasmania, due in part to its relative isolation, contains many of Australia's most ancient species, the descendants of plants that grew on Gondwana. That ancient landmass separated into Antarctica, Africa, South America, India, Arabia, and Australia some 180 million years ago.*

One of the largest conservation areas in Australia, this site, covering almost 20 percent of the island of Tasmania, is one of the last remaining areas of temperate wilderness in the world. It is an extremely wet, rugged, mountainous region of dense vegetation, with striking rock and land formations caused by glacial erosion. Home to marsupials, arboreal mammals and rodents, the site is also known for its specialized niches for rare plants. The tallest known flowering plant, swamp gum *Eucalyptus regnans*, forms the canopy in areas of pristine tall forest. The island's many endemic species include the famous Tasmanian devil, the world's largest marsupial carnivore; the extremely rare orange-bellied parrot; and the cave-dwelling Tasmanian glow-worm. The region contains rocks with rare plant and amphibian fossils and Pleistocene archaeological sites with evidence of human occupation in limestone caves.

*A nocturnal scavenger, the Tasmanian devil—the world's largest carnivorous marsupial—has powerful jaws and devours entire animals, whether prey or carcasses, including the bones and fur.*

PART I - THE NATURAL WORLD

# SUB-ANTARCTIC ISLANDS

The sub-Antarctic islands southeast of New Zealand lie in what are known as both the stormy latitudes (47 to 52 degrees south) and the albatross latitudes.

## New Zealand

**Total protected area:**

188,932 acres

### Significance:

The islands are home to 120 bird species, including the Southern Royal albatross, Gibson's albatross, antipodean albatross, Campbell mollymauk and white-capped mollymauk.

*"To be one of the few people who land on these islands each year is a privilege and a responsibility."*

—The Department of Conservation of New Zealand

This site in the Southern Ocean, southeast of New Zealand, is made up of five groups of highly biodiverse islands (the Snares, Bounty Islands, Antipodes Islands, Auckland Islands and Campbell Island). These remote, undisturbed islands are the nesting grounds of a large number of pelagic seabirds and penguins, and home to 120 species of birds. Much of the bird and plant life is unique to the islands, including endemic albatrosses and cormorants. A highly productive marine ecosystem, the region is also the breeding grounds of the Southern right whale, the rare Hooker sea lion, and the New Zealand fur seal.

Entry to the islands is strictly controlled. Visitors must obtain a permit and then must adhere to a strict minimum-impact code to minimize any effects on the islands' precious organisms, species and habitats.

Rarely seen on land, albatrosses gather in established island colonies to breed, forming large groups. The parents produce a single egg and take turns caring for the chick once it hatches.

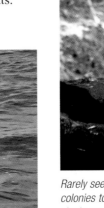

The albatross has a wingspan of 6 1/2 to 11 feet (2 to 3.4 m). They can glide on the ocean winds for hours without flapping their wings.

# MANOVO-GOUNDA ST. FLORIS NATIONAL PARK

Known for its rich wildlife, Manovo–Gounda St. Floris National Park is a vast stretch of savanna between East and West Africa. The region's varied habitats are home to black rhinoceroses, elephants, lions, wild dogs, red-fronted gazelles and buffalo, as well as some of Africa's most endangered mammal species: the small forest elephant, the leopard, and the cheetah. Various waterfowl species live in the park's northern floodplains.

The site was added to the World Heritage in Danger list because of the many elephants and black rhinoceroses that have been killed. The West African black rhinoceros population fell from an estimated 70,000 in the late 1960s to only 2,410 individuals in 2004. On July 7, 2006, the World Conservation Union (IUCN) announced the near extinction of the black rhino, which once ranged across the savannas of West Africa. Heavy poaching has also decimated the park's leopard and crocodile populations.

## WORLD HERITAGE IN DANGER

### Central African Republic

**Threat:**

The park's wildlife—including the rare black rhino—has been heavily poached.

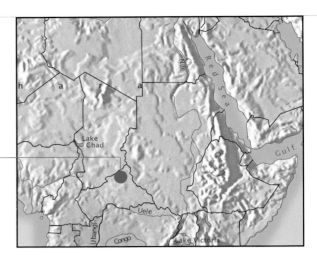

Spotted hyenas, the largest of the hyena species, are fast runners who hunt in packs, isolating a herd animal and then chasing it down.

Most female elephants give birth to a calf every two to four years. The cows live in family herds, raising young calves, while the adult males typically roam.

When hunting, cheetahs often scan the grasslands for signs of their prey, primarily antelopes. Their eyesight is extremely keen.

# ARABIAN ORYX SANCTUARY

The Arabian Oryx Sanctuary in Oman was removed from the World Heritage List in 2007 because of the country's decision to reduce the sanctuary to a tenth of its original size. The sanctuary is the only site to have been removed from the list. The World Heritage Committee considered the resulting loss of habitat to have destroyed the value of the site. The Arabian oryx, which had become extinct in the wild in 1972, was reintroduced in 1982 into the protected desert area, a site that is also home to Arabian wolves, honey badgers, ibex and the largest population of Arabian gazelle in the wild. Though the reintroduction of a free-ranging herd of oryx to the wild was initially a success, the population has since declined to fewer than 70 animals as a consequence of poaching and the development of nearby oil fields.

## Oman

**Total protected area:**
Approximately 6,795,400 acres

**Significance:**
The site is now the last home of the wild Arabian oryx.

The Phoenix Zoo in the United States is credited with having saved the Arabian oryx from extinction. Since starting the first captive-breeding herd with only 9 animals in 1962, it has had more than 200 successful births.

*"In October 1972, a motorized hunting party from outside Oman killed or removed this last herd of oryx. The oryx no longer occurred in the wild."*

—The Arabian Oryx Project

*Oryx were reintroduced after suffering extinction in the wild; once, they roamed the width of the desert in numerous small herds.*

*The largest indigenous mammal in the region, oryx can subsist on desert plants with no other source of water for months.*

*"The World Heritage Committee on Thursday took the unprecedented decision of removing a site from UNESCO's World Heritage List. The Arabian Oryx Sanctuary (Oman), home to the rare antelope, today became the first site to be deleted since UNESCO's 1972 Convention concerning the Protection of the World Cultural and Natural Heritage entered into force."*

—World Heritage Center, June 28, 2007

*Oryx eat various perennial grasses that grow sparsely on the stony desert plateau in central Oman along with acacia trees.*

# BELIZE BARRIER REEF RESERVE SYSTEM

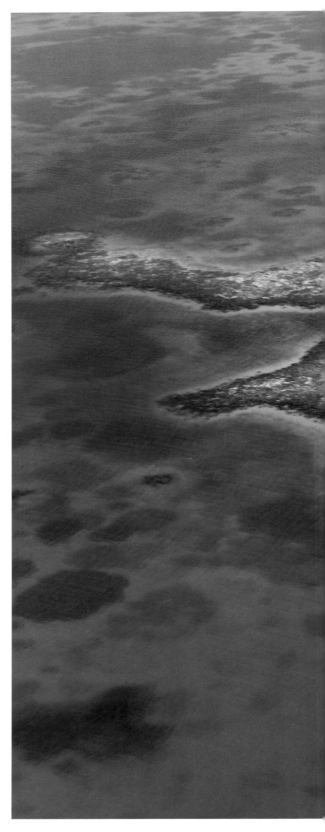

The seven sites that make up the Belize Barrier Reef Reserve System are each composed of the reef itself, which is the largest barrier reef in the northern hemisphere, as well as offshore coral atolls, sand cays, mangrove forests, coastal lagoons and estuaries. Together, these varied habitats represent the reef's evolutionary development, and display examples of fringe, atoll and barrier reef types. The reserve is an important refuge for marine turtles, manatees and American marine crocodiles, all threatened species.

The barrier reef ecosystem is threatened by over-exploitation by fishing and tourism. Overcollecting and damage from boat anchors has resulted in signs of stress on the reefs.

*Iconic of coral reef fauna, the Moorish idol prefers to feed from flat reefs, where it searches for sponges and aquatic invertebrates.*

## Belize

**Total protected area:**

237,962 acres

**Significance:**

This reef system is home to 70 hard coral species and 36 soft coral species.

*The Belize Barrier Reef is home to more than 500 species of fish, 65 varieties of stony coral and 350 types of mollusks.*

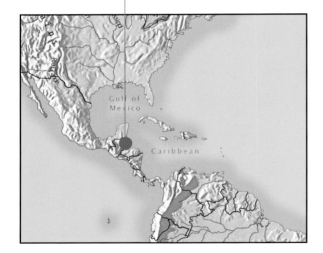

*"This government will ensure that the Belize Barrier Reef lives on for generations to come, and like you rightly pointed out, sometimes we, the politicians, lack the political will to ensure the well being of the reef but we will do all that is possible to ensure marine sustainability and a healthier reef."*

—Gaspar Vega, Deputy Prime Minister and Minister of Natural Resources and the Environment of Belize, March 2008

Sometimes mistaken for coral, brightly colored sponges are plentiful in the reef system.

Extending along Belize's coastline for 185 miles (298 km), the Belize Barrier Reef occupies a substantial portion of the Mesoamerican Barrier Reef System, which is second only to Australia's Great Barrier Reef in size.

"It is one of the few places left where you can observe nature at its best, but it is nonetheless under threat."

—Coral reef researcher Julianne Robinson, National Geographic Society

Angelfish are among the most plentiful fish found in the reef system. Gray angelfish, which feed on sponges, are a common sight.

# WHALE SANCTUARY OF EL VIZCAINO

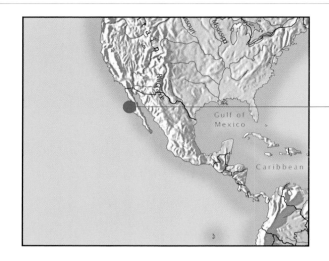

## Mexico

**Total protected area:**

916,637 acres

**Significance:**

The region is an important wintering site for gray whales.

The El Vizcaino sanctuary, halfway down the coast of the Baja California peninsula, was created in 1971 to provide a refuge for the migrating whales that gathered there. Gray whales make the long journey from the Bering Sea to Baja each year, starting out in October and reaching the site in early January, after traveling along some 12,500 miles (20,116 km) of coastline. The marine ecosystems protected by the site are exceptionally interesting. The coastal lagoons of Ojo de Liebre and San Ignacio shelter four endangered species of marine turtle, and are also major breeding and wintering sites for the gray whale, blue whale, harbor seal, California sea lion and northern elephant seal.

*"It's a unique site on a worldwide scale, for species habitat and for its natural beauty, which is also a value to be preserved."*

—Ernesto Zedillo,
president of Mexico, March 2000

*A coastal mammal, the California sea lion feeds on crustaceans such as shrimp, octopus and fish. When hunting, it dives underwater for up to 9 minutes at a time.*

*The brown pelican, which migrates south to Baja California, was listed as endangered in 1973. After declaring the bird endangered, biologists observed an increase in pelican nesting success, which has restored the birds' population.*

# THE GULF OF CALIFORNIA

## Mexico

### Total protected area:

4,541,580 acres

### Significance:

The Gulf of California is home to 39 percent of the world's total species of marine mammals.

*The common bottlenose dolphin—which makes its home in warm waters and tropical climates—communicates using ultrasonic pulses and sounds.*

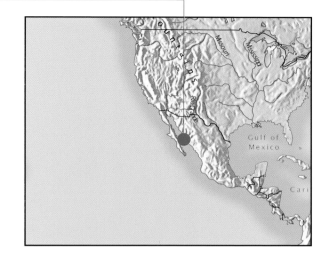

Located in northeastern Mexico's Gulf of California, the islands of the Sea of Cortez are an extraordinary natural laboratory for the study of speciation and oceanographic processes. The 244 islands, islets and coastal areas make up the third largest World Heritage marine site and are home to a third of the world's marine cetacean species and 39 percent of its marine mammals. The site contains 695 vascular plant species, more than any other World Heritage marine site, and 891 species of fish, as well as an abundance of bird species. The blue whale, humpback whale, killer whale, sperm whale and gray whale all visit the area.

*"It is the world's aquarium."*

—French explorer Captain Jacques Cousteau

*A peninsula protruding into the gulf across from the tip of Baja California, Mazatlan is known as the "Pearl of the Pacific."*

*The Loreto Bay Marine Park, located off the Gulf of California, was named a wildlife protected area in 1996 by the Mexican government.*

# LAKE BAIKAL

The oldest and deepest large lake in the world, Lake Baikal is also one of the most biologically diverse. Known as "the Galápagos of Russia," the lake has great scientific value and contains extraordinary fauna because of its isolation and its age (25 million years). Situated near the Mongolian border in southeast Siberia, and walled in by mountains, it is 5,577 feet (1,700 m) deep, and contains 20 percent of the world's unfrozen fresh water.

## Russia

### Total protected area:

21,745,000 acres

### Significance:

Lake Baikal is the oldest and deepest lake in the world and contains 20 percent of the world's unfrozen fresh water.

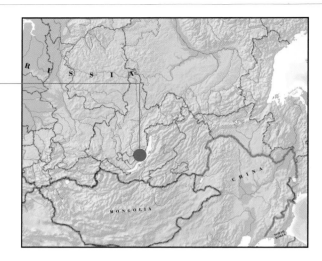

The white marble cliffs of Cape Burkhan lie on the western coast of Olhan Island, the largest island in Lake Baikal.

Lake Baikal's aquatic fauna is some of the strangest in the world, including 255 species of shrimp-like amphipods, 147 species of snail and 80 species of flatworm. The water is filtered by millions of tiny crustaceans, *Epischura baicalensis*, which form 96 percent of the zooplankton. The lake also has deep hydrothermal vents that are home to unique species of sponges. Sixty percent of the lake's 1,200 species are endemic, among them the nerpa, a freshwater seal that is found only in Lake Baikal.

*"I wish to congratulate President Putin for his decision. By altering the course of the oil pipeline, the Russian Federation shows its commitment to joining international efforts to protect the common heritage of humanity and to promote sustainable development. UNESCO and its World Heritage Centre appreciate the spirit of cooperation shown by the Russian Federation in seeking to protect its natural environment and freshwater resources."*

—UNESCO's Director-General Koïchiro Matsuura, April 28, 2006

Siberians who live on the shores of Lake Baikal practice shamanism. They will tie colorful bits of cloth to trees as signs of fortune, protection and healing.

# PLITVICE LAKES NATIONAL PARK

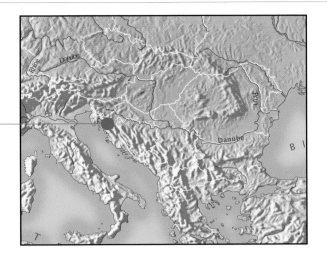

## Croatia

**Total protected area:**

72,850 acres

**Significance:**

Natural dams of travertine have created a series of beautiful lakes, caves and cascades.

*"The lakes were formed by the Black Queen, answering people's prayers by making the rain pour and pour in the valley after a sultry oppression sat over the fields and mountains for months, drying up the Crna Rijeka (Black River)."*

—Legend of the foundation of the Plitvice Lakes

Croatia's Plitvice Lakes, situated in a river basin of limestone and dolomite, consist of a series of 16 lakes created over the last 4,000 years as natural dams were formed by the river's slow deposition of travertine barriers. Linked by cascades and waterfalls, the variously sized lakes feature travertine-roofed and vaulted caves. The geological processes that sculpted the striking and characteristic shapes of the park's lakes, caves and waterfalls continue today. The lakes are also famous for their distinctive colors, which change regularly, ranging from azure to gray, depending on the organisms in the water, its mineral content and the angle of sunlight. The surrounding forests of beech and fir are home to bears, wolves, wild cats, otters and many types of rare birds.

With the outbreak of war in 1991, the site was deserted, then subsequently occupied, and many of the facilities were destroyed. It was placed on the World Heritage in Danger list in 1992 but withdrawn in 1996. Today, the numerous tourists who visit the lakes and waterfalls every year are the only threat to the unspoiled nature of the park.

*A chain of 16 continuous lakes linked by waterfalls, Plitvice Lakes National Park extends between the mountains of Mala Kapela and Licka Pljesevica.*

*The highest waterfall in Plitvice Lakes National Park is between 223 and 256 feet (68–78 m) high.*

# DANUBE DELTA

## Russia

**Total protected area:**

1,678,394 acres

**Significance:**

The delta is home to millions of birds that congregate from around the world during the migration seasons.

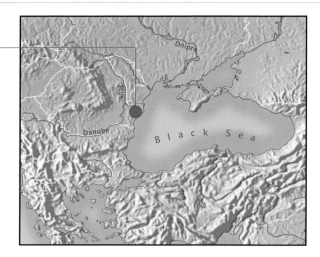

The Danube Delta expands seaward at a rate of 88 to 100 feet (24–30 m) each year.

As it reaches the Black Sea, the Danube River forms Europe's largest and best-preserved delta. The region is also the largest continuous marshland in Europe. Narrow channels rich with aquatic vegetation connect a series of freshwater lakes; to the south, a sandbar separates large, brackish lagoons from the sea. The Danube constantly carries alluvial deposits into the delta, reshaping the riverbanks and sandbars. The European Commission has recognized the river as the "single most important non-oceanic body of water in Europe."

The delta's habitat types include a great expanse of reed beds, willow and poplar forests, meadows and sandy and muddy beaches. Millions of birds come from all over the world to lay their eggs. The site hosts more than 300 species of birds, including cormorant, pelican, great white heron, red-footed falcon and ibis. Its numerous lakes and marshes are home to 45 freshwater fish species.

After beginning work on a channel in 2004 to create a new navigable link from the Black Sea to the Ukrainian section of the Danube Delta, Ukraine recently complied with the European Union's request that the project be shut down so it would not damage the delta's fragile ecosystem.

*"The last worthy deed of the Danube, so rich in marvels, is the Delta."*

—Romanian geographer
Simion Mehedinti (1869–1962)

The Danube Delta is home to an array of wildlife, including the endangered Dalmatian pelican, which breeds and winters in the wetlands.

# GLACIER BAY NATIONAL PARK AND PRESERVE

*Glacier Bay, which was designated a World Heritage site in 1992, contains the northern, southern and western slopes of Mount Fairweather (15,300 feet / 4,663 m).*

G lacier Bay National Park is part of a tremendous reserve of glaciers and high peaks situated on the border between Alaska and Canada. Mostly undisturbed wilderness, the region contains high mountain ranges, deep fjords, coastal beaches with protected coves and freshwater lakes. Rapid glacial retreat in Glacier Bay over the last 200 years has resulted in the formation of 16 tidewater glaciers. Eight marine mammals are found in the preserve, including harbor seals, Stellar sea lions and humpback whales—one of the region's only endangered species—which have been studied and monitored since the 1970s. In 1968, an attempt to reintroduce sea otters in the bay failed.

## United States and Canada

**Total protected area:**

23,969,000 acres

**Significance:**

Of the world's 30 tidewater glaciers, 16 are found in Glacier Bay National Park.

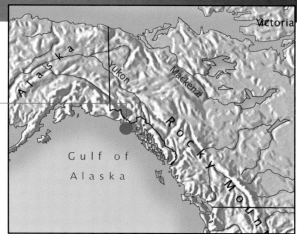

*"We found a compact sheet of ice as far as the eye could distinguish."*

—Captain George Vancouver, 1794

*The steep peaks and glacial valleys of Skagway, Alaska, were formed more than 115,000 years ago by advancing and retreating glaciers.*

The park has four terrestrial habitats: wet tundra, coastal forest, alpine tundra and glaciers and ice fields. It is home to gray wolves, brown and black bears, wolverines, Canadian lynx, black-tailed deer, river otters, moose and mountain goats.

European explorers and fur traders began visiting the area in the 18th century. In 1794 British explorer Captain George Vancouver reported that Glacier Bay was almost entirely iced over. Naturalist John Muir explored the area in 1879 and found that the ice had retreated dramatically. Scientific studies of glacial retreat were first undertaken in 1890.

# ILULISSAT ICEFJORD

## Denmark

**Total protected area:**

994,350 acres

**Significance:**

This is the site of one of the fastest moving and most active glaciers in the world.

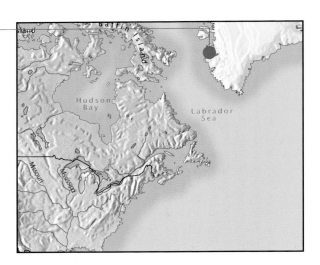

*Ilulissat is the third largest city in Greenland. This fishing haven lies 186 miles (300 km) north of the Polar Circle, on the coast of Disko Bay.*

The 99,435-acre (40,240 ha) Ilulissat Icefjord is the outlet to the sea of Sermeq Kujalleq, one of the fastest moving and most active glaciers in the world. North of the Arctic Circle on Greenland's west coast, it annually produces 10 percent of all of the calf ice in Greenland, more than any other glacier except those in Antarctica. The site consists of a huge ice sheet and a fast-moving glacial ice-stream that regularly calves into a fjord full of icebergs—a natural phenomenon that occurs only in Greenland and Antarctica. Scientific studies of the glacier have helped to develop our understanding of climate change and ice cap glaciology.

*Some of Greenland's fjords are as deep as 2,600 feet (800 m); their steep slopes can rise as high as 394 feet (120 m).*

*The Ilulissat Icefjord is an impressive remnant of the last ice age of the Quaternary Period, which occurred roughly 1.8 million years ago.*

*"Greenland was perceived as this huge solid place that would never melt. In the U.S., global warming is a tomorrow issue. For us working here, it hits you like a ton of bricks when you see it."*

—Dr. Robert Corell,
chair of the steering committee
for the Arctic Climate Impact Assessment

*The waters around Greenland are home to the majority of the icebergs in the North Atlantic.*

# GREAT BARRIER REEF

The Moorish idol is native to the shallow waters off the Australian coast. It uses its long snout to eat coralline algae in rocky reefs.

The most extensive stretch of coral reef in the world, the Great Barrier Reef is famous for its biological diversity and beauty. On Australia's northeast coast, the reef system, which extends to Papua New Guinea, comprises some 3,400 individual reefs, including 760 fringing reefs and approximately 300 coral cays. The reef contains over 1,500 species of fish, 400 species of coral, and 4,000 species of mollusk, as well as a variety of sponges, anemones, marine worms and crustaceans. The humpback whale, minke whale, killer whale and bottlenose dolphin all live around the reef. The area is also a major feeding ground for the dugong, and a nesting ground for the large green turtle, both of which are threatened by extinction.

The most significant threat to the Great Barrier Reef is climate change. In 1998 and 2002 massive coral bleaching events—thought to be the result of rising ocean temperatures—damaged roughly 5 percent of the reef. As many as 1.9 million tourists and some 4.9 million recreational visitors visit the Great Barrier Reef every year.

## Australia

**Total protected area:**

86,165,646 acres

**Significance:**

The world's largest collection of coral reefs, the Great Barrier Reef contains some 400 different types of coral.

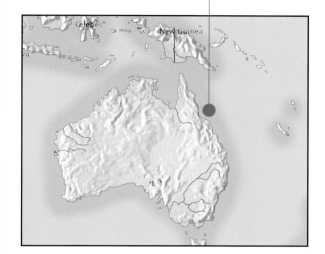

The green sea turtle, which makes its home in warm coastal waters around reefs and inlets, feeds on marine grasses and sea algae.

*"We were called up with the alarming news of the ship being fast ashore upon a rock, which she in a few moments convinced us of by beating very violently against the rocks."*

—Discovery of the Great Barrier; excerpt from English naturalist and botanist Joseph Banks' journal, when the ship *Endeavour* ran aground on the Great Barrier on June 11, 1770

The blacktip reef shark of Australia is relatively small, reaching a length of only about 4.5 feet (1.4 m).

Although threatened by coastal development and overfishing, the Great Barrier Reef contains an array of aquatic life, including the blue spine unicorn fish.

# IGUAÇU NATIONAL PARK

## Brazil and Argentina

**Total protected area:**

420,080 acres

**Significance:**

These two parks share 275 natural falls over which flow 6.5 million liters of water per second.

*One of the world's most impressive waterfalls,* Garganta del Diablo—*the Devil's Throat—plummets from more than 260 feet high (80 m) and emits a mist visible up to 4 miles (7 km) away.*

Brazil's verdant Iguaçu National Park and Argentina's neighboring Iguazú National Park contain some of the most spectacular waterfalls in the world. Forming 150 to 300 cataracts, the Iguazú River plummets over a massive semicircular ledge, continuously carving steps into the gigantic basalt staircase below. The cloud of spray and mist produced by the waterfalls creates a super-humid microclimate and a habitat for lush growth.

In the now-deforested river valley, the park forms an island of humid subtropical rain forest, with characteristic tree ferns, epiphytes and lianas. It is home to coatimundi, ocelots, jaguars, pumas and American tapirs. The park is also a refuge for rare and endangered species such as the harpy eagle, giant otter and giant anteater.

*"I had seen photographs many years ago, but no one can know how it is without coming here and seeing it. It is unbelievably beautiful."*

—U.S. president Bill Clinton, after visiting Iguaçu Falls in August 2001

*At a series of cataracts along the Iguaçu River, water pours over the falls at a rate of up to 450,000 cubic feet (12,700 cu m) per second during the rainy season.*

# MOSI-OA-TUNYA / VICTORIA FALLS

Victoria Falls, or as the locals call it, *Mosi-oa-Tunya*—"the smoke that rises"—is a magnificent series of waterfalls that forms the natural border between Zambia and Zimbabwe, where the Zambezi River cascades down a series of basalt gorges. When the river is in full flood (in February and March), the water pouring over the falls forms the largest sheet of falling water in the world. The plume of iridescent mist can be seen more than 12 miles (20 km) away.

Zambia's Mosi-oa-Tunya National Park contains the banks of the Zambezi River above the falls and a series of deep zigzag basalt gorges below them. The herds of elephants that live in Zimbabwe's neighboring Zambezi Park cross the river into Zambia during the dry season. The parks are also home to buffalo, giraffe, wildebeest, zebra, baboons and occasional lions and leopards. Large populations of hippopotamuses and crocodiles occupy the river above the falls. The gorges below the falls house 35 species of raptors, including black eagles and peregrine falcons, as well as black storks.

*The Victoria Falls (Zambezi) Bridge spans the gorge and connects the nations of Zambia and Zimbabwe, providing access for train, automobile and foot traffic.*

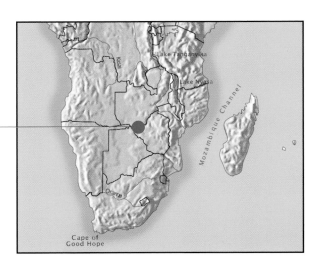

*Twice as wide and deep as Niagara Falls, Victoria Falls plunges to a maximum drop of 355 feet (108 meters) into a chasm.*

*"... scenes so lovely that they must have been gazed upon by angels in their flight."*

—Scottish explorer Dr. David Livingstone, who visited the falls in 1855 and named them for Queen Victoria

## Zimbabwe and Zambia

**Total protected area:**

16,950 acres

**Significance:**

The massive Victoria Falls is perhaps the most spectacular waterfall in the world.

# LAKE MALAWI NATIONAL PARK

Traditional fishing methods are allowed in Lake Malawi National Park because up to 40,000 Malawians depend upon fishing for their livelihood.

## Malawi

**Total protected area:**

23,227 acres

**Significance:**

Lake Malawi contains the largest number of fish species of any lake in the world.

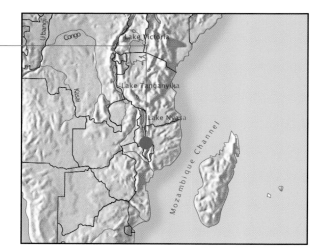

Lake Malawi is extraordinary for the sheer number of fish species it contains—more than any other lake in the world—most of which are found nowhere else in the world. There are an estimated 900 species of cichlids in the lake, of which more than 90 percent are endemic. Cichlids are very territorial, brightly colored fish that are sought after in the aquarium trade. They are comparable to the Galapagos Islands' finches in their importance to the study of evolution, because the numerous species that have developed are outstanding examples of adaptive radiation.

Lake Malawi is also extremely deep and clear. The national park, at the southern end of the lake's great expanse, protects much of the lake's rich aquatic life, but deforestation, erosion and over-fishing have degraded some of the freshwater habitats.

Many cichlids that have been released outside of their natural range have become nuisance species, as is the case with tilapia in the southern United States, which compete with native fish and, by eating certain types of aquatic plants, affect the local flora.

Established as a national park in part to protect the area's aquatic life, the freshwater lake contains 30 percent of all known cichlid species.

The ninth-largest lake in the world, Lake Malawi extends for 348 miles (560 km) and accounts for one-fifth of the area of the nation of Malawi. The lake lies within Africa's Western Rift Valley.

# SHARK BAY

A stop on the migration routes of humpback and southern right whales, Australia's Shark Bay is especially rich in marine fauna. There are large populations of sharks, particularly hammerheads and tiger sharks. Dugongs also inhabit the bay, as do various rays, including manta rays.

At the westernmost point of the Australian continent, Shark Bay is a group of inlets and bays, divided by islands and peninsulas, on the Indian Ocean. It is exceptional for its vast sea grass beds, the largest and richest in the world; its salinity, which is almost twice that of normal seawater; and its abundance of "living fossils," microorganisms that form microbial mats and cement together to form stromatolites. Among the oldest forms of life on earth, stromatolites are mineralized colonies of algae that form hard, dome-shaped deposits. Along the coastline of the bay are high cliffs, sandy plains, and narrow sandy beaches. The ecosystems of the region have developed over a long period in isolation. Some of Australia's threatened mammals are found on the islands in Shark Bay: burrowing bettongs, hare-wallabies, bandicoots and Shark Bay mice.

Tourism is important to the Australian economy. Today, Monkey Mia, where wild dolphins have been approaching humans since the 1960s, is Shark Bay's most popular and spectacular tourist attraction.

## Australia

**Total protected area:**

5,429,647 acres

**Significance:**

Shark Bay is known for its vast sea grass beds, its high degree of salinity, and its abundance of "living fossils."

Twenty-eight species of shark can be found in Shark Bay, including the world's largest fish—the whale shark—which can grow to a length of 39 feet (12 m).

*"The sea fish that we saw here are chiefly sharks. There is an abundance of them in this particular sound, and I therefore give it the name of Shark's Bay."*

—English explorer William Dampier, the first European to visit the bay, in July 1699

Shark Bay dolphins trap fish on shore and then purposefully beach themselves to catch their prey. More than 2,000 wild dolphins inhabit the bay.

The high salt content of Shark Bay's Hamelin Pool makes it is one of only three places in the world where marine stromatolites live.

# LOS GLACIARES NATIONAL PARK

## Argentina

**Total protected area:**

1,101,843 acres

**Significance:**

The park contains the Patagonian Ice Field, the largest mantle of ice outside of Antarctica, as well as hundreds of glaciers.

*Los Glaciares contains the third largest ice cap in the world (after Greenland and Argentina) and an impressive freshwater reserve.*

Los Glaciares National Park, in the Southern Argentine Andes, is a mountainous area of exceptional beauty, home to both Patagonian forest and steppe. The park also contains the Patagonian Ice Field, the largest mantle of ice outside of Antarctica. In addition to the ice field's 47 glaciers, 13 of which feed into the Atlantic, there are some 200 smaller glaciers. Lake Argentino is one of the park's many glacial lakes, where the glaciers converge and, as huge pieces break off, launch icebergs into the water. Excursion boats and organized tours regularly visit Lake Argentino and some of the park's large glaciers, such as Upsala.

Los Glaciares National Park combines two distinct areas: forests and grassy plains in the east and large glaciers in the west.

*"In my wanderings in the south during those years, I saw exceptionally beautiful places and more than once pondered on the importance that the Nation set aside portions for present and future generations."*

—Argentine Explorer Dr. Francisco Pascacio Moreno (1852–1919)

*The Perito Moreno glacier rises to a height of 190 feet (60 m) and is 14,800 feet (4,500 m) wide.*

# EAST RENNELL

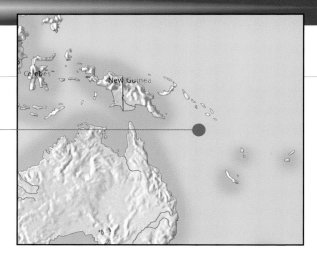

## Solomon Islands

**Total protected area:**

91,500 acres

**Significance:**

Rennell is the world's largest raised coral atoll.

East Rennell is the southern portion of Rennell Island, the largest raised coral atoll in the world. The southernmost of the western Pacific's Solomon Islands, Rennell has an extremely high number of endemic species for an island of its size. Its fauna is important because of the many unique species that have developed in geographic isolation there. The East Rennell site contains all of the larger island's habitats and most of the endemic bird species. It is mostly undisturbed forest. Lake Tegano, a brackish lake on the atoll that also contains many endemic species, is the largest lake in the insular Pacific. Its large basin was once a lagoon within the atoll.

*The large coral atoll of Rennell Island was formed during the Pleistocene period. During that time, tectonic movements raised the ocean floor sufficiently to allow coral growth.*

*With the exception of Papua, New Guinea, the Solomon Islands contain the greatest diversity of fauna species in the Pacific.*

*Lake Tegano, at 18 miles (29 km) long and 6 miles (10 km) wide, is the largest body of enclosed water in the insular Pacific.*

PART I - THE NATURAL WORLD

# TUBBATAHA REEF MARINE PARK

The lionfish, one of Tubbataha Reef's 483 species of fish, uses its long venomous spines to puncture its enemies.

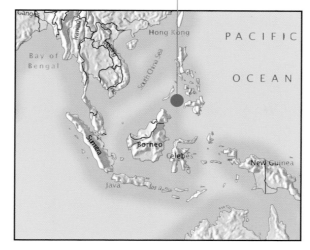

## Philippines

**Total protected area:**

82,000 acres

**Significance:**

This site is home to a pristine coral reef with a high density of marine species.

Tubbataha Reef Marine Park in the Philippines protects a pristine coral reef with a high density of marine species. The park consists of two coral atolls, North and South Reef, divided by a 5-mile (8 km) wide channel, as well as lagoons with beds of sea grass and coralline-sand cays that are nesting sites for birds and turtles. Approximately 400 species of fish, 6 species of shark, including both whitetip and blacktip sharks, 9 species of marine mammals and various marine turtles, including hawksbill and green turtles, inhabit the marine park. Tubbataha, which means "a long reef exposed at low tide" in Samal, has remained relatively pristine, despite its popularity as a diving destination, because of the reef's inaccessibility. Besides ecotourism, no other activities are allowed in the park, which is guarded by armed rangers 24 hours a day, 7 days a week.

By the mid-1990s damage to the reefs from boat anchors was so severe that the coral could not repair itself between dive seasons. In 1996, the government of Japan and the Philippine Department of Tourism funded the installation of 12 concrete blocks to be used as moorings, and in 2003 additional blocks were installed through funds provided by the World Wide Fund for Nature–Philippines.

> *"Tubbataha Reef Marine Park in the Philippines is home to a diversity of marine life that matches or exceeds any other diving location in the world."*
>
> —World Wide Fund for Nature

Tubbataha Reef contains 24,700 acres (10,000 ha) of coral reef. The sea turtles that inhabit the area are known in the Philippines as pawikan.

Dynamite fishing had caused the clownfish to become almost extinct in the Tubbataha Reef. Since becoming protected, the fish have repopulated the area.

# FRASER ISLAND

Named for Captain James Fraser, who survived a shipwreck there in 1836, Fraser Island, just off the eastern coast of Australia, is the largest sand island in the world, at 454,672 acres (184,000 ha). Its combination of tall sand dunes and tropical rain forest scattered with freshwater lakes forms a unique ecosystem. The dune lakes are very unusual in terms of their number, diversity and age. There are 40 "perched" lakes that lie above the water table, which is more than half the number of known perched lakes in the world. Originally formed in wind-scoured depressions, these lakes collect organic matter and over time become impermeable. Some are thought to be up to 300,000 years old.

Nearly 50 species of fern are found on Fraser Island. It is rich in reptile fauna, such as populations of acid frogs and breeding colonies of loggerhead and green turtles. The population of dugongs in the area has fallen off, and overfishing is a concern.

*Fraser Island has been a forest reserve since 1908; it produces kauri and hoop pine, blackbutt and satinay timber.*

*Abundant in reptile fauna, the island harbors lizards, acid frogs, snakes and freshwater river turtles, as well as 354 species of bird, including the endangered ground parrot.*

*Fraser Island's perched lakes, including Lake McKenzie, are up to 300,000 years old and comprise more than half of the known perched lakes in the world.*

## Australia

**Total protected area:**

420,894 acres

**Significance:**

Fraser is home to 40 perched lakes that hold some of the cleanest water in the world.

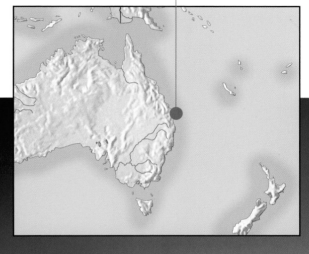

*Lake McKenzie, settled on a sand dune, stretches across more than 370 acres (150 ha) and is more than 16 feet (5 m) deep.*

*Rain forests grow on sand dunes at elevations of 656 feet (200 m), a phenomenon unique to Fraser Island.*

# THE GRAND CANYON

PART I - THE NATURAL WORLD

*The Colorado River has been carving the Grand Canyon for roughly 6 million years. The rock at the base of the canyon is more than 2.5 billion years old.*

**United States**

**Total protected area:**

1,218,420 acres

**Significance:**

The Grand Canyon is the most spectacular gorge on Earth.

The Grand Canyon is one of the best-known natural sites in the world. Carved over millions of years by the Colorado River, the vast gorge plunges to a depth of 6,000 feet (1,828 m) and at its widest points spans a distance of 15 miles (24 km). For both hikers and geologists, the canyon presents a record of the North American continent's early geologic history. Traversing the canyon trail, one travels back in time through the horizontal strata of the four major geologic eras. Both terrestrial and marine fossils from the Paleozoic era can be seen, as well as fossil remains of Cenozoic mammals.

The park is home to rare, endemic and protected plant and animal species, including the California condor, which until recently faced extinction. The last wild condor was captured for a breeding program managed by the San Diego Wild Animal Park and the Los Angeles Zoo, and in 1996 biologists successfully reintroduced the condor in the Grand Canyon.

*"Thus the Grand Canyon is a land of song. Mountains of music swell in the rivers, hills of music billow in the creeks, and meadows of music murmur in the rills that ripple over the rocks. Altogether it is a symphony of multitudinous melodies. All this is the music of waters."*

—John Wesley Powell,
first Grand Canyon expedition, 1869

*Numerous animals call the Grand Canyon home, including the California condor, bighorn sheep, myriad reptiles and many types of rodents, some of which are quite rare.*

# THE CANADIAN ROCKY MOUNTAINS

## Canada

**Total protected area:**

5,713,610 acres

**Significance:**

The parks that make up the Canadian Rockies are home to spectacular mountain peaks, glaciers and lakes, as well as fossil remains.

The Canadian Rocky Mountains are renowned for their glorious scenery and their extraordinary geologic and evolutionary history. They are the northernmost and most heavily glaciated of the Rockies, resulting in a landscape of peaks and U-shaped valleys, lakes and towering waterfalls created by melting glacial ice, and canyons and limestone caves. The Burgess Shale, a fossil site discovered in the mountain strata in 1909, is one of the richest fossil troves in the world, with extremely well-preserved specimens dating back 560 million years to the Cambrian era. About 100,000 fossils have been collected since its discovery, including fossils of long-extinct, previously unknown creatures.

The site combines the national parks of Jasper, Banff, Kootenay and Yoho, as well as four provincial parks. The parks are home to alpine species, such as Rocky Mountain goats and bighorn sheep, and forest mammals, such as moose and caribou. Carnivores include gray wolves, grizzly bears, black bears, lynx and wolverines. The Rockies are also an ideal habitat for birds, such as the golden eagle, the three-toed woodpecker and the mountain bluebird.

*Bighorn sheep live in groups on mountainous ledges. Rams can develop horns more than 3.3 feet (1 m) long.*

*"Wonder, reverence, the feeling that one is nearer the mystery of things—that is what one feels in places of such sublime beauty."*

—J. B. Harkin, Canada's first Commissioner of National Parks, about the Rockies

*Established in 1885, Banff National Park, located in Alberta, Canada, is a majestic Rocky Mountain wilderness, featuring numerous peaks that soar above 8,000 feet (2,400 m).*

The Canadian Pacific Railway built the Fairmont Chateau Lake Louise during the early 1900s. It soon became a magnet for wealthy vacationers.

Moraine Lake is a jewel in Banff National Park's Valley of the Ten Peaks. Seasonally melting glaciers deposit rock flour into the lake, coloring the water turquoise.

# VOLCANOES OF KAMCHATKA

One of the most active volcanic areas on earth, Russia's Kamchatka peninsula contains 200 volcanoes, 30 of which are active. Klyuchevskaya Sopka, at 15,584 feet (4,750 m) is the region's highest volcano. Kronotsky is the most striking example of the symmetrical conical shape worn by many of the Kamchatkan volcanoes. It is a strikingly beautiful region of glaciers, lakes and unpolluted rivers, with unusually diverse wildlife, including large populations of sea otter and brown bear, which live off the salmon that spawn in the area. The rivers of Kamchatka, major spawning grounds, have the greatest concentration of salmonid fish species in the world. Colonies of seabirds, such as Stellar's sea eagle, nest along the coast of the Bering Sea, and many migratory birds use the site as a wintering ground. Kamchatka is home to white-tailed eagles, gyr falcons and peregrine falcons, which all feed on the spawning salmon.

**Russia**

**Total protected area:**

10,818,557 acres

**Significance:**

Kamchatka is among the world's most volcanically active regions.

*Many of Kamachatka's volcanoes are spectacularly active. Over time, mountainside lava flows have transformed the volcanoes into near-perfect cones.*

*The volcanoes Kluchevskoj and Kamen loom above the Kamchatka wilderness. Soaring to 15,042 feet (4,585 m), Kamen is the second-largest volcano on the peninsula, after Klyuchevskaya Sopka.*

# HAWAII VOLCANOES NATIONAL PARK

*Formed by volcanoes, Hawaii is consistently reformed by them. Over the years, lava flows have consumed roads and villages.*

**United States**

**Total protected area:**
229,644 acres

**Significance:**
This national park contains two of the world's most active volcanoes, as well as rare birds and forests of giant ferns.

*A red-hot lava flow from Kilauea spills into the Pacific Ocean, where it hardens amid steam and boiling water. The volcanic edges of the Hawaiian islands regularly collapse into the ocean.*

Established in 1916, Hawaii Volcanoes National Park is a geological showcase of 70 million years of volcanism, migration, and evolution. The park contains two of the most active volcanoes in the world, Mauna Loa and Kilauea. At 13,680 feet (4,170 m), Mauna Loa is an enormous, flat-domed shield volcano that was formed by layers of lava flow. It is considered to be the best example of its type in the world. The region is a continually transforming landscape shaped by volcanic eruptions and lava flows. The site is also known for its rare birds and lush forests of giant ferns. Hawaii is home to a third of the endangered species in the United States.

*"There was a time in the mysterious past when the air was surrounded with spiritual beings and a thin veil divided the living from the dead, the natural from the supernatural. During that time, Pele, goddess of the volcano, came to Hawaii."*

—Hawaiian legend

# MOUNT KENYA

## Kenya

**Total protected area:**

350,939 acres

**Significance:**

This national park contains two of the world's most active volcanoes, as well as rare birds and forests of giant ferns.

*Mount Kenya's main peaks were formed by lava flows which, over time, plugged the vent atop the volcano and were subsequently eroded.*

An extinct volcano that was active more than 2.5 million years ago, Mount Kenya is Africa's second highest peak, rising to 17,057 feet (5,199 m). It has 12 glaciers, which are rapidly receding at the summit, deep glacial valleys, small glacial lakes and forested lower slopes. A snow-capped mountain that straddles the equator, Mount Kenya features regions of rich alpine flora and bamboo forests at its higher altitudes.

Several of the species that live in this afro-alpine ecosystem are found nowhere else in the world. In the lower forest and bamboo zone, white-tailed mongooses, elephants, black rhinoceroses and leopards (which have also been reported in the alpine zone), are all found. The local Kikuyu and Meru peoples consider Mount Kenya holy.

*The Kikuyu and Meru, native peoples of the east African equatorial region, hold Mount Kenya sacred. Its three peaks—Lenana, Batian and Nelion—all soar above 16,000 feet (4,800 m).*

# ULURU-KATA TJUTA NATIONAL PARK

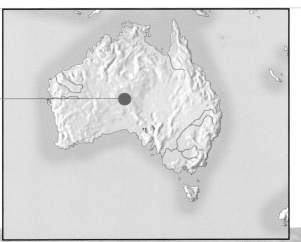

## Australia

**Total protected area:**

327,578 acres

**Significance:**

Uluru—a vast monolith rising from the Australian desert—is perhaps the best known such formation in the world.

*"Uluru is both sacred site and physical wonder. A giant red rock rising from the floor of the vast inland Australian desert, glowing in the face of the sun."*

—Peter Garrett, Australian politician and lead singer of the band Midnight Oil

*Rising 1,142 feet (348 m) above the surrounding flatlands and spanning nearly 6 miles (9.6 km) in circumference, Uluru is the lonely remnant of a prehistoric mountain range.*

This site in central Australia features colossal geologic formations rising from a landscape of red sand plains, dunes and alluvial desert. Uluru is an immense, smooth monolith; Kata Tjuta, west of Uluru, is a group of steep-sided rock domes. Both landforms are sacred to the Pitjantjatjara and Yankunytjatjara, the aboriginal peoples of the area, which are among the oldest human societies in the world. Ancient paintings on Uluru testify to how long the Aborigines have inhabited the region.

The park is considered an outstanding example of traditional hunting-and-gathering patterns of settlement and land use. A network of tracks, said to mark the paths of mythical and ancestral journeys, also cross the park and link Uluru and Kata Tjuta. The park is home to native Australian mammals, such as dingoes, red kangaroos and wallaroos, as well as all five Australian reptile families.

*Uluru's striated sandstone bulk is spectacularly framed by the big sky and barren land of central Australia.*

# THREE PARALLEL RIVERS OF YUNNAN PROTECTED AREAS

## China

**Total protected area:**

4,196,837 acres

**Significance:**

This region of protected areas is at the very epicenter of Chinese biodiversity.

Three of Asia's great rivers—the Yangtze (Jinsha), Mekong and Salween—run through this mountainous region in northwest Yunnan Province, which is one of the most biodiverse temperate regions in the world. Consisting of eight protected areas within the Three Parallel Rivers National Park, the site features deep parallel river gorges at the feet of high, glaciated peaks.

The site is outstanding geologically, with unusual alpine karst caves and sandstone landforms and more than 400 glacial lakes. The region has over 6,000 species of higher plants, a quarter of which were discovered there. It also contains more than 25 percent of the world's animal species and more than 50 percent of China's, with a concentration of rare and endangered animals, such as the Yunnan snub-faced monkey, Asian black bear, red panda and the snow and clouded leopards.

*"Because of its high elevation and the deep gorges of the three rivers, the ecosystem in this region is extremely fragile, and once damaged, is almost impossible to restore."*

—The World Wide Fund for Nature

*The third-longest river in the world, the Yangtze winds roughly 3,900 miles (6,300 km) from the Tibetan Plateau to the East China Sea.*

*The Three Parallel Rivers Protected Area exhibits profound biological and geological contrasts: gorges and peaks, numerous types of rock, and both temperate and tropical flora and fauna.*

# WEST NORWEGIAN FJORDS

## Norway

**Total protected area:**
168,887 acres

**Significance:**
Southwestern Norway is home to many of the world's most spectacular fjords.

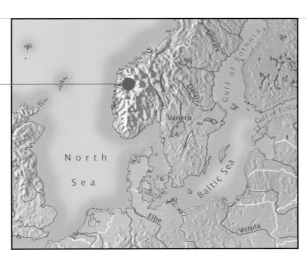

The waters of the Geirangerfjord and the Nærøyfjord are deep; the fjord walls can extend 1,600 feet (490 m) below the water.

Two of the world's longest and deepest fjords, Geirangerfjord and Nærøyfjord, in southwestern Norway, are considered classic fjords of stunning beauty. Waterfalls cascade down the sheer faces of the fjords' crystalline rock walls, which rise out of the sea into a landscape of rugged, wooded mountains and glaciers. Above the tree line, the birch and pine woods and alpine grassland give way to rock, scree and snowfields.

The fjords and their surrounding landscape are known not only for their spectacular scenery, but also as outstanding examples of active glaciation. All of Norway's native deer, including three kinds of reindeer, are found here, as well as Arctic fox, brown bear, lynx, wolverine and otter. The great variety of birds equals the variety of habitats and range of altitudes.

The sheer rock walls of the Geirangerfjord and the Nærøyfjord can reach heights of nearly 4,600 feet (1,400 km) above the Norwegian Sea.

*"We need to protect the Nærøyfjord and Geirangerfjord for our children and all future generations. The fjords are precious and they inspire me. It's so wonderful that they will now be protected for posterity!"*

—British long-distance swimmer Lewis Gordon Pugh, commenting on the fjord's inscription on the World Heritage List

Sightseeing boats cruise the fjords, allowing droves of tourists to witness the hidden splendor of the region.

# JUNGFRAU·ALETSCH·BIETSCHORN

## Switzerland

**Total protected area:**

133,274 acres

**Significance:**

In addition to its outstanding natural beauty, this site offers significant information about how mountains and glaciers are formed.

*Switzerland is famous for its Alps, which rise to more than 15,000 feet (4,600 m) and support unique alpine flora.*

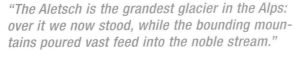

This spectacular site in Switzerland's High Alps contains Europe's largest glacier, the Aletsch, and the most glaciated region of the mountain range, with classic glacial features such as U-shaped valleys, cirques, horn peaks and moraines. There is a wide range of alpine and subalpine habitats. Below the glacial region of rock and snow-covered peaks, the slopes of the mountains are forested by beech, spruce and Scots pine.

The site is known for its excellent examples of plant succession, where plants colonized the land as the glaciers receded. The phenomenon can be seen where forests now meet the moraine left in the wake of the Aletsch Glacier in 1850.

*The 13,642-foot (4,158 m) Jungfrau is served by a cog railway system that negotiates a steep, 4-mile (6.4 km) tunnel to reach the Jungfraujoch station, Europe's highest railway station.*

*"The Aletsch is the grandest glacier in the Alps: over it we now stood, while the bounding mountains poured vast feed into the noble stream."*

—Physicist and glacier explorer John Tyndall, 1860

*The Aletsch Glacier winds through the Alps, ending at an elevation of a little more than 5,000 feet (1,524 m). Ridges of rock and debris mark its ice stream.*

# DORSET AND EAST DEVON COAST

One of the most important geological sites in the world, the cliffs along the Dorset and East Devon coast of Great Britain reveal some 185 million years of the earth's history. Triassic, Jurassic and Cretaceous geological strata are all exposed in the coastal cliffs, as well as classic examples of landforms created by coastal erosion. The site's Jurassic rocks are renowned for the vertebrate fossils that they contain, as well as evidence of marine life during the Jurassic period, when the sea covered the region.

There is also great scientific interest in the site's beaches and their development and other coastal geological features, such as bays, lagoons and landslides. Chesil Beach, one of the most famous of England's pebble beaches, encloses the Fleet lagoon, a huge saline lagoon that is one of the most significant in Europe. Important paleontological discoveries include one of the earliest flying reptiles and marine reptiles, such as ichthyosaurs and pterosaurs.

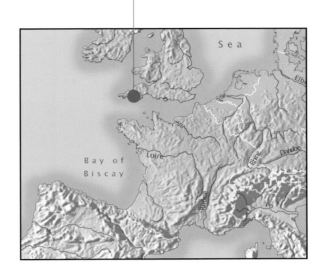

## United Kingdom

**Total protected area:**
6,301 acres

**Significance:**
Devon's coastline is one of the most iconic in the world.

*The lighthouse of the village of Sidmouth has long warned ships off the treacherous cliffs of the Devon coast.*

*The South West Coast Path spans the entirety of the Devon coast; travelers must be careful of the fragile and steep ledges.*

*Imposing and beautiful, the high cliffs of the Devon coast preserve a wealth of fossils and exhibit millions of years of geologic history.*

# YELLOWSTONE NATIONAL PARK

## United States

**Total Protected Area:**

2,220,726 acres

**Significance:**

Its concentration of geysers and hot springs, its wildlife, and landscape make Yellowstone one of the most spectacular parks in the world.

Dotted with hot springs and punctuated by geysers, Yellowstone possesses the largest volcanic system in North America and experienced a super-volcanic eruption 640,000 years ago.

Yellowstone is noted for its herds of wild bison. Some herds spend winters near the warmth of Yellowstone's geysers and hot springs.

Most famous for its geysers, Yellowstone National Park is an extraordinary natural museum of geothermal phenomena, with more than 10,000 examples. An incredible two thirds of the world's geysers are there (approximately 3,000), as well as lava formations, hot springs, mud pots, and fumaroles. It is a "volcanic hot spot" in the most seismically active region of the Rocky Mountains.

Established in 1872 in Wyoming, the park also preserves a natural forest ecosystem that is large enough to support populations of grizzly bear, elk and bison, and perpetuate their survival. Once numbering between 30 and 60 million throughout North America, wild bison populations in the park had increased from fewer than 50 in 1902 to 4,000 by 2003. The threatened whooping crane, bald eagle, and trumpeter swan are also found there. The park is home to mountain lion, lynx, coyote and gray wolf, which was reintroduced in 1994.

Paleontologists have discovered the bones of the prehistoric ancestors of the gray wolves in one of Yellowstone's caves. Nearly 200 species of petrified plants have been found. They are relics of the 25 million years of volcanic ashflows and mudflows that would periodically blanket and petrify the forest.

*"Yellowstone would forever be dedicated and set apart as a public park or pleasuring ground for the benefit and enjoyment of the people."*
—U.S. president Ulysses S. Grant, 1871

A popular park attraction, Morning Glory Pool is so named because its blue water and funnel shape resemble the morning glory flower. Bacteria cause the hot spring's distinctive hue.

# YOSEMITE NATIONAL PARK

## United States

**Total protected area:**

761,783 acres

**Significance:**

One of the first wilderness parks in the U.S., it is known for its enormous granite formations.

At Yosemite, millions of years of geologic uplift and glacial movement have sculpted a deep, U-shaped valley, marked by deep canyons and towering granite domes and monoliths.

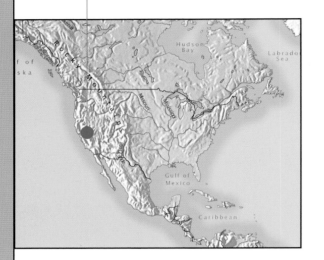

El Capitan rises 7,569 feet (2,307 m) from the Yosemite Valley. Rock climbers come from near and far to test their mettle against the world's largest granite monolith.

Yosemite National Park, in California's Sierra Nevada Mountains, is a gem. One of the United States' first wilderness parks, it contains spectacular waterfalls, cliffs, hanging valleys, lakes and huge granite formations, all carved by glaciers. The enormous rounded granite domes Sentinel Dome and Half Dome rise 3,000 feet and 4,800 feet (900 m and 1450 m), respectively, above the Yosemite Valley floor. El Capitan, a 3,000-foot (1,000 m) vertical rock formation in the valley, is a destination for rock climbers from all over the world.

The park is also home to diverse flora and fauna, including groves of the giant sequoia, the world's tallest-growing species of tree.

Naturalist John Muir, who came to California in 1868, helped spark scientific interest in the Yosemite region and worked to have federal laws passed to protect it. On September 25, 1890, the Yosemite Act was passed, making the sequoia grove and the area outside the valley a national park, the first time land was set aside by the federal government as protected wilderness.

*"The level bottom seemed to be dressed like a garden, sunny meadows here and there, and groves of pine and oak; the river of Mercy sweeping in majesty through the midst of them and flashing back the sunbeams."*

—Environmentalist John Muir (1838–1914), describing the site in 1869

Half Dome—a sheer granite face of 8,836 feet (2,693 m)—is perhaps Yosemite's most prominent landmark.

Autumn in Yosemite is temperate and dry, giving way to a mild but snowy winter. Summer brings witness to persistent thunderstorms.

# GIANT´S CAUSEWAY

North
Sea

### United Kingdom

**Total protected area:**

173 acres

**Significance:**

The 40,000 basalt columns that comprise Giant's Causeway have inspired legends and advanced the knowledge of earth sciences.

*"The giant Finn McCool built the causeway to walk to Scotland to fight his Scottish equivalent Benandonner."*

—Irish legend

*Giant's Causeway's basalt columns can reach heights of 36 feet (12 m). They were formed when the lava plateau they composed cooled.*

The Giant's Causeway is an extraordinary geological formation sweeping along a stretch of coast in Northern Ireland at the foot of high basalt cliffs. Some 40,000 massive black basalt columns thrusting up out of the sea form an enormous promontory of huge polygonal paving stones. This dramatic landscape, which has inspired legends of giants striding over the sea to Scotland, was created some 50 to 60 million years ago by volcanic activity during the Tertiary Period.

Many of the formations are named for objects they resemble: the Giant's Organ and Giant's Boot, the Giant's Eyes, the Shepherd's Steps, the Honeycomb, the Giant's Harp, the Chimney Stacks, the Giant's Gate and the Camel's Hump. An extremely important site in the history of earth science, the Giant's Causeway was introduced to the world in 1693 in a paper presented to the Royal Society by Sir Richard Bulkily, a fellow of Trinity College, Dublin, and was the cause of major controversy in geology in the 18th century.

*The predominantly hexagonal columns of the Giant's Causeway are home to an assortment of unique plant life, including vernal squill and sea spleenwort.*

# TSINGY DE BEMARAHA

n a landscape of undulating hills, abrupt cliffs and limestone pinnacles, this nature reserve in western Madagascar features limestone uplands cut into sharp peaks that form a "forest of rocks." The word *tsingy*, which means pointed peaks in the local Madagascan language, describes the unusual needlelike formations. At the eastern edge of the limestone plateau is the Manambolo River's spectacular gorge and dramatic cliffs. The dense, dry forest is characteristic of the karst region in Madagascar, with species of ebony and wild banana that are found only there. Tsingy de Bemaraha's undisturbed forests are also the habitat for rare and endangered lemurs and birds.

*This precarious bridge spanning the limestone karst is now little used, since only scientists are allowed in Bemaraha Reserve. Some families do reside illegally within the park.*

*Founded as a nature reserve in 1927, Tsingy de Bemaraha is arguably Madagascar's most important biological reserve.*

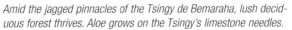

*Amid the jagged pinnacles of the Tsingy de Bemaraha, lush deciduous forest thrives. Aloe grows on the Tsingy's limestone needles.*

## Madagascar

**Total protected area:**

375,600 acres

**Significance:**

This reserve's spectacular karstic landscapes and limestone plateaus are home to rare and endangered animals.

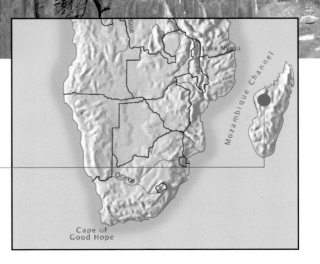

# DINOSAUR PROVINCIAL PARK

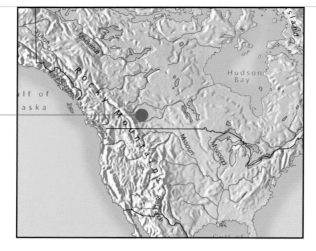

## Canada

**Total protected area:**

18,515 acres

**Significance:**

The fossil beds in this park are the largest in Canada.

*Eons of wind and water eroded the badlands of Dinosaur Provincial Park, exposing millions of years of sedimentary rock and hundreds of dinosaur skeletons.*

*"I was climbing up a steep face about 400 feet high. I stuck my head around a point and there was this skull leering at me, sticking right out of the ground. It gave me a fright."*

—Joseph Tyrrell,
discoverer of the first *Albertosaurus*, 1884

East of Calgary in Alberta's Badlands, Dinosaur Provincial Park contains major fossil discoveries that date back 75 million years. The remains of at least 35 different dinosaur species have been found there, including specimens from every group of dinosaurs from the Cretaceous period. The fossil beds are the biggest in Canada. More than 300 dinosaur skeletons have been excavated from a 17-mile (27 km) stretch of land. Fossil remains of fish, turtles, marsupials and amphibians have also been found at the site. The region is also known for the Badlands' outstanding collection of hoodoos, pinnacles, mesas and buttes—landforms created by erosion in the aftermath of the ice age 15,000 years ago.

*A hoodoo protrudes atop a badlands butte. Coyotes, pronghorn antelopes, mule deer, and cottontail rabbits live on the prairie and amid the distinctive rock formations.*

PART I - THE NATURAL WORLD

# WATERTON GLACIER

Straddling the border between Canada and the United States, to the east of the Continental Divide, Waterton Glacier International Peace Park was created in 1932 by joining Glacier National Park in Montana with Waterton Lakes National Park in Alberta. Dedicated to world peace by Sir Charles Arthur Mander on behalf of the Rotary Club International, the park was created to celebrate peaceful relations and goodwill between Canada, the United States and the Blackfoot Confederacy. The park's mountain ranges rise suddenly from a prairie landscape of rolling grasslands. Its valleys, basins and lakes are of glacial origin. Rich in plant and mammal species, the park contains gray wolf, coyote, cougar, black bear and mink, as well as a population of grizzly bear.

## Canada

**Total protected area:**

671,941 acres

**Significance:**

This park was created to celebrate the friendship among Canada, the United States, and the Blackfoot Confederacy.

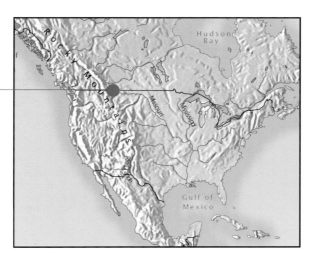

The official symbol of Glacier National Park, the mountain goat is a common sight on the ridges and slopes of Montana and Alberta's Rocky Mountains.

The picturesque Prince of Wales Hotel, built in the 1920s by the Great Northern Railway, graces Waterton Lake, the deepest lake in the Canadian Rockies.

# SANGAY NATIONAL PARK

I n eastern Ecuador, just south of the equator, Sangay National Park contains ecosystems ranging from the tropical rain forests of the Amazon basin to alpine tundra on the mountains of South America's Cordilleras. The topography rises from alluvial fans to foothills to the rugged volcanic zone of the High Andes. Two of the park's three volcanoes—Tungurahua and Sangay—are still active. In 2006 a major eruption resulted in the deaths of a family and two scientists and the destruction of several small villages. It recently erupted again in the

## Ecuador

### Total protected area:

671,941 acres

### Significance:

The park's diverse ecosystems range from tropical rain forest to alpine tundra and include two active volcanoes.

*The turbulent, 17,159-foot (5,230 m) Sangay volcano overshadows tropical rain forests home to jaguar, ocelot, tapir, and pudu deer and countless tropical birds. On Sangay's other sides are canyons which were formed by volcanic ash and considerable rainfall.*

winter of 2008. The site has a rich diversity of species in each region of the park, from the peaks' Andean fox, puma and mountain tapir to the lower forests' spectacled bear, giant otter and jaguar. Sangay is home to rare endemic birds, as well as condor, giant hummingbird and king vulture.

*In 1999 Tungurahua began erupting again after decades of dormancy. The volcano continues to erupt—2006 was a year of particularly violent activity.*

*Tungurahua erupting in November 2006. The 16,479-foot (5,023 m) volcano was once a destination for climbers but has become too dangerous.*

# CANAIMA NATIONAL PARK

**C**anaima National Park in southeastern Venezuela is known for its distinctive tepui, or tabletop, mountain formations, which cover about 65 percent of the park. The tepuis, with their sheer walls and flat tops, rise above the surrounding forested plateau.

## Venezuela

**Total protected area:**

7,400,000 acres

**Significance:**

Canaima is home to the world's highest waterfall and distinctive tabletop mountains.

Water flowing from their summits forms hundreds of waterfalls, including the famous Angel Falls, the highest waterfall in the world at 3,208 feet (978 m), with an uninterrupted drop of 2,648 feet (807 m). So many of the plants that grow on the tepuis' summits are endemic that the region has been recognized as a separate biogeographical entity. Various carnivorous plants are found there, as are more than 3,000 species of ferns and an estimated 500 species of orchids.

*Unknown to the wider world for centuries, Angel Falls is still difficult to vist. Deep in the Venezuelan jungle, the falls can be reached only by airplane, followed by a boat trip upriver.*

*A tepui towers above Canaima National Park. Composed of sandstone and quartzite, tepuis were standing when South America was connected to Africa.*

*The Pemon Indians, indigenous to Canaima National Park, call Angel Falls* Kerepakupai merú, *which means "waterfall of the deepest place."*

*"While on a solo flight November 14, 1933, Angel flew into Devil's Canyon and saw for the first time what was to become known to the world as Angel Falls."*

—Niece of Jimmie Angel and president of the Jimmie Angel Historical Project

# TE WAHIPOUNAMU

Southwest New Zealand's Te Wahipounamu—Maori for "the place of green stone"— is known for its fjords, rocky coasts, towering cliffs and waterfalls, all formed by the mountainous region's successive glaciations. The site contains some of the world's most imposing mountains, including Mount Aspiring, Mount Tasman and Aoraki/Mount Cook, and the fjords of Fiordland National Park, such as Milford Sound, Doubtful Sound and Dusky Sound, some of the finest examples of glaciated landforms in the southern hemisphere.

The forests that cover two-thirds of the park are a mix of beech and podocarps (southern hemisphere conifers), some of which are over 800 years old. Te Wahipounamu is home to two extremely rare birds: the kea, the only alpine parrot in the world, and the endangered takahe, a large flightless bird that was thought to be extinct for 50 years. The New Zealand fur seal, also once hunted to near extinction, now breeds along the southwest coast in huge colonies.

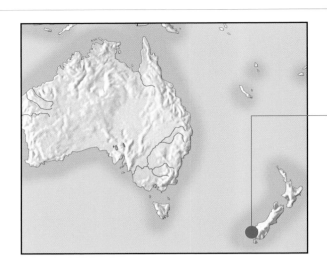

*A panorama of Te Wahipounamu reveals the diverse and rugged landscape of the park, which was formed by tectonic shifts over the past 5 million years.*

*The highest mountain in New Zealand, Aoraki, or Mount Cook, pierces the clouds at 12,316 feet (3,754 m). It was first summited in 1894.*

*A thin, temporary waterfall, the result of tumultuous rainfall, rushes into Milford Sound, on the Tasman Sea. The area is the wettest in New Zealand.*

## New Zealand

**Total protected area:**

6,424,740 acres

**Significance:**

The site contains some of the world's most spectacular scenery, including mountains, fjords, towering cliffs and waterfalls, and rare animal species, including the world's only known alpine parrot.

*The Southern Alps of New Zealand range along nearly the entirety of the South Island of New Zealand. More than 300 glaciers cover these peaks.*

# PURNULULU NATIONAL PARK

## Australia

**Total protected area:**

592,368 acres

**Significance:**

Purnululu is home to impressive beehive-shaped sandstone formations formed by years of erosion.

This national park in Western Australia contains the Bungle Bungle Range—beehive-shaped formations that are outstanding examples of sandstone cone karst and the processes of erosion. The towers of quartz sandstone, with steep sides and domed summits, were formed over a 20-million-year period on a plateau of Devonian sandstone that is approximately 360 million years old. The formations have dark gray stripes, alternating with the orange of the sandstone, which are horizontal bands of crust formed by cyanobacteria (ancient single-celled photosynthetic organisms) and iron oxide on the rock.

Purnululu also contains forested gorges, where palms, orchids and ferns grow, and arid sand plains. Aboriginal Australians have lived in the region for 40,000 years.

*"You can't see what's holding them together. I don't know how to describe it. It is like a place not from this earth."*

—Canyon expert Richard D. Fisher, about the Bungle Bungles of Purnululu

*Numerous creeks run around and through the Bungle Bungle Range. The watercourses in the Purnululu region have supported aboriginal societies for millennia.*

*The sedimentary rock composing the Bungle Bungle Range was deposited some 350 million years ago.*

# KILIMANJARO

Africa's Kilimanjaro is one of the Seven Summits, a group of the seven continents' tallest mountains.

## Tanzania

**Total protected area:**

186,201 acres

**Significance:**

One of the most iconic mountains in the world, Kilimanjaro is also the highest point in Africa.

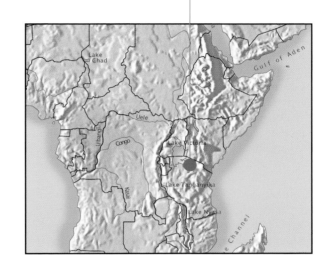

At 19,340 feet (5,895 m), the highest point in Africa, Kilimanjaro is one of the biggest volcanoes in the world. This ice-capped volcanic massif, skirted by forest, rises above the surrounding savanna. It has three main volcanic peaks: Shira, now a plateau; Mawenzi, a craggy peak with steep cliffs overlooking two deep gorges; and Kibo, the most recently active (in the Pleistocene), which has two craters and minor fumaroles, the openings through which hot volcanic gases escape. A plateau known as the Saddle lies between Kibo and Mawenzi, which is a large region of high-altitude tundra. The national park includes the mountain above the tree line and some of the belt of forest that circles the mountain below. Seven of the larger forest mammals have been seen above the tree line, including the Kilimanjaro tree hyrax, grey duiker and eland. Leopards live in the montane forest, and elephants are sometimes seen on the higher slopes. It is a habitat for three primate species: blue monkey, western black and white colobus and bushbaby.

Sitting slightly south of the equator, and rising to 19,340 feet (5,895 m), Kilimanjaro is a site of diverse ecosystems. Jungles flank its lower slopes, and savanna rings its base, which is home to elephants, among other species.

*"That mountain is the most mystical, magical draw to people's imagination. Once the ice disappears, it's going to be a very different place."*

—Douglas R. Hardy, geologist at the University of Massachusetts, about the effect of global warming, February 2001

The Tanzanian government placed this sign on the summit of Kilimanjaro. Some 15,000 people attempt to scale Kilimanjaro every year; roughly 40 percent succeed.

# SAGARMATHA

The summit of Mount Everest—the highest mountain in the world at 29,028 feet (8,848 m)—rises majestically above Sagarmatha National Park in the Himalayan highlands of northeastern Nepal. Sagarmatha, the Nepalese name for Everest, means "goddess of the sky," or "mother of the universe." The site is one of the planet's most beautiful and geologically interesting regions, with high peaks, deep valleys and glaciers. The park contains seven peaks over 23,000 feet (7,000 m) and, in fact, most of the park is above the tree line. Its rivers, fed by glaciers, flow into the Ganges River system.

The rare snow leopard and lesser panda are found in the park, though the number of mammalian species that live in the geologically young Himalayas is low.

The Sherpas, a few thousand of whom live in the area, have a long history serving as guides and porters to climbers and explorers of the Himalayan region. Sir Edmund Hillary established the Himalayan Trust to help improve the lives of the Sherpas by funding schools and hospitals, planting forests and repairing monasteries.

## Nepal

**Total protected area:**

283,677 acres

**Significance:**

In addition to being the site of the highest mountain in the world, Sagarmatha National Park is one of the world's most beautiful and geologically interesting regions.

*Lukla Airport, now officially named Tenzing-Hillary Airport, is a gateway to Mount Everest—most prospective climbers land at Lukla before heading to base camp.*

*"For in my heart, I needed to go … the pull of Everest was stronger for me than any force on earth."*

—Nepalese Sherpa Tenzing Norgay, first man to reach Everest's summit, with Sir Edmund Hillary, May 1953

*Mount Everest was created by the collision of the Indo-Australian Plate and the Eurasian Plate some 70 million years ago.*

*Well-adapted to the high-altitude environment of Sagarmatha, Sherpas are considered among the most capable mountain climbers in the world.*

*Though Hinduism is the chief religion of Nepal, Buddhism has a long history in the nation, and stupas—Buddhist monuments—dot the Sagarmatha region.*

*A mountain of many names: known as Sagarmatha in Nepal and Chomolungma in Tibet, Westerners first knew it simply as Peak XV. In 1865, it was dubbed "Mount Everest," after Sir George Everest, the British surveyor-general of India, who first recorded its height and location.*

# NANDA DEVI

## India

**Total protected area:**

154,347 acres

**Significance:**

This remote Himalayan park is home to several rare and endangered animals such as the Asiatic black bear, snow leopard and blue sheep.

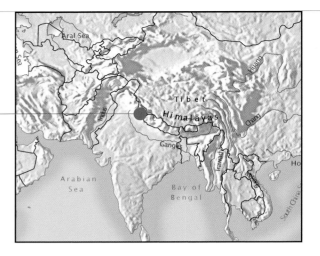

This site, a region of spectacular and rugged wilderness near the Tibetan border in the Himalayas, is dominated by Nanda Devi's pyramidal peak, which rises to over 25,590 feet (7,800 m). No humans live in the park, which has remained more or less untouched because of its inaccessibility. A remote gorge leads to a vast glacial basin, encircled by mountain peaks. Below the upper and lower Rishi river valleys, known as the Inner and Outer Sanctuaries, the river, fed by glaciers, runs into a deep and narrow gorge that is virtually inaccessible. It is the habitat of several endangered mammals, including the snow leopard, Himalayan musk deer and blue sheep. The entire sanctuary, including the main summit, was closed to human activity in 1983 after becoming inundated by climbing expeditions, but it was reopened for regulated ecotourism in 2003.

*"Today, on October 14, 2001, in front of our revered Nanda Devi, and drawing inspiration from Chipko's radiant history, we dedicate ourselves to the transformation of our region into a global center for peace, prosperity and biodiversity conservation."*

—Extract from the Nanda Devi Biodiversity Conservation and Ecotourism Declaration

*Though no humans live within Nanda Devi National Park, the region itself is home to the Gahrwali and Kumaoni people, as well as Punjabis, Nepalis, Tibetans and Bengalis.*

*Domesticated yaks are used in many ways: their milk and meat is consumed, and their hair is made into yarn. They transport goods and people as well.*

*The Himalayas of Nanda Devi National Park soar to incredible heights: numerous mountains rise more than 20,000 feet (6,100 m).*

# OLYMPIC NATIONAL PARK

*Spectacularly beautiful, the Hurricane Ridge is also known for turbulent weather—ocean winds churn among the mountains, and snow can fall in any season.*

*The rugged coastline of Washington state is characterized by giant rock formations rising from the seafloor.*

Known for its glacier-capped mountains, rare temperate rain forest and stretch of undeveloped rocky Pacific coastline, Olympic National Park sits on a peninsula in Washington State, separated from the land to the south by the high mountain range.

One of the wettest regions in the United States, the park is a habitat for giant conifers, massive moss-covered maple trees and lush ferns. The old-growth forests of Douglas fir and western hemlock are a refuge for the northern spotted owl, which depends upon them as its habitat. The primeval forest the park protects is one of the only remaining large tracts in the country. Because of the region's isolation, much of the park's wildlife is unique to the Olympic Peninsula. Endemic species include the Olympic marmot, Olympic snow mole and Olympic torrent salamander.

*The temperate rain forests of the Pacific Northwest constitute the largest such habitat in the world. Some absorb more than 120 inches (300 cm) of rain per year.*

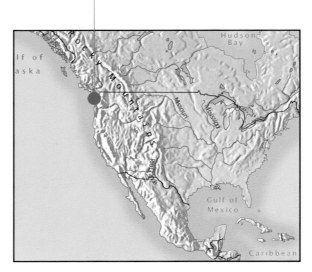

## United States

**Total protected area:**

913,447 acres

**Significance:**

Olympic National Park is notable for its rain forest, its glacier-capped peaks, and wildlife.

*"In closing, I would state that while the country on the outer slope of these mountains is valuable, the interior is useless for all practicable purposes. It would, however, serve admirably for a national park..."*

—Lieutenant Joseph O'Neil, 1890

# RWENZORI MOUNTAINS NATIONAL PARK

## Uganda

**Total protected area:**

246,117 acres

**Significance:**

The region is home to about half the total glacier area in Africa and offers spectacular scenery.

The rugged Rwenzori Mountains rise from vast savanna that is home to lions, water buffalo, elephants and antelope. The mountains themselves support numerous species of monkeys and birds.

Rwenzori Mountains National Park, located in southwestern Uganda, contains some of Africa's highest peaks and a beautiful alpine region of glaciers, waterfalls and lakes. The site's high-altitude flora, unique to the mountains' unusual cloud forests, is known among botanists as "Africa's botanic big game." The giant heathers and lobelias that grow there are examples of the rarity and outstanding range of the region's species.

Rising steeply above dry plains, the Rwenzori Mountains—also known as "the Mountains of the Moon"—are higher than the Alps. Extremely rugged and wet, with upland bogs that absorb the rain, they are the highest and most permanent source of the Nile, which is fed by 11 rivers.

*"There has been hidden to this day a giant amongst mountains, the melting snow of whose tops has been for some 50 centuries most vital to the people of Egypt."*

—Henry Morton Stanley, first European sighting of the Ruwenzori, 1889

*Though seen here on a clear day, clouds often shield the humid Rwenzori Mountains—some believe that cloud cover may have prevented early European explorers from seeing the mountains.*

PART I – THE NATURAL WORLD

# AÏR AND TÉNÉRÉ NATURAL RESERVES

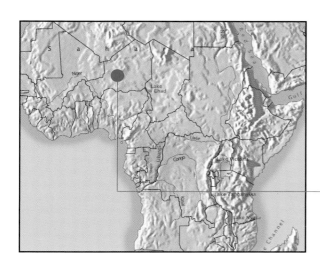

*Able to carry heavy cargo and travel long distances, dromedary camels have long been the most efficient form of transportation in the Sahara region.*

## WORLD HERITAGE IN DANGER

### Niger

**Threat:**

Military conflicts as well as civil disturbance prompted UNESCO to place the reserves on the World Heritage in Danger list.

*The temperature of the Ténéré can rise as high as 108°F (42 °C) in summer months. Such a bleak, arid landscape is a far cry from its prehistoric state as an ocean floor.*

The Aïr and Ténéré Reserves—which together make up the largest protected region in Africa and the third largest reserve in the world—feature the volcanic massif of the Aïr Mountains, an ecological island in the Sahara desert. The diversity of the reserves' landscapes and wildlife is outstanding. Nine rugged, flat-topped mountains rise above a heavily eroded rocky plateau with ancient canyons and green, wooded wadis—valleys or streambed areas with seasonal or intermittent water flow.

The Aïr reserve is home to important populations of threatened species, such as dorcas gazelle; damas gazelle; addax, an endangered desert antelope; and aoudad, a desert sheep. The eastern section of the site contains an expanse of the plains and huge sand dunes of the Ténéré desert, one of the Sahara's biggest "sand seas."

*Some species are so well adapted to the desert climate that they do not drink, getting all of the water they need from food.*

# CAPE FLORAL PROTECTED AREA

Cape Floral's fynbos vegetation supports no large animals; however, it does support small wildlife, including many varieties of endemic butterflies and other insects.

"Biodiversity in the Cape Floristic Region is under threat from the spread of invasive alien species, land-use transformation due to agriculture and urbanisation, unsustainable harvesting and poor land-use planning."

—Cape Action for People and the Environment (C.A.P.E.)

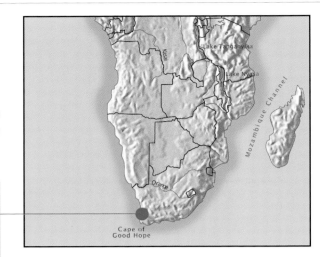

## South Africa

**Total protected area:**

1,366,493 acres

## Significance:

The 8 areas in this site combine to make one of the richest regions for plants in the world. Although comprising less than half of 1% of the continent's area, the Cape Floral Region is home to approximately 20% of Africa's plant life.

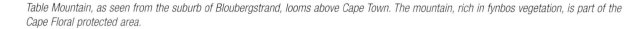

Table Mountain, as seen from the suburb of Bloubergstrand, looms above Cape Town. The mountain, rich in fynbos vegetation, is part of the Cape Floral protected area.

Nearly 1,000 species of daisy thrive in the Cape Floral Protected Area. Particularly noteworthy are the orange and yellow Namaqualand daisies that bloom in droves during spring.

This site in Cape Province, South Africa, comprises eight protected areas and contains 20 percent of the plants found on the continent. It is one of the richest and most important botanical regions in the world, both for the unique reproductive strategies and adaptations to fire that the plants display and for its extraordinarily high diversity and endemism. The density of species found there is also among the highest of any site in the world. There are 9,000 plant species in the region, 1,435 of them threatened. The distinctive fine-leaved Cape Floral vegetation that withstands the region's periodic fires is called *fynbos*, Afrikaans for fine bush.

# uKHAHLAMBA—DRAKENSBERG PARK

Originally home to the hunter-gatherer San people, the Drakensberg region was overtaken by livestock-raising Europeans during the 19th century. Angora goats are among the animals raised today as livestock.

Atop Cathedral Peak, at 9,856 feet (3,004 m), is a wide vista of the distinctively shaped, rugged Drakensberg.

The Drakensberg, or "Dragon's Mountains," are the highest peaks in southern Africa, rising to an elevation of 11,422 feet (3,482 m) at Thabana Ntlenyana. These high, jagged peaks are called *uKhahlamba*—"the barrier of spears"—in Zulu.

The landscape, with such natural architectural forms as basaltic buttresses, sandstone ramparts and the foothills' towering cliffs, is exceptionally beautiful. The region's diverse habitats include grasslands, river valleys and rocky gorges. The summit plateau is an island of alpine tundra. Thousands of rock paintings depicting animals and humans have been found in the mountainous region's many caves and rock shelters. Made by the late–Stone Age San people, who lived in the area for at least 4,000 years, the paintings are the largest collection of rock art in sub-Saharan Africa.

## South Africa

### Total protected area:

600,000 acres

### Significance:

These, the highest mountains in South Africa, are home to diverse habitats as well as thousands of rock paintings from the late Stone Age.

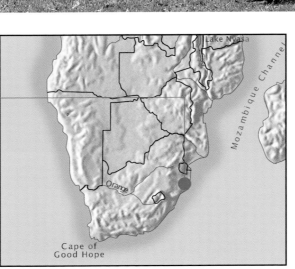

The Drakensberg sees many hikers each year, and skiers flock to the region during the winter, when temperatures plunge and snow falls on the mountains.

# HA LONG BAY

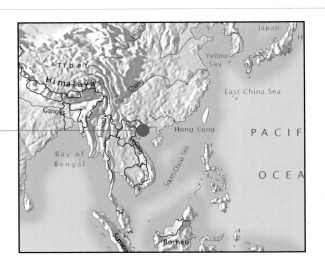

**A**pproximately 1,600 islands and islets are clustered in Ha Long Bay, or Bay of the Descending Dragon, in the Gulf of Tonkin. Covered with thick vegetation, the limestone islands look like rounded monoliths, or lush floating hills, with steep, sheer sides that rise abruptly out of the water. Few are inhabited, but some support fishermen. The islands are outstanding examples of limestone karst and of the natural formations created by erosion. They are famous for their caves and grottoes, which have names such as "Three Palace Grotto" and "Heavenly Residence Grotto." The largest grotto, a series of three large chambers full of stalagmites and stalactites, is called "Wooden Stakes Cave."

## Vietnam

**Total protected area:**

370,658 acres

**Significance:**

The approximately 1,600 limestone islands, most uninhabited, create a spectacular seascape.

*Fishing is the chief occupation in Ha Long Bay. Roughly 200 species of fish are found in the bay.*

*"... dragons landed and shot a stream of pearls from their mouths that turned into thousands of stone islands in the water. The invaders' fast war ships were not able to stop, and crashed into the islands, and so Vietnam survived the invasion."*

*—Vietnamese legend*

*Ha Long bay is a premier tourist attraction in Vietnam—people are drawn both to the splendor of the bay and to nearby Ha Long City.*

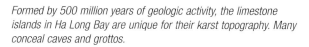

*Formed by 500 million years of geologic activity, the limestone islands in Ha Long Bay are unique for their karst topography. Many conceal caves and grottos.*

## Slovenia

**Total protected area:**

1,021 acres

**Significance:**

Skocjan is one of the most famous sites in the world for the study of karstic phenomena—natural formations that occur in limestone.

*Geologically spectacular, the Skocjan Caves are also notable for their archeological wealth. The caves held symbolic power for ancient peoples from all over southern Europe.*

This site is an exceptional system of well-preserved limestone caves, with subterranean passages, grottoes and chasms that have been carved by the Reka River, as well as underground lakes and waterfalls. Located on the Kras plateau in Slovenia, it is one of the most famous sites in the world for the study of karstic phenomena, the stunning natural formations that occur in limestone. The caves contain one of the largest underground canyons in the world. The river disappears into the caves and then flows through the underground passage for 21 miles (34 km) to the Adriatic Sea. This underground canyon branches off into five enormous side galleries, which are considered among the wonders of the caving world.

*Like the Reka River, the Rak River disappears into the Skocjan Caves. It eventually flows into the Pivka River somewhere beneath the rocks.*

# HIERAPOLIS-PAMUKKALE

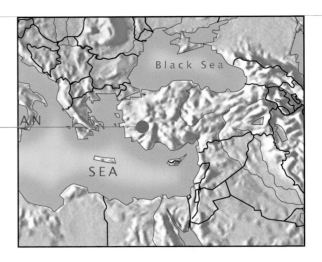

In the foothills of the Cokelez Mountains in southeast Turkey, mineral-rich water from thermal springs flows over high travertine cliffs into a series of natural travertine terraces. The waterfalls spilling into the stepped, semi-circular pools deposit a white coating of calcium carbonate, which over time has formed petrified waterfalls and mineral forests. The site also contains the ruins of the ancient Roman town of Hierapolis, which include the old thermal baths, fed by the hot springs, tombs, a monumental gate and a theater.

## Turkey

**Total protected area:**

Not available

**Significance:**

The otherworldly landscape at Hierapolis–Pamukkale was created by hot springs rich in calcites.

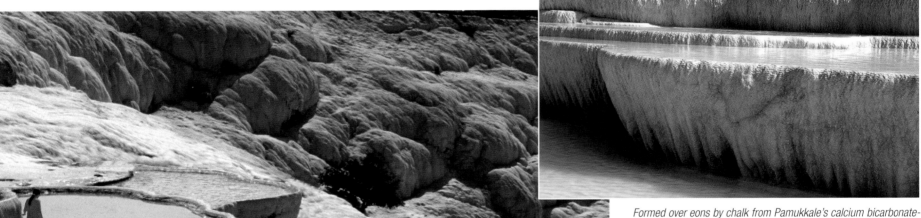

*Formed over eons by chalk from Pamukkale's calcium bicarbonate-laden water, these terraces are continually refinished to a bright white by new deposits.*

*The limestone and travertine terraced basins of Pamukkale in the foothills of the Cokelez Mountains fill with cascading water from the thermal springs in the high cliffs above.*

*The sun sets on Pamukkale, one of Turkey's most distinctive landforms, and a magnet for tourists from around the Mediterranean.*

# WESTERN CAUCASUS

*The rugged and forbidding Caucasus Mountains were formed by the collision of the Arabian plate and the Eurasian plate some 28 million years ago.*

## Russia

**Total protected area:**

868,872 acres

**Significance:**

This remote area in the Russian Federation is one of the world's few regions untouched by humans or domesticated animals.

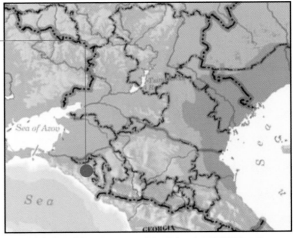

*The Caucasus Mountains, seen here from the summit of Mount Elbrus, possess numerous peaks above 16,000 feet (4,800 m).*

The Western Caucasus, northeast of the Black Sea, is one of Europe's only mountain ranges to have large tracts of montane forest undisturbed by humans or domesticated animals. Some of the protected site's more remote regions are inaccessible except by helicopter. There are vast beech forests and virgin fir forests with 300-year-old trees. The area is known as a center of plant diversity, with ecosystems ranging from lowland to subalpine habitats. Above the forest line, there are alpine meadows and, at higher altitudes, snow-covered terrain. The geology of the site is also diverse. In the north, are many limestone caves, including Russia's largest. Most of the region has the moraines, U-shaped valleys and mountain lakes of a glaciated landscape. The glacier-fed rivers form a series of waterfalls as they flow into the Black Sea.

# GREAT SMOKY MOUNTAINS

Straddling North Carolina and Tennessee in the heavily forested southern Appalachian Mountains—among the oldest mountains in the world—Great Smoky Mountains National Park is known for its beauty and old-growth forests. Although it is the most-visited national park in the United States, the forests, which contain 130 tree species, are relatively pristine. It is the largest tract of unbroken forest remaining in the eastern United States. The park is a refuge for black bear and elk, which were reintroduced into the park in 2001. River otter and peregrine falcon have also been successfully reintroduced into the park. The site is also known as the "Wildflower National Park." More kinds of flowering plants grow in the Great Smoky Mountains than in any other national park on the continent. Since the Smoky Mountains were too far south to be overtaken by glaciers during the last ice age, they became a refuge for plants and animals displaced from their northern habitats.

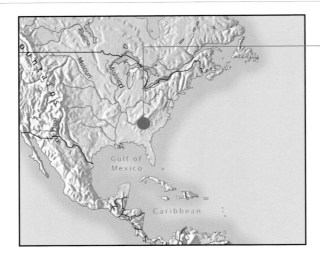

Once the homeland of the Cherokee Indians, the region was established as a national park in 1830, when President Andrew Jackson signed the Indian Removal Act and the Cherokee were forcibly removed along the "Trail of Tears" to what is now Oklahoma.

## United States

**Total protected area:**

516,450 acres

**Significance:**

The Great Smoky Mountains is the most-visited national park in the United States. Despite this, it is also relatively pristine.

*A tree stands alone in the foggy splendor of Cades Cove, a remote valley in Tennessee's section of the Great Smoky Mountains.*

*A summer storm approaches Newfound Gap, a mountain pass on the border of Tennessee and North Carolina. The Appalachian Trail runs through the pass.*

PART I - THE NATURAL WORLD

The Saami use reindeer for a variety of purposes, including sport. Here, two reindeer race each other—off camera, a Saami jockey follows on skis.

*"As long as we have water for the fish to live in, as long as we have land for reindeer to graze and wander, as long as we have grounds for the wild beasts to hide in, there is comfort on this earth."*

—Sami poet Paulus Utsi (1918–1975)

This wooden dwelling is built in the conical shape of a traditional Saami lavvu, which utilizes wood only for the frame; skin is wrapped around that frame to form the structure.

During winter, reindeer eat snow to hydrate themselves. They also eat lichen, a slow growing plant found on rocks and trees.

Saami have herded reindeer for hundreds of years and consume both reindeer meat and milk.

# TOKAJ

## Hungary

**Total protected area:**

33,171 acres

**Significance:**

The vineyards and traditions of Tokaj have been sustained for over 1,000 years.

*"… his kingdom of Hungary was one of the finest countries in the world; it was most fertile, producing in great abundance wines of various sorts, all excellent, though Tokaj was the best."*

—John Adams, 2nd U.S. president

*The wine of Tokaj is the pride of Hungary. The region's vineyards are mentioned in the Hungarian national anthem.*

The vineyards and traditions of Tokaj, a small town in northeastern Hungary renowned for its wine, have been sustained for over a thousand years. The region's winemaking methods, still in use today, have been regulated for almost 300 years to assure the quality of the famous wine. The grapes are harvested completely by hand. In 1737, by royal decree, the site was declared a closed wine region, the first in the world. The famous yellow muscat grape, one of the oldest and most distinctive varieties in the world, has been cultivated in Tokaj for centuries. The cultivation of grapes and production of wine have shaped the development of the landscape and patterns of settlement over the centuries. Beneath the region's farms and villages there are deep, ancient wine cellars carved out of the rock.

*Tokaji Aszu is aged for many years before it is finally bottled. A world-renowned dessert wine, it has a high alcohol content compared with other wines.*

he production of wine has been the traditional mainstay of landholders in Portugal's Alto Douro wine region for the past 2,000 years. Port, the region's most famous wine dating back to the 18th century, continues to be successfully produced using traditional methods. Alto Douro is one of Europe's most admired traditional wine-producing regions, both for the beauty of its landscape and the excellence of its product. The region has distinctive terraced vineyards and farms called quintas, large clusters of buildings dedicated to the production of wine.

### Portugal

**Total protected area:**

60,787 acres

**Significance:**

Wine has been produced in this area of Portugal for 2,000 years.

MEDITERRANEA

*The Douro River Valley has a climate of extreme summer heat followed by profound cold during the rest of the year. This contrast, combined with the rich soils of the region, creates optimal conditions for grape growing.*

*"Here the green tints outdo the colours of the rainbow"*

—Portuguese poet Miguel Torga (1907–1995), writing about the Douro region

*Different aging processes make different kinds of port. Wines aged in wooden barrels have different flavors than wine aged in tanks.*

# SAINT-ÉMILION

*The landscape of the Jurisdiction of Saint-Émilion has remained unchanged for centuries.*

## France

**Total protected area:**

19,388 acres

**Significance:**

This medieval town overlooking the Dordogne valley is the oldest wine producer in Bordeaux—arguably the most famous wine region in the world.

This beautiful medieval town overlooking the Dordogne valley is the oldest wine producer in Bordeaux, perhaps the most famous wine region in the world. Vineyards planted by the Romans in what was then the Roman province of Aquitaine were flourishing by the fourth century AD. Saint-Émilion has been known for its distinguished wines since at least the 12th century, when it was designated a special wine jurisdiction. It is a landscape of chateaux and vineyards that have been cultivated for centuries. The town itself contains a Romanesque church, a 13th-century gateway that is a remnant of the medieval town's fortifications, and half-timbered architecture dating from the 15th century.

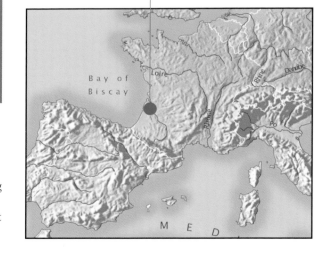

*Saint-Émilion was named after a traveling monk who settled in the region during the 8th century. Monks who later followed Émilion began carving this church from regional limestone in the 9th century.*

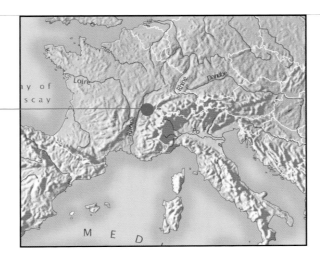

## Switzerland

**Total protected area:**

2,000 acres

**Significance:**

The vineyards of Lavaux provide an overview of the changes in wine production over the last 1,000 years.

*The well-harmonized terraces of Lavaux primarily grow Chasselas, a white grape that makes a dry, full wine, and is sometimes blended with Sauvignon Blanc.*

Built by Benedictine and Cistercian monks in the 11th century, these terraced vineyards cover 2,050 acres (830 ha) of the mountain's lower slopes on Lake Geneva's northern shore. Lying between the Chateau de Chillon, which also dates to the 11th century, and Lausanne, the well-preserved terraces have been continuously in use for at least 800 years. Lavaux's beauty and productivity have been valued since the monks first began growing grapes. The wine produced by Lavaux, nearly all of which is bought by the Swiss, has had a major role in the region's history and economy.

*The vineyards of Lavaux, seen here near Vevey with the Chablais region looming across Lake Geneva, are protected indefinitely from further development.*

# VAL D'ORCIA

## Italy

**Total protected area:**

Not available

**Significance:**

Val d'Orcia has come to represent the iconic Renaissance agricultural landscape.

On the outskirts of Siena in Tuscany, Val d'Orcia preserves the Renaissance agricultural landscape of spare chalk plains, cypress trees, and hilltop settlements familiar from Italian Renaissance paintings. An accomplishment of the city-state of Siena, the well-managed landscape was as much a product of civilization as of nature and seems to represent Renaissance ideals of beauty, order and harmony with nature. The site includes a section of the Via Francigena, the medieval pilgrimage route from Rome to Canterbury, and the local abbeys and monasteries that were stops along the way.

*A grove of cypress trees graces a field in Val d'Orcia. The tall, pointed form of the cypress is distinctive of the landscape.*

*"This valley ... where ancient, verdant woodlands strewn with flint, stone and bronze axes bear witness to the first step taken by man."*

—Excerpt from a tourist guide written in the early 1900s by Fabio Bargagli Petrucci

*The sparsely settled, rolling landscape of Val d'Orcia is seamed by old Roman roads, which are collectively called* Via Francigena.

# ORTO BOTANICO DI PADOVA

## Italy

**Total protected area:**

5.5 acres

**Significance:**

Orto Botanico is the world's first botanical garden.

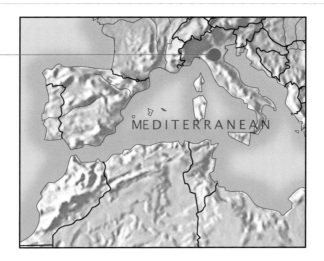

*This greenhouse near the north gate of the park contains the Goethe palm, a Mediterranean dwarf palm that has traditionally grown along the seacoast.*

*This print depicts the garden as it appeared in the 16th century. The garden's presumed designer was Daniele Barbaro, a learned Venetian nobleman and cardinal.*

The first botanical garden in the world, the Orto Botanico di Padova was created in 1545 by the University of Padua as a center for research on medicinal plants. The garden's original layout—four quadrants with a circular central plot representing the world, surrounded by a ring of water—has been preserved. The scientific investigations undertaken in the 16th century at the Orto Botanico, which continues to be used today for research, resulted in important contributions to botany, medicine and chemistry. Many of the rare plants that the garden acquired as specimens were later introduced into Europe.

*The Orto Botanico di Padova contains plant species from around the world. The garden was regularly burglarized in earlier times; thieves found that medicinal flora could fetch high prices.*

# PART II - HUMAN CULTURE

Scientists are still trying to unravel the mystery of when life first appeared on earth. Intriguing clues in the form of fossils and bones give us a glimpse of how the earliest plants and animals might have appeared. These remains deepen our understanding of what the Earth was like from many millions to just a few thousand years ago.

But what of our earliest ancestors? They too left behind fossils and bones for our study, enriching our knowledge of where we came from and how we changed and developed. Perhaps even more telling are the ancient paintings and monuments created by our distant and not-so-distant ancestors—for they tell us how their day-to-day life might have been lived.

*The Neolithic site Stonehenge, located on the Salisbury Plain in Wiltshire, was built between 3200 BC and 1600 BC.*

# KAKADU

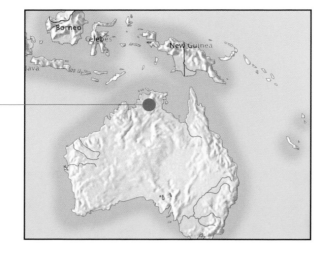

## Australia

**Period:**

From 40,000 years ago

**Significance:**

The park is home to 20,000-year-old Aboriginal rock paintings.

Kakadu National Park in Australia's Northern Territory sprawls almost 120 miles (200 km) north to south and 60 miles (96 km) east to west. Within this vast area are not only a huge range of landscapes—rivers, floodplains, waterfalls, grasslands and harsh rocky outcrops—but also a series of remarkable Aboriginal cave paintings, some dating back 20,000 years. They constitute an exceptional record of a culture and way of life that, until the arrival of Europeans in the 19th century, remained essentially unchanged since the appearance of the first Aboriginal peoples in what is now Australia 40,000 years ago.

It is easily argued that these paintings, with their abstract, flowing lines, have a religious significance. Yet the paintings also record and seem to celebrate the teeming natural world that inspired their ancient makers.

*Aboriginals believe that Mimi spirits rose out of cave cracks at Ubirr and painted red and yellow figures on the ceilings.*

*"Some Creation Ancestors put themselves on rock walls as paintings and became djang (dreaming places). Some of these paintings are andjamun (sacred and dangerous) and can be seen only by senior men or women; others can be seen by all people."*

—Warradjan Aboriginal Cultural Centre

*An Aboriginal territory situated in the wet-dry tropics, Kakadu National Park extends over an area of 7,646 square miles (19,804 sq km).*

*Aboriginal people frequently painted the animals that they hunted, such as this fish, which is on a rock at Ubirr.*

The creation ancestor known as Namondjok, shown here on a rock from the Nourlangie site, is thought by Aboriginal peoples to appear only at night as a dark spot in the Milky Way.

According to tradition, Aboriginal creation ancestors formed the Nourlangie rock site when they took the form of wallabies and cut two crevices in the rock.

Aboriginal peoples have been using the Anbangbang rock shelter for the past 20,000 years. The large overhang provides protection from the elements, which is a chief reason that these cave paintings have survived.

# MESSEL PIT FOSSIL

## Germany

**Period:**

From 50 million to 60 million years ago

**Significance:**

Messel Pit is one of the world's most important fossil sites.

This open-cast shale mine in Germany, 22 miles (35 km) southeast of Frankfurt, is the unlikely setting for one of the most important fossil sites in the world. When mining began at Messel in 1859, it became clear that the oil-rich earth was a near-perfect environment for the preservation of a huge variety of fossils—vegetable and animal—from the Eocene period, 50 to 60 million years ago.

The remains of horses, bats, crocodiles, rodents, a variety of fish and birds and numerous insects have all been discovered among the thousands of fossils so far unearthed. More than 30 different types of plant have also been found. No less remarkable is that on occasion individual hairs and feathers have been preserved, as have the stomach contents of some animals.

*At 3,290 feet (1,000 m) long and 2,300 feet (700 m) wide, Messel Pit holds more than 40,000 fossils, including those of the primitive horse Propalaeotherium parvulum.*

*Many rare specimens have been excavated at Messel Pit, including an extinct species of water frog and a pregnant mare.*

*Messel Pit comprises the remains of a lake bed containing 280 million-year-old red sandstone deposits, in which delicate imprints of hair and feathers have been preserved.*

# MONTE SAN GIORGIO

An extraordinary window is opened on the distant past at Monte San Giorgio in southern Switzerland. More than 10,000 fossils from the Triassic period, 245 to 350 million years ago, chiefly of marine animals, though including some land-based species, have been discovered at this exceptional site.

What today is an alpine landscape more than 3,000 feet (900 m) above sea level was in the Triassic a shallow, tropical lagoon, teeming with life. Thirty species of marine and terrestrial reptiles, 80 different species of fish, and hundreds of invertebrate species have been discovered in the course of more than 100 years of excavations. The result is that Monte San Giorgio remains by some measure the single most important site from the Triassic yet discovered anywhere in the world.

*Compound layers of ash in the Triassic carbonate formations of Monte San Giorgio have preserved numerous specimens of plants, invertebrates, fish, and reptiles.*

*Monte San Giorgio is a rocky, wooded mountain that rises to an elevation of 3,599 feet (1,097 m).*

## Switzerland

**Period:**

From 245 million to 350 million years ago

**Significance:**

More than 10,000 fossils of the Triassic period are preserved at this site.

# MIGUASHA NATIONAL PARK

## Canada

**Period:**

Approximately 350 million years ago

**Significance:**

Fossils here date from the "Age of Fishes."

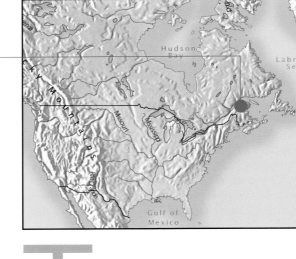

The Devonian period, which occurred some 350 million years ago, represented a key moment in the evolution of animal life on Earth. It was then, in this "Age of Fishes," that marine life took its first, tentative steps on land, in time giving rise to the first air-breathing animals. Of these "lobe-finned" amphibians, six species have been discovered, no fewer than five of them in Québec's Miguasha National Park.

The first fossils were discovered in 1842 by a local geologist, Abraham Gesner. In this pre-Darwinian age, their significance was almost entirely overlooked. It was not until later in the 19th century that the true importance of the site began to be appreciated. More than 5,000 of these fossils have since been discovered.

*The remnants of the great extinction that occurred during the Devonian period can be seen in the preservation of boreal tree species such as fir and birch.*

*Located on the southern side of the Gaspé Peninsula, Miguasha is home to 20 species of fossilized fish, including the jawless fish.*

*Rich fossil beds at Miguasha preserve an abundance of marine life. The great barrier reefs that were once plentiful here contained stromatoporoid, a variety of coral that has since become extinct.*

*Canada's Miguasha National Park contains fossilized remains of the first flowering plant as well as 10 species of the first vascular plants of the Devonian forests.*

The art produced during the Bovidian (cattle herder) period, from 4500 to 2500 BC, featured scenes of nomadic herders.

Although the Acacus is one of the most arid areas of the Sahara desert, it does contain vegetation such as the callotropis plant.

# SERRA DA CAPIVARA

## Brazil

**Period:**

12,000 BC to AD 100

**Significance:**

Site of the oldest rock paintings in the Americas.

Located in northeastern Brazil, Serra da Capivara National Park is home to many ancient caves bearing paintings, some of which are more than 25,000 years old. Discovered in the 1960s, the paintings are an outstanding testimony to one of the oldest human communities in South America. Subjects of the art include flora, animals, hunting and scenes of rituals, violence, sex and family life. The site is administered by FUMDHAM—Museum of the American Man Foundation (Fundação Museu do Homem Americano). The museum, located near the site in the city of São Raimundo Nonato, exhibits artifacts that were found near the rock paintings during the archaeological digs within the park.

At Serra da Capivara National Park, 60,000 cave paintings and engraved figures are found in caverns, burrows, and canyons.

Ancient inhabitants used animal hair, plants and natural fibers to paint animals, such as horses, paleo-llamas and aquatic birds.

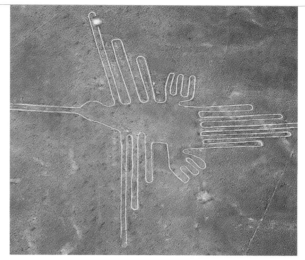

## Peru

**Period:**

Between 500 BC and AD 500

**Significance:**

Nazca is the site of enormous ancient geoglyphics that can be seen clearly only from the sky.

*Over 300 lines, geometrical figures and drawings, such as the hummingbird, are etched on the dry surface of Peru's coastal plain.*

The arid Nazca desert in southern Peru, one of the driest places on Earth, contains one of the world's most remarkable and mysterious outpourings of human creative endeavor, the Nazca Lines, created between about 500 BC and AD 500 by the so-called Nazca peoples.

They consist of a series of immense drawings (technically known as geoglyphs) of varying degrees of complexity scratched into the soil. Some are no more than straight lines, the longest of which is 8 miles (13 km) long. Others are simple geometric shapes. Yet more than 70 are immense and highly stylized images of animals, humans and plants. The largest is up to 900 feet (roughly 275 m) long.

*Archeologists believe that the concentration and arrangement of the figures and lines were created through extensive labor that took place over several periods of cultural change.*

*Even though engravings such as the Candelabra are exposed to the elements, they have been preserved due to the plain's dry climate and minimal wind erosion.*

# THEBES

## Egypt

**Period:**

Between 2030 and 1070 BC

**Significance:**

Thebes reflects the apogee of Ancient Egypt's power and glory.

*Anubis, god of mummification and the afterlife, is depicted here in a fresco in the temple of Queen Hatshepsut, the first female pharaoh.*

*Each of the Colossi of Memmon represents Amenhotep III, whose opulent mortuary temple they originally guarded. Little of the pharaoh's tomb remains but its sentinels.*

Although it was not the administrative capital of Egypt, Thebes on the east bank of the Nile emerged as a major center from 1552 BC, the beginning of the New Kingdom. This was primarily because it was here in the Valley of the Kings that the New Kingdom pharaohs were buried. Ancient Egyptian society placed as great a premium on deliberate grandeur as it did on preserving the mortal remains of its rulers, themselves considered gods, with as much splendor as possible: hence the epic scale of the Valley of the Kings.

The god Horus bestowed divinity upon pharaohs. Queen Hatshepsut used this association to consolidate power by claiming to be the child of the gods Amon and Hathor.

*"I found it near the remains of its body [Rameses II] and chair, with its face upwards, and apparently smiling on me, at the thought of being taken to England."*
—Italian explorer Giovanni Battista Belzoni, 1815

Queen Hatshepsut's temple was damaged and her image removed from its walls following the revolt that ended her 20-year reign.

Ramses II, the most powerful of the pharaohs, transformed Thebes by ordering his likeness carved over those of his predecessors. His tomb is in the Valley of the Kings.

# ABU SIMBEL

Ancient Egypt, a civilization that remained essentially unchanged for almost 30 centuries, is conventionally said to have reached the peak of its power and prestige under the New Kingdom pharaoh Ramses II, who ruled from 1290 to 1224 BC. Yet in reality, whatever the splendors of his rule, Egypt was more vulnerable to outside conquest than its apparent strength might have suggested. Beginning in 1069 BC, the country endured 400 years of foreign domination.

That said, even in Egypt few monuments rival the largest of seven temples built by Ramses II at Abu Simbel on the upper reaches of the Nile. Abu Simbel is dominated by four immense seated statues of the pharaoh himself, each 67 feet (20.4 m) high, their imperturbably blank features matched by their over-poweringly formal monumentality. As ever in Egyptian art, size is a direct reflection of status: the larger the figure, the greater his or her importance. As with the temple they guard, all the statues at Abu Simbel were carved directly from the living rock.

No less remarkably, in 1968 the entire temple was moved from its original location when it was threatened by flooding after the construction of the High Aswan Dam began in 1960.

*Philae is considered one of the possible final resting places of Osiris. The god's murder was avenged by his son, Horus, whose statuary appears in a chapel on the island.*

*Two seated figures of Ramses II were among the enormous carvings of Abu Simbel relocated between 1964 and 1968 to avoid submersion.*

## SUCCESS STORY

### Egypt

**The Challenge:**

The construction of the Aswan Dam created a reservoir that would have permanently submerged the monuments of Abu Simbel.

**The Solution:**

The monuments were painstakingly dismantled and then relocated to higher ground.

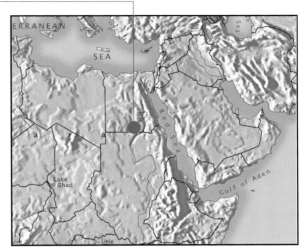

Hawks were symbols of the god Horus, personified by the pharaoh.

*"Every morning I waked in time to witness that daily miracle. Every morning I saw those awful brethren pass from death to life, from life to sculptured stone."*

—Novelist Amelia B. Edwards,
*A Thousand Miles Up the Nile* (1877)

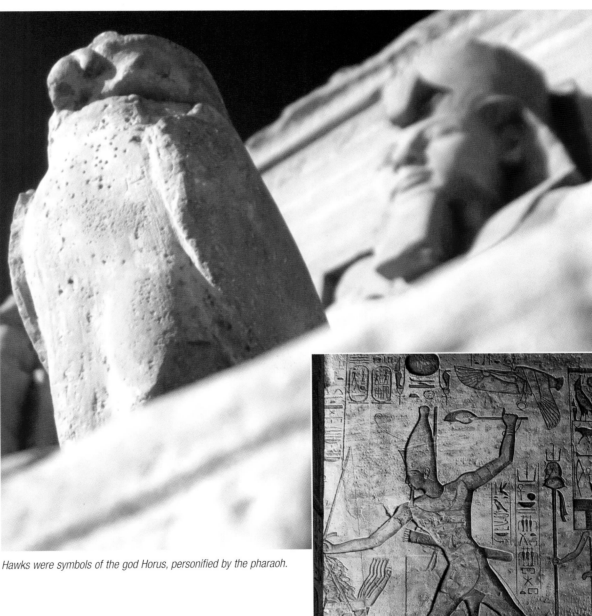

Hieroglyphics at Abu Simpel depict offerings to the gods and Ramses II, victorious over his enemies.

# PYRAMIDS OF GIZA

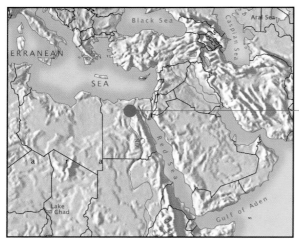

## Egypt

**Period:**

2560 BC

**Significance:**

The Pyramids of Giza are the most iconic symbols of the civilization of ancient Egypt.

*The relationship between the Great Sphinx and the nearby pyramids continues to be debated.*

No structures are more instantly identified with ancient Egypt than the pyramids at Giza, just outside Memphis, administrative capital of Old Kingdom Egypt and today some miles south of the modern capital, Cairo. These were not the first pyramids; the first was a step pyramid built for the pharaoh Zoser around 2650 BC. Yet within 60 years the pharaoh Khufu was building what today is known simply as the Great Pyramid, the largest of three smooth-sided pyramids at Giza. The other two were built at approximately the same time for the pharaohs Khafre and Menkaure.

The Great Pyramid is a monumental structure in every sense. It contains 2 million limestone blocks, each weighing about 32,000 pounds (14,515 kg). For 43 centuries, its summit, 480 feet (146 m) above the desert, made it the tallest structure in the world. Its construction, estimated to have taken 20 years, involved not just impressive feats of organization but also slave labor on a monumental scale.

*The pharaoh Khafre erected what appears to be the tallest of the pyramids at Giza. In fact, it is second in size to that of his father, Khufu; it was built on a mound to suggest a greater height.*

*"From the heights of these pyramids, forty centuries look down on us."*

—Napoleon Bonaparte

*The pyramid of Khufu, or Great Pyramid of Cheops, is the only extant example of the Seven Wonders of the Ancient World. For nearly 4,000 years, it was the world's tallest human-made structure.*

# GEBEL BARKAL

The ruins of Gebel Barkal are situated atop a small flat-topped mountain, commanding views of the Nile valley below.

## Sudan

**Period:**

900 BC to AD 350

**Significance:**

Five archeological sites stand as testimony to early Kush cultures.

The largest temples on the hill of Gebel Barkal in the Republic of Sudan have always been considered sacred by the local people.

Though under intermittent Egyptian rule as a southern buffer state, by the end of the New Kingdom in ca. 1150 BC, Nubia was beginning to emerge as an independent entity, Kush.

Whatever its claims to independence, Kush, located on the Nile, today in northern Sudan, remained culturally subservient to its much larger neighbor. The remaining structures at Gebel Barkal, itself a 300-foot (91.4 m) high, flat-topped rocky outcrop, make clear the debt to Egypt. This is most obviously true of the region's pyramids, dating from various periods from the first millennium BC. They are more slender than the Egyptian originals, as well as substantially smaller, but owe a clear debt to Egypt nonetheless.

There are also 13 temples and three palaces in and around Gebel Barkal, lonely outposts still only partly excavated in a harsh desert environment.

Although similar in construction to the pyramids at Gebel Barkal, the pyramids at Meroë were built over chambers containing bodies that had been buried or burned rather than mummified.

# MONASTERY OF SAINT CATHERINE

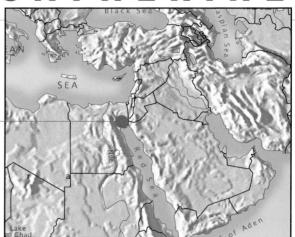

Saint Catherine's Monastery sits in the Sinai peninsula in Egypt at the foot of Mount Sinai, where Moses is said to have received the Ten Commandments. It is among the most remarkable monasteries in the world. In part, this is a matter of its stark desert setting. It also has the distinction of being the second-oldest continuously inhabited monastery in the Christian world.

## Egypt

**Period:**

6th century

**Significance:**

On Mount Sinai, a site sacred to Christianity, Islam and Judaism, this remote monastery is one of the earliest Christian monastic communities.

*For centuries, pilgrims have come to Mount Sinai seeking to follow in the steps of Moses and have left relics behind.*

*Inside the monastery walls are a basilica, bell tower, mosque and archive containing religious manuscripts and icons.*

It was built from 527 by the emperor Justinian on the site of a small chapel, itself reputedly built on the site of the burning bush through which God first spoke to Moses.

Then as now, it was a notable center of scholarship. Its library contains the largest and most important collection of early Christian manuscripts outside the Vatican. It also lays claim to a dazzling collection of more than 2,000 icons.

From the outside, it appears as much fortress as place of worship. Its heavily buttressed walls are nine feet (2.75 m) thick and in places 60 feet (18.25 m) high. In fact, for many years, visitors and supplies

had to be hoisted up to a small door high off the ground in order to gain entrance to this heavily protected monastery..

No less intriguing, St. Catherine's also contains a mosque, built to commemorate its giving shelter to Muhammad himself, who thereafter extended his personal protection to the monastery.

*"God came down on Mount Sinai, to the peak of the mountain. He summoned Moses to the mountain peak, and Moses climbed up."*

—Genesis 19:20

## Lebanon

**Period:**

1200 to around 332 BC

**Significance:**

This Phoenician city was once a major maritime power.

*These columns are thought to have been part of a palaestra, a Greek wrestling school with a central courtyard and adjoining rooms.*

*The restored Triumphal Arch of Tyre and an aqueduct system that served the city are among the remains from Roman times.*

Tyre, today in southern Lebanon, is among the most significant ancient cities of the Near East. Although the accuracy of Herodotus' claim that it was founded in 2750 BC is doubtful, certainly by about 1300 BC, it was clearly emerging as one of the major ports of the Levant. Later, as one of the leading ports of the seafaring Phoenicians, it played a key role in the establishment of the Phoenician, later Carthaginian, maritime empire in the western Mediterranean.

As the tides of war and conquest surged back and forth across the region, the city inevitably felt their effects. In 332 BC, it was taken by Alexander the Great after a seven-month seige. Almost 300 years later, it was the victim of Roman conquest. And almost 12 turbulent centuries later, it fell in an orgy of bloodletting to the Crusaders. Muslim rule was reimposed by the Mameluks with the final expulsion of the Crusaders in 1291. By the 16th century, it was firmly within the orbit of the rapidly expanding Ottoman empire. Only in 1920, with Lebanese independence, did the city reemerge under native rule.

*"And they shall destroy the walls of Tyrus and break down her towers."*

—Ezekiel 26:4

# BAALBEK

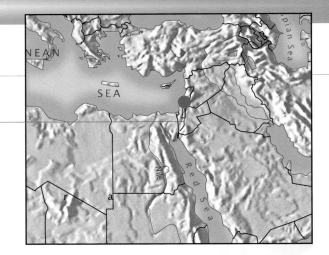

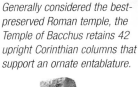

The ancient Phoenician city of Baalbek in Lebanon—Heliopolis to the Romans after its conquest in the 1st century BC—is remarkable not only for its antiquity but also for the unusual quality and quantity of its Roman buildings. The most impressive, if only by virtue of its startling size, is the Temple of Jupiter—the largest temple in the entire Roman empire. It was begun in the mid-1st century AD during the reign of Nero. Today, all that remains are six immense Corinthian columns (there were originally 42) stretching skyward almost 70 feet (21 m) and bearing a richly carved entablature, or lintel. But the sheer scale of even these fragmentary remains makes instantly clear the reach of Rome at its height.

## Lebanon

**Period:**

From 2000 BC

**Significance:**

This Phoenician city is home to some of the world's finest examples of Imperial Roman architecture at its peak.

*Generally considered the best-preserved Roman temple, the Temple of Bacchus retains 42 upright Corinthian columns that support an ornate entablature.*

Next to the temple is the 2nd-century AD Temple of Bacchus, considerably smaller but much better preserved. The opulence and precision of its carving, weathered though it may be, is no less striking a reminder of the abundant resources available to the Romans and of the aggressive determination with which they deployed them.

*"UNESCO has already launched two urgent appeals to the belligerents to ensure that the hostilities spare the site and its surroundings, which are part of the ancestral heritage of humanity, and avert the total destruction feared by all."*

—Koïchiro Matsuura, Director-General of UNESCO, launching an alert on August 12, 2006, to protect heritage in Lebanon and Israel during the summer 2006 war

*Jupiter, Venus and Bacchus were each honored by temples. These six columns are all that remain of the Temple of Jupiter, once the largest in the Roman empire.*

*The Great Court was originally surrounded by 128 stone columns, of which only 6 remain.*

## Syria

**Period:**

2000 BC

**Significance:**

Aleppo contains vestiges of the civilizations of its many rulers, including the Hittites, Assyrians, Arabs, Mongols and Ottomans.

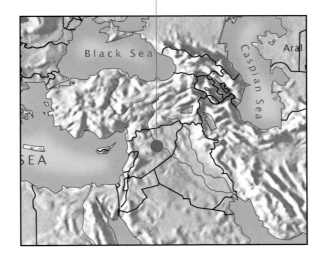

*The ruins of the Simonis Abbey still stand in the old city of Aleppo.*

*Built in the 13th century on a large hill overlooking the city, the Citadel of Aleppo is among the oldest and largest castles in the world.*

Aleppo in northern Syria is one of the oldest continuously inhabited cities in the world, its origins dating back to the beginnings of civilization in the Middle East almost 6,000 years ago. Its location in the Fertile Crescent—between the Mediterranean and the Euphrates—explains its importance. At the crossroads of several major trade routes between east and west for millennia, its importance, and its wealth, lasted at least to the end of the Middle Ages. It was only with the discovery of the sea route to India around the Cape of Good Hope that Aleppo found itself bypassed, subsiding into a sedentary backwater of the Ottoman empire.

*The bridge at the entrance to the Citadel was also an aqueduct that provided water to the walled fortress.*

# JERUSALEM

## Israel and Palestine
## (currently disputed)

### Period:

From 3000 BC

### Significance:

Jerusalem has been a holy city throughout history in Judaism, Christianity and Islam.

*A night view of a narrow street in the Old City.*

*Facing south over the Old City, one stands at the Muslim Quarter, with the Christian Quarter at right. Beyond the center, the Jewish Quarter is at left and the Armenian Quarter at right.*

# OLYMPIA

The Ionic columns of the palaestra surrounded a courtyard used for wrestling. The enclosed rooms at right were used for undressing, conversing and storing oil.

Olympia, in south-central Greece, is a crucially important Greek religious site. It is the site not merely of the Olympic games but also of one of the largest and most sumptuous temples dedicated to Zeus in the Greek world. The site itself was largely destroyed by the Emperor Theodosious I in AD 394. As emperor of a newly Christian Rome, in 394 he banned the Games because of their pagan connotations. Yet enough artifacts remain to make clear the status of Olympia.

Their origins shrouded in mystery, the Games probably began in 776 BC and were thereafter held every four years. They were as much artistic gatherings as they were sporting events. Poetry competitions, for example, were regular features. There were also a series of elaborate religious rituals. Yet athletics, originally just running races and later expanded to include throwing, jumping, chariot races, boxing and wrestling, were at the heart of the Games.

Only free-born Greek men were allowed to compete, always naked, though later Roman competitors were admitted. The winners typically were awarded laurel wreaths. The Games were closed by a banquet for all the competitors at which 100 oxen, sacrificed to Zeus at the start of the competition, were served.

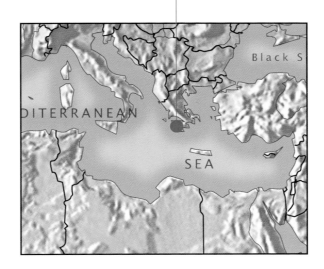

## Greece

**Period:**

10th century BC

**Significance:**

Olympia was the birthplace of the Olympic games and the site of one of the largest temples dedicated to Zeus.

*Ancient Olympia, as rendered in the late 19th century.*

*"People used to gather in Olympia both to make a pilgrimage to the past and to demonstrate faith in the future. This should also be the case with modern Olympiads."*

—Pierre Frédy, Baron de Coubertin, founder of the modern Olympic Games

# RHODES

The rocky Greek island of Rhodes, just off the coast of Turkey, is the largest of the Dodecanese, the string of islands scattered across the waters of the eastern Aegean. Its history is a typical mixture of the blood-soaked and the peaceful, the island falling variously under the sway of outside conquerors, as well as enjoying extended periods of prosperity. Yet it is notable as the site of the Colossus of Rhodes, an

## Greece

**Period:**

11th century BC

**Significance:**

Rhodes was the location of the bronze Colossus of Rhodes—one of the Seven Wonders of the Ancient World.

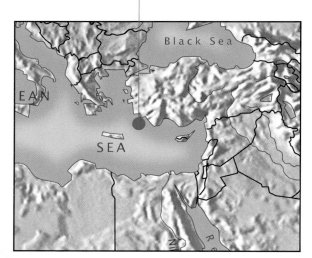

Published in 1493, this woodcut of Rhodes by Hartmann Schedel is one of the earliest printed images of a city.

After losing control of the Holy Land in the Crusades, Christian knights retreated to Rhodes, where they built the Palace of the Grandmaster in the 14th century. When the island was captured by the Ottoman Empire in 1522–23, the palace became a fortress.

immense bronze statue more than 100 feet (30.5 m) high, built between 292 and 280 BC, that towered over the ancient harbor. It remained in place only until 226 BC when an earthquake brought it crashing down. It was nonetheless one of the Seven Wonders of the Ancient World, a stupendous feat of engineering as much as of sculpture.

The island's other claim to fame came much later, in 1309, when Rhodes became the headquarters, indeed the property, of the Knights Hospitaller, or Knights of Rhodes. This was a religious order, founded in Jerusalem in 1080. Its primary concern was to tend

the sick. After the establishment of the Latin states of the Holy Land after the First Crusade in 1096 and the conquest of Jerusalem three years later, it became one of the most important upholders of the increasingly beleaguered Crusader states in the Holy Land.

With the final expulsion of the Crusaders in 1291, the Knights Hospitallers moved to Rhodes, establishing themselves there with papal permission in 1309. And here they proceeded to create one of the most memorable medieval complexes in Europe, its grave, understated beauty achieving a kind of architectural perfection.

Situated above a modern town, the acropolis of Lindos was fortified by successive powers, each leaving its mark on the site.

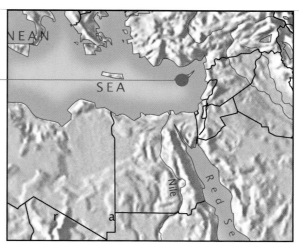

## Greece

**Period:**

12th century BC

**Significance:**

This Cypriot town is the mythological birthplace of Aphrodite.

The archaeological site Kourion, located near Paphos, includes a restored amphitheater overlooking the Mediterranean.

Paphos, nestled in the southwest corner of Cyprus, is indelibly associated with Aphrodite, the Greek goddess of love. It was here, according to legend, that she was born, emerging from the foaming seas. In fact the island had been associated with various fertility cults for 5,000 years. Yet it was Aphrodite, to whom an enormous temple was built, who made the island a focus of pilgrimage across the Greek world. Earthquakes and the inevitable depredations of the centuries mean that little more than the foundations of the temple remain today.

The town subsequently passed under Byzantine, then Venetian control before it fell to the Ottomans in the 16th century. Today, it presents an exceptionally vivid record of this turbulent history, the whole beguilingly beautiful—much like Aphrodite herself. Even in Greece, few places more instantly exude this obvious sense of the past.

*"Not only did Aphrodite start the war by offering Helen of Troy to Paris, but the abduction was accomplished when Paris, seeing Helen for the first time, was inflamed with desire to have her."*

—Myth of Aphrodite being the original cause of the Trojan War

# NEMRUT DAĞ

## Turkey

**Period:**

62 BC

**Significance:**

This tomb of King Antiochus I is among the ancient world's most ambitious constructions.

I n the 1st century BC, the briefly independent kingdom of Commagene in the barren mountains of southeast Turkey gave rise to an audacious attempt to ensure a kind of improbable immortality on the part of its king, Antiochus I. Though little more than a gangster ruler, vengeful and brutal, he had a series of 30-foot (9-m) high representations of himself and a variety of Greek and Persian deities planted in the dusty wastes of this isolated mountainside. They were to be not merely his tomb but also a permanent reminder of his rule. Human vanity has rarely been more precisely—or memorably—recorded.

Statues of eagles and lions, symbols of power and nobility, were placed to stand guard over the king's burial mound.

Syncretic deities of Greek and Persian extraction were erected alongside the king's ancestors in honor of King Antiochus Theos.

*"Those who come to visit my grave should wear their most beautiful clothes and the most fragrant perfumes. I will give them happiness and prosperity for generations on these lands."*

—King Antiochus, 50 BC

There are no ancient references to Nemrut Dağ, which was discovered in the late 19th century and has not been fully excavated. It has recently been restored with fallen fragments, still impressive despite their ruinous state, erected where they were found.

## Turkey

**Period:**

12th century BC

**Significance:**

This city in western Turkey may be Troy, the ancient Greek city and site of the Trojan War.

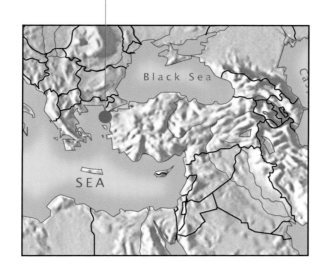

*The historical existence of Troy was doubted until its rediscovery by archaeologist Heinrich Schliemann in the 1870s.*

The ancient Greek city of Troy, today Hisarlik in western Turkey, continues to exert an extraordinary hold on Western imaginations. The reason is that it was Troy that provided the starting point for Homer's epic poems, the *Iliad* and the *Odyssey*, the former the story of the Trojan War, the latter of Odysseus's 20-year quest to return home. The extent to which these sprawling masterpieces can be thought, even tangentially, to relate historical episodes is doubtful. It is not even clear whether Homer himself, conventionally said to have lived in the 8th century BC, was a real figure. The poems themselves, a heady conflation of gods, humans, monsters and fabled beings, almost certainly stem from an older oral tradition of storytelling. Nonetheless, they were believed by the Greeks themselves to have been true and form the bedrock of Western literature.

Repeated efforts have been made to identify the site of Troy. From the available evidence, Hisarlik is as convincing a candidate as any. The site itself has been continuously occupied for millennia, progressively built and rebuilt following fires, earthquakes and, probably, wars to form a series of archaeological layers. One of these city layers, the prosaically named Troy VII, not only dates to approximately the right period—ca.1300 to 950 BC—but also suggests a substantial, fortified settlement.

*The fabled Trojan horse, recreated as a tourist attraction near the site.*

*Helen's beauty so transfixed her suitor Menelaus that he dropped his weapons upon seeing her. The legend was depicted on this krater—a Greek pottery vessel—centuries after the fall of Troy.*

# ROME

## Italy

**Period:**

753 BC to AD 410

**Significance:**

This ancient city was the heart of the Roman Empire.

The rise of Rome was certainly remarkable; it was an obscure crossing point on the river Tiber in central Italy, yet came to form the heart of the largest empire the world had then known. Not just the entire Mediterranean world, but the ancient Near East, Spain, France and Britain were all ruled from Rome. The city itself—"I found a city of bricks," asserted the first emperor, Augustus, "I left

The Elian Bridge was built over the Tiber river by the Emperor Hadrian (AD 117–138). Saint Peter's Basicila, dominating the skyline beyond, was completed 15 centuries later.

a city of marble"—was suitably imposing, displaying the Roman genius for public works on a stupendous scale: baths, temples, theaters, palaces, triumphal arches and aqueducts. Their architectural language may have been borrowed from Greece, but their splendor and daring was authentically Roman. Even ruined, they inspire awe. Little wonder later peoples took the city for the work of giants.

Yet Rome, reduced to a squalid backwater in the Middle Ages, was to rise again after the Renaissance, the heart of the Roman Catholic Church largely recast by a series of energetic popes able to make full use of the energies of a series of no less ambitious architects of genius. Baroque Rome saw a series of vast new buildings, chiefly churches, and public spaces teeming with heroically dynamic statues and, a key hallmark of the Baroque, sumptuous fountains. It was town planning on an audacious scale.

Ancient Rome developed around the Forum, which included an amphitheater, basilicas, shrines and temples, such as the Temple of Saturn, seen at right. The Forum thus served as an economic, political, social and religious center all at once, and remains a crowd-pleaser today.

*"As long as the Coliseum stands, so shall Rome. When the Coliseum falls, so shall Rome. When Rome falls, so shall the world."*

—The Venerable Bede (672–735)

*When completed during the reign of Augustus (27 BC–AD 14), the Theater of Marcellus could seat 11,000 spectators.*

# PONT DU GARD

### France

**Period:**

Middle of the 1st century AD

**Significance:**

The aqueduct is an engineering feat of the Roman Empire.

*Recent renovations, including the addition of a museum, serve the thousands of visitors who make the Pont du Gard one of the five most popular tourist attractions in France.*

PART II - HUMAN CULTURE

*No mortar was used to build the aqueduct bridge that spans the Gardon River. Instead, stones were cut and raised to fit into place.*

t is often said of the Romans that they were not so much architects as engineers. Certainly, it is the case that much Roman architecture has a kind of ponderous opulence in which more was always intended to mean better. It is perhaps no surprise that the Romans not only invented concrete but also rapidly became adept in its use. Yet the Pont du Gard in southern France, constructed between AD 40 and 60, proves that Roman engineering could produce structures that were both elegant and durable.

It is a purely utilitarian aqueduct, part of a 30-mile (48-km) structure that brought water from natural springs at Uzès to the thriving, rapidly expanding Roman city of Nîmes. A precise measure of its exacting construction reveals that it is gravity fed despite dropping by only 40 feet (12 m) over its full length. It is just as impressive that it was built with no mortar: the precut blocks fit precisely over its length, with the upper of its three arched tiers rising 155 feet (47 m) above the rocky river bed below.

*In 1743, a second bridge was built along the lower level of the Pont du Gard to accommodate curious pedestrians.*

# POMPEII AND HERCULANEUM

## Italy

**Period:**

79 AD

**Significance:**

Buried under ash after the eruption of Mount Vesuvius in AD 79, Pompeii has since been excavated and provides invaluable insight into life in 1st-century Roman Italy.

The eruption of Vesuvius in the late summer of AD 79 buried the two towns at its feet, Pompeii and Herculaneum, under ash almost 10 feet thick. The destruction was such that the towns were abandoned and never rebuilt. The result, in effect, was to freeze them in time. Only in the 18th century were they rediscovered; in the 19th century excavation revealed them once again.

Pompeii in particular yielded a rich harvest. It was a seaside town, one largely given over to pleasurable pursuits. A number of the larger houses, decorated with elaborate mosaics, wall paintings, and extensive gardens, underline the luxury of upper-class life in 1st-century Roman Italy.

*"… darker, and larger, and mightier, spread the cloud above them. It was a sudden and more ghastly Night rushing upon the realm of Noon!"*

—Excerpt from *The Last Days of Pompeii* by Edward Bulwer-Lytton, 1834

*The streets of Pompeii were paved with cobblestones.*

*Archeologists unearthing Pompeii in the 1860s found human-shaped voids in the volcanic ash. They used plaster to cast molds of the voids, recreating the bodies of animals and humans—many of them in futilely protective positions—killed by the eruption.*

# AQUILEIA

## Italy

### Period:

Since 180 BC

### Significance:

One of the largest and wealthiest cities in the Roman Empire, Aquileia has been left almost completely untouched, and so provides a nearly complete example of an early Roman city.

*Fourth-century mosaics cover the floor of the Cathedral of Aquileia, with columns in the Gothic style built 1,000 years later.*

Aquileia, at the northern end of the Adriatic in Friuli-Venezia Giulia, is a relative rarity among the Roman cities of Italy, having been founded in 180 BC as a garrison town to protect Rome's new allies, the Veneti. Though hardly a frontier town, it nonetheless quickly established itself as a key staging post on the route to Rome's European territories to the northeast.

In 452, the city was all but annihilated by Attila's Huns. In part, its archaeological significance today rests in the fact that, still only partially excavated, Aquileia is potentially an archaeological treasure house. Its other claim to fame is its cathedral, built in 1379 and shimmering with mosaics.

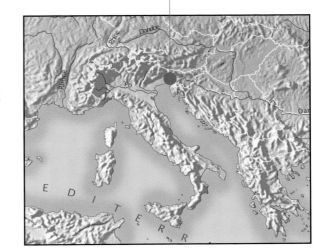

*For centuries, the stones of visible ancient Roman remains at Aquileia were pillaged by locals for use in buildings.*

# VOLUBILIS

## Morocco

**Period:**

3rd century BC

**Significance:**

This North African city was an important outpost on the western edge of the Roman empire.

Grand facades, such as that of the Decumanus Maximus, suggest the transformation of an agrarian outpost into a provincial center.

T he reach of Rome was such that it was able to maintain its rule in North Africa with only a single legion of about 6,000 men. The *Pax Romana* duly imposed, North Africa became one of the richest provinces in the empire, cities such as Volubilis in Morocco growing wealthy on the grain and oil produced in this fertile region. Even with the collapse of Rome, the city, almost uniquely, continued to thrive. It was only with the lightning Muslim conquest of North Africa in the 7th century that this once elegant provincial outpost was extinguished.

The Triumphal Arch honored Emperor Caracalla, who granted citizenship to the residents of Volubilis and exempted them from taxation.

*"Just when you think you are at the world's end, you see smoke rising from east to west as far as the eye can turn ... one long, low, rising and falling, and hiding and showing line of towers ... that is the wall."*

— British author Rudyard Kipling, from *Puck of Pook's Hill*

Hadrian's wall was built from east to west, with regular forts and towers—garrisoned by Roman troops—along the way.

20th century, its stones were still being carried off for use in local buildings—substantial sections of this extraordinary construction remain, snaking its way over its moorland landscape.

Sycamore Gap is known popularly as "the Robin Hood tree," because it was featured in a film about the legendary figure.

# B A T H

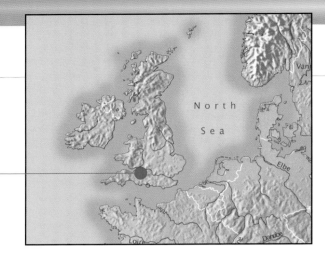

## United Kingdom

**Period:**

AD 43

**Significance:**

This British town served as a retreat for wealthy Romans, who took advantage of the city's natural thermal waters.

The aptly named city of Bath in Somerset, in the softly rolling land-scapes of southwest England, rapidly became a key Roman city. The Romans took advantage of the city's naturally hot thermal waters, with their apparent medicinal properties. These steamy, muddy waters—which still bubble and thrust upwards—were all but

*The Great Bath is largely reconstructed over remaining Roman pillars. Restoration and reconstruction of the Roman bath have occurred at various stages since the 12th century, as successive generations basked in the supposedly salubrious waters.*

*Connecting Bath to Bathwick over the Avon river, Pulteney Bridge is one of only four in the world designed with shops lining each of its sides.*

irresistible to the Romans, precisely as they would be to later generations of visitors.

To the Romans, Bath was known as *Aquae Sulis*, the Waters of Sulis Minerva, the city's presiding goddess. Characteristically, a Great Bath, heavily restored in the 18th and 19th centuries, was built. Here, high-born Romans could ease their aching

*Water heated by geothermal energy to a consistent 114°F rises from the Sacred Spring, associated with the Roman goddess Sulis.*

bones and console themselves for having been dispatched to so remote an outpost of the empire, secure in the knowledge that reliable Roman plumbing and central heating was always on hand.

Its fragmentary Roman ruins aside, Bath is justly celebrated today as a model late 18th-century English town. It is made up of a series of uniform crescents and terraces, understated in their elegance, which reinforces a vision of town planning unmatched in Great Britain.

*Surplus water flows from the Sacred Spring via a brick tributary, constructed in Roman times, still functional despite its age.*

# TIVOLI

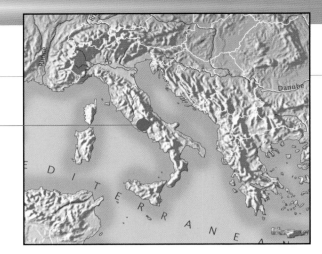

Tivoli, conveniently a few miles south of Rome, is home to two of the most extravagant villas in Italy: one, the 2nd-century AD complex built for the emperor Hadrian; the other the late-Renaissance gardens of the Villa d'Este, constructed in conscious emulation of its antique predecessors. Each, lavish and opulent, represents conspicuous consumption on a deliberately epic scale.

For Hadrian, the goal was to recreate in miniature the ancient world's most celebrated buildings. The result was a series of marble-clad masterpieces clustered around a series of exactly landscaped pools, lakes and artificial islands. Even today, largely ruined, it retains an improbably extravagant grandeur.

The Villa d'Este was no less deliberately grand, a summer house justified above all by its lavish, sprawling gardens. Statuary, fountains and artfully sited buildings, the whole intended to evoke a lost Roman world as much as to proclaim a Rome reborn, were laid out. Extravagance was the whole point of these endlessly opulent creations.

## Italy

**Period:**

2nd century

**Significance:**

Tivoli is recognized as a World Heritage site for its two grand villas: Adriana and Este.

*Three rectangular fish ponds extend into the garden of the Villa d'Este, separated from the estate by the arching waters of the Fountain of Neptune, Roman god of the sea.*

*Musical tones are produced by water and air channeled through the pipes of the recently restored Organ Fountain, which features statues of Apollo and Diana.*

## France

**Period:**

1st century

**Significance:**

Arles is an excellent example of the adaptation of an ancient city to medieval European civilization.

Built 125 years after Rome colonized Arles, the Arena is still used today—testament to its construction—for concerts, opera, theater and bullfights, including the prestigious annual Cocarde d'Or.

The Mediterranean coast of France, long a magnet for early Greek settlers, as well as for the later Romans as they spread their stern rule across the Mediterranean, is among the most captivating in the world. The seafaring Greeks established a colony here as early as the 6th century BC. Later, for the Romans, its subjection was an imperative. Arles, a near-model city, thrived under the rule of Rome. A series of substantial public buildings—theaters, baths and temples—proclaimed its status as a stable, orderly and prosperous Roman colony. In the Middle Ages, it thrived again, a crucial trading center in a France that was slowly reasserting itself.

Archways are repeated throughout the Arena's three tiers.

# LOIRE VALLEY

Early Renaissance France was a land increasingly aware of its cultural significance. For its ruling families and nobility above all, this meant an elaborately intricate courtly code, an extension of the medieval knightly virtues of chivalry. History was on their side: French victory in the seemingly intractable struggle with England—the 100 Years' War—allowed castles to be given over to this vision of civilized living rather than the grimmer arts of warfare.

And it was in the fertile and temperate valley of the country's longest river, the Loire, that precisely these courtly virtues were taken to new heights. It was the king, François I, who set the tone in 1519, commissioning the immense Château of Chambord, where he was later to install the aging Leonardo da Vinci, who may have been responsible for the extraordinary double-helix spiral staircase. Under the building's profusion of turrets and towers, 2,000 people could be accommodated. It took 12,000 horses to transport king and court to and from this vast palace.

Other architectural highlights in the valley are the jewel-like Azay-le-Rideau; Catherine de Medici's Chenonceau, its elegant lines reflected in the waters of the little river Cher over which it was built; Ussé, where Charles Perrault wrote *The Sleeping Beauty*; and Valençay, with its spreading acres of formal gardens, punctuated with fountains. But the Loire Valley is a region of elegant, historic towns, too: Blois, Orléans, Amboise and Angers, all standing on the banks of the broad, shallow river.

In the 17th century, Louis XIV may have wrested the focus away from the Loire, transferring it instead to Versailles outside Paris, where he was eventually to build a palace larger even than that at Chambord.

*"The Loire is a queen and kings have loved her."*
—French aphorism about the Loire Valley

## France

**Period:**

Since the 10th century

**Significance:**

Loire Valley is noteworthy for its architectural heritage in such historic towns as Blois, Chinon, Orléans, Saumur and Tours, particularly in its 300 castles.

*Constructed as a showpiece rather than a fortification, the Château de Chambord is a masterpiece of the French Renaissance, with more than 400 rooms and an astonishing 365 fireplaces.*

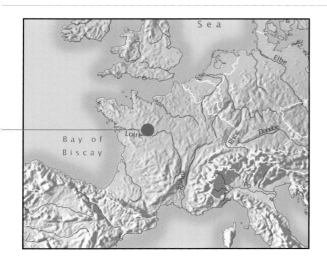

*Spanning the Cher River is the Château de Chenonceau, a remarkable construction resting on four major arches and two smaller ones.*

*The world-famous gardens of Château de Villandry were painstakingly reconstructed in the early 20th century, because the original Renaissance gardens were destroyed the century before.*

# EDINBURGH

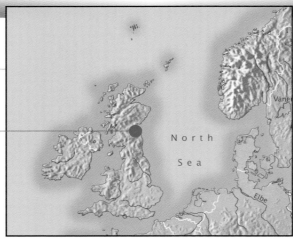

## United Kingdom

### Period:

Capital of Scotland since 1437

### Significance:

The Scottish capital since the 15th century, Edinburgh has two distinct areas: the Old Town, dominated by a medieval fortress, and the neoclassical New Town, whose development from the 18th century onward had a far-reaching influence on European urban planning.

*Edinburgh Castle perches atop a volcanic rock, called Castle Rock, which formed some 340 million years ago. Archaeological digs suggest the first fortress there arose in about 600 AD.*

No city in Britain matches Edinburgh for the drama of its setting. The Scottish capital is built on an extinct volcano, whose steep crags loom over the city center and provide an unmatched setting for the medieval Old Town, crowned at one end by Edinburgh Castle. From the castle, the Royal Mile, one of the most compelling medieval streets in Europe, leads past the ancient cathedral to Holyrood Castle, still the monarch's official residence in Scotland.

Yet the glory of Edinburgh is found just as much in the 18th-century New Town, the most imposing collection of Georgian buildings in Britain, harmonious, elegant and measured, not just a precise counterpoint to the Old Town but a fitting reflection of the rapidly growing status of the 18th-century city. Impoverished and provincial for much of its history, Edinburgh was transformed in the 18th century. It was more than a matter of economic prosperity: the city underwent an intellectual revolution that more than justified the tag commonly applied to it of "the Athens of the North."

*The flag of Scotland displays the white cross of Saint Andrew.*

# THE PALACE OF WESTMINSTER

The Palace of Westminster in London, site of both the House of Commons and House of Lords, can legitimately claim to be the "Mother of Parliaments." The process by which England's, later Britain's, parliament came to exercise powers—previously the purview of the monarch—was fitful at best, as was the emergence of a fully representative democracy. It was only in 1918 that every British man was given the vote and not until 1928 that all women were. But that Britain can claim to be among the world's most dependably democratic countries is beyond doubt.

Appropriately, the building itself, completed in 1860 after an 1834 fire destroyed the medieval original, is perhaps the best-known in London, certainly the most instantly recognized. Its Thames-side setting and richly detailed Gothic exterior, framed by the 336-foot-high Victoria Tower to the south and Big Ben—actually the name of one of its bells; properly, it is the Clock Tower—to the north are iconic.

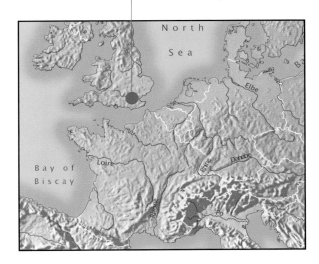

## United Kingdom

### Period:

Early 11th century, rebuilt in the 19th century

### Significance:

Westminster Palace, sited on the west bank of the River Thames in London, is the site of the House of Commons and the House of Lords.

*A statue of one of Great Britain's most famous prime ministers, Winston Churchill, overlooks Westminster's clock tower.*

*"What touches all, should be approved of all, and it is also clear that common dangers should be met by measures agreed upon in common."*

—King Edward I on November 13, 1295, at the first official Parliament of England

*Once the home of Great Britain's royal family, the Palace of Westminster took on its current Parlimentary duties following a fire during the reign of Henry VIII (1509–1547).*

# WELSH CASTLES OF KING EDWARD

From 1277, Edward I of England—also called "Longshanks" in honor of his unusual height—began a ruthless subjection of neighboring Wales, a country at least nominally independent but in reality fragmented into various houses, chieftainships and tribes. By 1284, his brutal control of Wales was complete. As a visible and permanent mark of his conquest, Edward then built a series of immense castles in Wales, chiefly in the mountainous north of the country: at Beaumaris, Harlech, Caernarfon, Conwy and Kidwelly among other places. It was the largest and most ambitious program of building in Britain since the construction of Hadrian's Wall, and an emphatic reminder of the military might of the Plantagenet war machine.

*Ingeniously designed to defend its inhabitants from outside attack, Beaumaris Castle featured a series of obstacles, such as a surrounding moat and arrow slits in the thick walls. The fortress, however, was never finished.*

*Caernarfon Castle. Edward I's heir, also Edward, was born at Caernarfon in 1284, and in 1301 his father bestowed upon him the title Prince of Wales. The investiture of Charles, the current Prince of Wales, took place at the castle in 1969.*

*Dating from between 1283 and 1289, Conwy Castle was built as part of Edward I's second campaign in north Wales.*

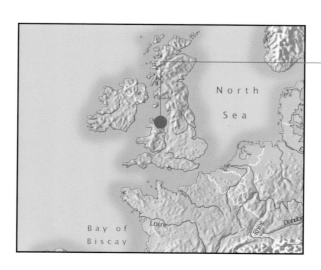

## United Kingdom

**Period:**

13th century

**Significance:**

These extremely well-preserved monuments are examples of the colonization and defense projects carried out throughout the reign of Edward I.

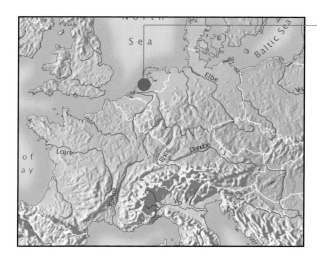

Windmills dot the low-lying Dutch landscape, where for centuries they provided the major power source for draining land, as well as milling grain, sawing lumber, and other labor-intensive activities.

## The Netherlands

**Period:**

1740

**Significance:**

This mill network, an innovation in the drainage and protection of an area by the development and application of hydraulic technology, began in the Middle Ages and has continued non-stop to the present day.

In traditional Dutch windmills, workers have to rotate the blades manually to take advantage of the prevailing wind's direction.

Small, densely populated Holland has long had to confront the geographical reality of those areas of the country—approximately 25 percent—that lie below sea level. From at least the Middle Ages, draining and protecting them has been an absolute priority, a relentless struggle with nature demanding ingenuity and determination.

If dikes are the principal means of holding back water, at least until the 19th century and the development of steam pumps, windmills were the principal means of pumping out the water. At one point, there were more than 10,000 windmills in the country, adding an instantly distinctive element to Holland's flat, canal-laced landscapes.

Today, few remain, but at Kinderdijk, or "Child's Dike," some 10 miles from Rotterdam, 19 windmills, the largest such concentration in Holland, have been preserved. The oldest, destroyed by a fire in 1997 but since rebuilt, dates from 1521; eight date from 1738; a further eight from 1740; and one from 1760. All are still operational though are used for only a few, symbolic days of the year.

Yet whatever the determination of the Dutch not merely to reclaim land from the sea but to preserve it, floods have been a regular and frequently fatal feature of Dutch history. As late as 1953, storms in the North Sea overwhelmed the country's sea defenses and left 1,835 dead.

*"During the Saint Elizabeth flood of 1421, the cradle with a child on the waves was kept in balance by a cat and stranded on the slope of a dike."*

—Legend behind the name "Kinderdijk"

For many years, residents of low-lying Kinderdijk relied on the village's 19 windmills to keep it above water. Today, they use powerful pumps to stay dry.

# LA GRAND-PLACE

## Belgium

**Period:**

Late17th century

**Significance:**

La Grand-Place is the central market square of Brussels.

*In the middle of Brussels' historic market square is the town hall, with its Gothic tower holding a statue of St. Michael.*

Across the Low Countries—essentially modern-day Holland and Belgium— medieval cities that had become prosperous from the wool trade competed to build ever more lavish and substantial civic buildings. Where in France and Italy, such emphatic statements of local pride mostly found expression in religious buildings, in northern Europe, markets, warehouses, town halls and guild halls proliferated.

None is more spectacular than the central market square of Brussels, La Grand-Place, dating mainly to the late 17th century but dominated by the medieval town hall, begun in 1402 and completed in 1455. Its central tower surges 318 feet (96 m) high from its steeply pitched roof. Opposite is the hardly less ornate 16th-century Maison du Roi.

*Because the European Union's administrative center is located in Brussels, the town is unofficially known as the "Capital of Europe."*

*"The most beautiful theater in the world."*
—French filmmaker Jean Cocteau (1889–1963), about La Grand-Place

*Brugge Town Hall, built around 1400, has an ornate carved ceiling and 19th-century murals that illustrate the town's history.*

Medieval Brugge was among the most powerful and prosperous of the cities of northern Europe's Hanseatic League. Trade was its lifeblood, its leading citizens among the richest families in the world, complacently disposing of vast fortunes. Projecting this sense of self-worth and civic pride was increasingly a priority, one that naturally found expression in public buildings of ever greater size and splendor.

The Cloth Hall in Brugge, for example, begun in 1282, boasts a tower that still dominates the historic heart of the city, rising 260 feet (85 m) skyward. For the period, it was an exceptionally daring structure, easily the equal of any cathedral. Private houses, too, reached levels of comfort and ostentation that almost outdid the private palaces of contemporary Venice or Florence. The comparison with Venice is apt. Like the Italian city, Brugge is a city of canals. Their placid, bottle-green waters add enormously to its charms.

Medieval Brugge, spared development because of the city's decline, has survived intact. By the 19th century, it was an economic has-been, forgotten and overlooked, grass growing in its cobbled streets.

## Belgium

### Period:

12th to 15th centuries

### Significance:

Brugge is an outstanding example of a medieval settlement that has maintained its historic fabric as it has evolved over the centuries.

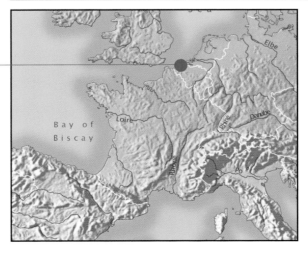

*The canals that weave through Brugge once connected the city to the North Sea for trade. The entry is now blocked by mud and silt.*

*Brugge has many well-preserved examples of medieval brick Gothic architecture. Belfries are common sights.*

# PARIS

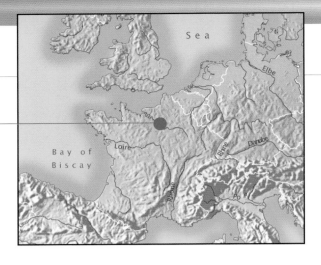

## France

**Period:**

Since the 10th century

**Significance:**

Of the world's greatest cities, Paris is the most elegant and culturally vital.

Paris effortlessly retains its status as the most elegant and civilized of the world's great cities. It is more than a matter of 2,000 years of history, more even than a matter of the city's superb buildings and parks, or even of the central role France has played in shaping the world today. Above all, it is a matter of style. Paris is permanently chic, permanently sophisticated, permanently assured.

From the Seine looping through the heart of the city, dividing the Left Bank from the Right; the grand boulevards and large squares of Haussmann's

*Commissioned by Napoleon in 1806, the Arc de Triomphe is engraved with the names of major and minor victories during the Revolutionary and Napoleonic periods.*

immensely influential city-planning scheme; the imposing grandeur of the Louvre and splendor of the Champs Elysées, with the Arc de Triomphe at its western end; the Gothic glories of the Ile de la Cité; the iconic Eiffel Tower and the aristocratic hauteur of the Marais or the Place des Vosges, Paris is a stunning collection of cultural and architectural landmarks in the history of Western Europe.

There is no period of Western architecture of the last 1,000 years without at least one good example, including the cathedrals of Notre Dame and La Sainte Chapelle, masterpieces of medieval architecture. The city's parks, too, are perfect urban oases of precise formality.

Built in 1889 to commemorate the 100th anniversary of the French Revolution, the Eiffel Tower stands about 1,000 feet (305 m) tall.

*"An artist has no home in Europe except in Paris."*

—Friedrich Nietzsche. German philosopher

Construction of Notre Dame began in 1163, when Pope Alexander III set the foundation stone in place, and continued off and on for the next two centuries.

# MONT SAINT-MICHEL

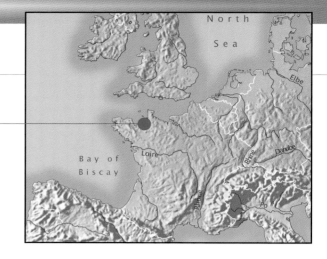

*"The archangel Michael appeared to St. Aubert, bishop of Avranches, in 708 and instructed him to build a church on the rocky islet. Aubert repeatedly ignored the angel's instruction, until Michael burned a hole in the bishop's skull with his finger."*

—The legend of Mont Saint-Michel

## France

### Period:

Built between the 11th and 16th centuries

### Significance:

Built over 500 years, on a natural site that posed formidable challenges, the abbey is an artistic and technical tour de force.

Mont Saint-Michel is one of the enduring wonders of France: the Benedictine abbey rises from a tiny granite island just off the coast of Normandy, in the midst of vast silt-rich mudflats. It is linked to the mainland by a small causeway. At its base are clustered the tiny, gray streets of the village that grew up in the shadow of the monastery. These in turn give way to the massive masonry that supports the church. The whole then climaxes in the tapering spire of the abbey church itself, as it reaches skyward. Victor Hugo called Mont Saint-Michel "a miraculous pyramid."

That so dramatic a site should have been a destination for medieval pilgrims, treading the "path to paradise," is hardly a surprise. Yet the monastery's history has been checkered. It was frequently under siege by the English during the Hundred Years' War, even if its symbolic significance was rather greater than its strategic importance. By the time of the French Revolution at the end of the 18th century, the abbey was forcibly closed and converted into a prison. Only in 1874, by which point its obvious architectural importance had been recognized, was the abbey reopened.

*Mont Saint-Michel abbey, dedicated to the archangel St. Michael, sits on a granite island between Normandy and Brittany.*

*According to the lore of Mont Saint-Michel, the Bishop of Avranches received orders to build the abbey from the archangel Michael in the year 708.*

# VERSAILLES

Garden designer André Le Nôtre (1613–1700) turned what was once a swamp into the gardens of Versailles.

## France

**Period:**
Construction began in 1624

**Significance:**
Versailles was the principal residence of the French kings from Louis XIV to Louis XVI.

*"There is an intimate relation between the King and his château. The idol is worthy of the temple, the temple of the idol...for a cathedral, it is the idea of God. For Versailles, it is the idea of the King. Its mythology is but a magnificent allegory of which Louis XIV is the reality."*

—Baron Arthur Léon Imbert de Saint-Amand

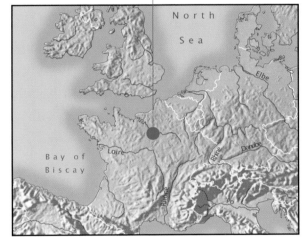

In 1661, the youthful Louis XIV, king of France since 1638 when he was only five years old, assumed full control of the French state. Among his earliest decisions was to rebuild his father's modest 20-room hunting lodge at Versailles, some miles south of Paris. In 1682 he went further: to the astonishment of the court, forced to give up the pleasures of Paris for a house in the country, he made Versailles the seat of the French government.

Louis seems genuinely to have been in love with Versailles. Yet that so unpromising a building could be transformed into the greatest palace in Europe scarcely seemed probable. But this is precisely what this remarkable ruler achieved.

Just as France was for Louis clearly the greatest and most naturally blessed country in Europe, so he was clearly the greatest, most naturally blessed of its kings. It followed that his court, a slave to etiquette, should eclipse all others.

The work itself took place in several distinct stages that lasted well into the next century. On occasion it came close to bankrupting the overstrained state. The first phase, complete by 1670, was to enclose the original hunting lodge in a new structure. This created both the formal entrance, the Cour d'Honneur, in the main (east) façade, and the central element of the main (west) garden façade. Simultaneously, the gardens themselves, a vast pleasure park studded with lakes, fountains and trim parterres, were first laid out.

The second phase saw the extension of the garden façade. When completed in 1708, it measured 1,318 feet (402 m). At the same time, the glittering Hall of Mirrors and the elegantly sumptuous Chapelle Royale were created. Further work was continued under Louis XVI, including the little *hameau*, or hamlet, built for Marie-Antoinette in 1783, in whose delightfully fake rustic surroundings she would play at being a milkmaid.

When the gardens were constructed in the 1600s, a network of iron water pipes fed some 1,400 fountains, including the mammoth Apollo fountain (foreground).

Some 36,000 workers toiled from 1660 to 1685 to build the Palace of Versailles. It served as the home of kings for more than a century.

# B E R N E

## Switzerland

**Period:**

15th and 16th centuries

**Significance:**

Berne, capital of Switzerland, was in the late Middle Ages the biggest and most powerful city-state north of the Alps.

Berne, federal capital of Switzerland, has long been overshadowed by Zurich to the east and Geneva to the west. Yet Berne is one of the most appealing and beautiful late-medieval cities in Europe.

Its location is dramatic, a rocky escarpment overlooking a steep bend in the fast-flowing river Aare, which almost encircles the old town. As a natural strongpoint, it was always a logical place to lay out a town, a point clearly not lost on its founder,

*The River Aare snakes its way through Berne, a heavily populated but small city of approximately 125,000 residents.*

PART II - HUMAN CULTURE

Duke Berchtold V of Zähringen, credited not just with its foundation in 1191 but its name, a corruption of bär, the German for bear, one of which he is traditionally said to have killed on the site.

The main attractions include the ornate Zytglogge, or clock tower, complete with an immense, richly colored clock; the dour 15th-century cathedral; and a series of elegant arcaded streets—four miles in all—that appeal to visitors and locals alike.

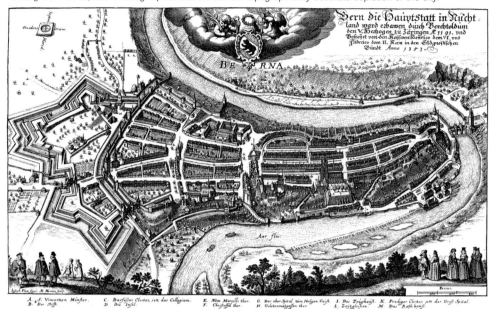

*Dating from 1549, this drawing represents the earliest topographically accurate depiction of the city.*

*"It is great here in Berne, an ancient, thoroughly comfortable city, in which one can live just as in Zurich. Both sides of the roads are completely lined by old arcades, so that one can stroll from one end of the city to the other in the worst downpour without getting noticeably wet…"*

—Albert Einstein, writing to Mileva Maric, February 4, 1902

*Berne residents take pride in the city's well-preserved historic center, which is known as "Old Town."*

# BELLINZONE

## Switzerland

**Period:**

15th century

**Significance:**

These three medieval castles on the border of Switzerland and Italy are among the most exceptional in Europe.

*Then and now, travelers have used the Saint Gotthard route through Bellinzone to take them north to the Alps and south to Italy.*

Bellinzone, nestled in the shadows of the Alps in the Italian-speaking canton of Ticino in southern Switzerland, claims three of the most remarkable castles in Europe. By any measure, they are an exceptional ensemble.

Location is key to Bellinzone and its castles. It controls the routes to no fewer than four Alpine passes. When in the 15th century Switzerland sought to protect its southern flank against Italian incursions, capturing Bellinzone, then controlled by the Sforza dukes of Milan, became a priority. The Milanese responded by turning the little town into today's fortress. The Swiss had their way, awarded Bellinzone by treaty in 1503. The castles, however, witnesses to centuries of warfare, remain.

*Castelgrande, overlooking the Ticino valley, is at the center of the fortifications built to protect the town and guard the alpine pass.*

*"They are the doors and keys of Italy."*

—War Officer Azzo Visconti,
describing the Bellinzone castles in 1475

High atop the hill, the Hohensalzburg Fortress overlooks the Salzach River. The castle's construction began in the 11th century and continued for several hundred years.

## Austria

**Period:**

From the 15th century

**Significance:**

Salzburg is among the greatest Baroque cities of the world.

Salzburg lies in western Austria, straddling the Salzach river, the Alps to its south, rolling plains to its north. It is among the most elegant of the world's cities, with a profusion of church towers and domes, and an historic center filled by handsome 17th- and 18th-century buildings. Over it all looms the impressive bulk of the Festung Hohensalzburg, the city fortress, first built in the 11th century, and then progressively enlarged over the succeeding centuries.

The site has been inhabited since well before it fell to the Romans in 15 BC. But it was from the Renaissance onward that Salzburg prospered. Salzburg means "salt castle" and it was salt—more particularly taxes levied on barges carrying salt past the city—that underpinned its prosperity.

For most people today Salzburg means Mozart, its most famous son. He was born here in 1756, and it was in Salzburg, too, that he worked between 1773 and 1777 for the city's ruler, the prince-archbishop. It was never a happy relationship. Mozart found provincial Salzburg increasingly stifling and the prince-archbishop condescending and petty. The city has more than made up for its offhand treatment since. Tributes to and memories of Mozart are everywhere in Salzburg.

*"Of all the lovely regions I have seen, none can compare to Salzburg's striking natural beauty."*

—Wolfgang Amadeus Mozart

Wolfgang Amadeus Mozart was born in Salzburg in 1756. His birthplace and family home on Getreidegasse is now a museum.

# GRAZ

## Austria

**Period:**

From the 14th century

**Significance:**

Graz's "Old Town" is one of the best-preserved city centers in Central Europe.

*A third of all Austrians live in its five largest cities, one of which is Graz. Many residents live in multistory apartment buildings.*

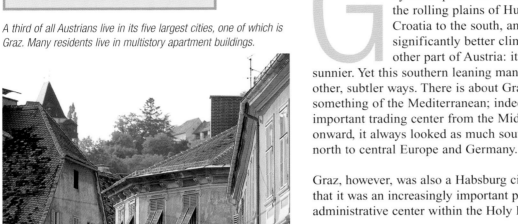

Graz in southeastern Austria is shielded by the Alps to the west and open to the rolling plains of Hungary and Croatia to the south, and so enjoys a significantly better climate than any other part of Austria: it is warmer and sunnier. Yet this southern leaning manifests itself in other, subtler ways. There is about Graz almost something of the Mediterranean; indeed, as an important trading center from the Middle Ages onward, it always looked as much south to Italy as north to central Europe and Germany.

Graz, however, was also a Habsburg city, meaning that it was an increasingly important political and administrative center within the Holy Roman Empire, that loose confederation of mainly German-speaking lands that sprawled across much of central Europe for almost 1,000 years until Napoleon imperiously disbanded it as a medieval relic in 1806.

The historic center of Graz—crossroads to the Balkans and the Mediterranean for hundreds of years—is notable as a World Heritage site in part because its buildings were designed by some of the greatest artists and architects of their times.

*The three bells of the clock tower in Graz have been accurately striking the hour since 1712.*

*"The devil promised the people of Graz to make their local mountain, the Schöckl. Satan flew over Graz with a huge rock from Africa in his hands. He threw the rock onto the town. The rock broke in two parts. Today, the smaller one is Austein with its Calvary. The bigger one is Schlossberg."*

—Legend of the Graz Mountains

*Its Baroque fountains may bring visitors to Graz today, but a teaching job drew astronomer Johannes Kepler to town in the 1590s.*

ienna was central Europe's imperial city par excellence. As capital of the sprawling, multilingual Austro-Hungarian empire in the 19th century, including the whole of modern Hungary, most of the Balkans, much of northeast Italy, as well the Czech Republic, Slovakia and even parts of Poland, it was acutely conscious of its imperial status. This was a city built to overwhelm.

The Hofburg, the one-time imperial palace, has almost 3,000 rooms. The principal art museum, the Kunsthistorisches Museum, rivals the Louvre in its sheer size. Running through the city's heart are two pedestrian-only shopping streets—Graben and Kärnterstrasse—built on a similarly colossal scale.

Yet Vienna at its 19th-century peak was also a city of music and cafés, one that had taken the arts of civilized urban life to new heights.

*A gilded statue of Johann Strauss II stands in Vienna's Stadtpark, where Strauss performed in the 1860s, soon after it opened.*

## Austria

**Period:**

From the 15th century

**Significance:**

Vienna, heart of the Holy Roman Empire, became the capital of the Austro-Hungarian Empire and musical capital of Europe.

*Vienna, shown here in 1609, has been a major port on the Danube River for centuries.*

*Constructed from 1872 to 1883 in the Gothic style, Vienna's city hall is still used today as the municipal center.*

# MIDDLE RHINE VALLEY

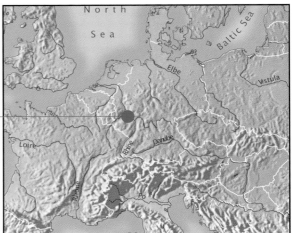

No other European river rivals the mythic Rhine. Natural barrier, natural frontier, natural conduit of trade, the Rhine flows through Europe's history just as it flows through the continent's heart. Rising deep in the Swiss Alps, it circles north and west before, gathering force all the while, it heads north at the Swiss city of Basel. From here it briefly marks the frontier between France and Germany before carving its majestic course past castle-studded heights and vine-clad slopes, flowing finally into the North Sea in Holland.

It is this German stretch that is the Rhine of legend. Parts consist of landscapes that are almost dreamlike. This is the Rhine of the Lorelei, the bewitching Rhine maidens who lured sailors to their death where, the river narrowing dramatically as it sweeps past the Lorelei itself, a vast rocky outcrop, the current speeds and swirls treacherously. This, too, is the ring of Wagner's epic operatic cycle, *The Ring of the Nibelungen*, drawn from the myths that the river has always spawned.

Yet, not much farther north, great industrial cities sprang up, powered by the great river. The industrial cities of the Rhineland may present a stark contrast with the wine-growing areas to the south. But they explain much about Germany's economic muscle.

## Germany

**Period:**

From the 12th century

**Significance:**

The river valley is home to more than 40 medieval castles.

*The Eltz Castle, which sits 230 feet (70 m) above the water, has remained in the same family since it was built in the 12th century.*

The ruins of the Ehrenfels Castle rise above the Binger Loch. The castle stood for centuries before the French destroyed it in the late 1600s.

*"The river breaks through and the rocks recede and look down with astonishment and bewilderment…"*

—Prussian author and playwright Heinrich von Kleist, during his 1803 Rhine journey

*Historically, nations have battled time and again for control of parts of the 820-mile (1,320 k) Rhine River.*

# AACHEN CATHEDRAL

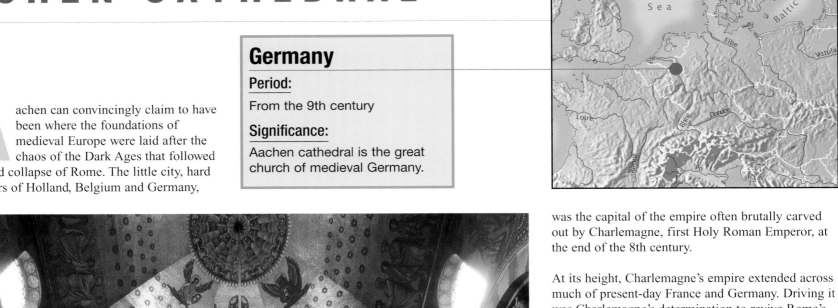

**A**achen can convincingly claim to have been where the foundations of medieval Europe were laid after the chaos of the Dark Ages that followed the protracted collapse of Rome. The little city, hard on the borders of Holland, Belgium and Germany,

## Germany

**Period:**

From the 9th century

**Significance:**

Aachen cathedral is the great church of medieval Germany.

was the capital of the empire often brutally carved out by Charlemagne, first Holy Roman Emperor, at the end of the 8th century.

At its height, Charlemagne's empire extended across much of present-day France and Germany. Driving it was Charlemagne's determination to revive Rome's power and learning in a properly Christian context. Charlemagne's cathedral in Aachen may be modest by the standards that followed, but its importance cannot be overstated.

*Constructed near the site of a former Roman spa, the cathedral contains one of Europe's most important ecclesiastical treasuries.*

*"In Aachen I have seen the well-proportioned pillars, with their beautiful capitals from porphyry green and red granite, which Carolus ordered to be taken from Rome and placed in this building."*

—Albrecht Dürer, German artist, 1520

*The palatine chapel, with its gilded paintings and ornate Barbarossa chandelier, remains an outstanding example of Carolingian architecture.*

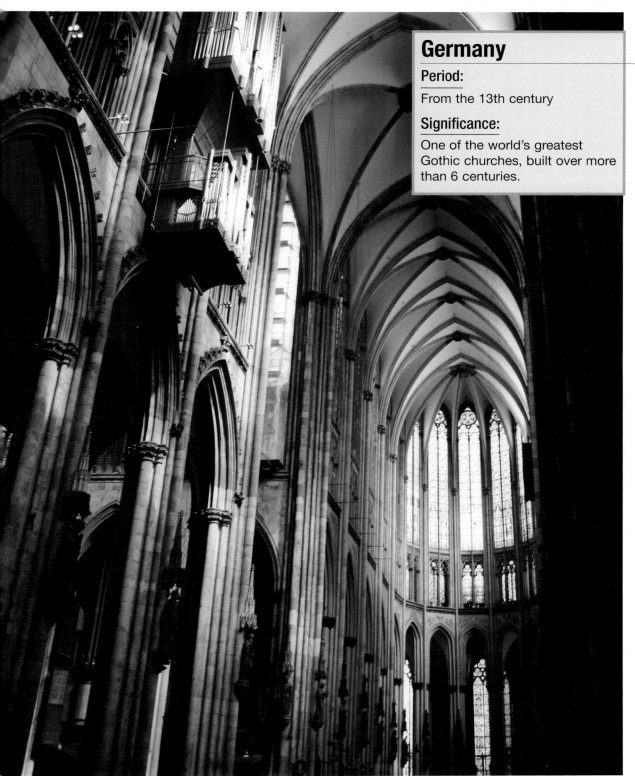

## Germany

**Period:**

From the 13th century

**Significance:**

One of the world's greatest Gothic churches, built over more than 6 centuries.

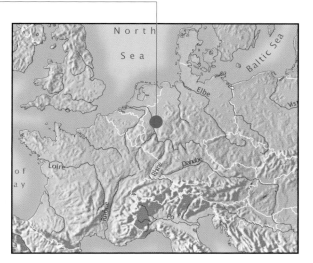

The nave of Cologne Cathedral, featuring one of the highest Gothic vaults ever constructed, was modeled on Amiens Cathedral in France.

The Gothic aspiration to build cathedrals that were larger, longer and above all higher came to a climax at Cologne on the banks of the Rhine in Germany. Taking their cue from France, the builders of this extraordinary monument to the medieval vision of a version of heaven on earth produced perhaps the most startling, and certainly the most elaborately decorated, Gothic cathedral in Europe.

This was 13th-century technology at its most audacious. The choir, or area behind the main altar, soars 150 feet (46 m). The transepts—the "wings" of the church—are 275 feet (84 m) wide. Just how daring

this was is underlined by the fate of the contemporary 13th-century cathedral at Beauvais in France, whose choir, 157 feet (48 m) high, collapsed in a heap of rubble and dust in 1284, only years after it had been completed.

Cologne cathedral, finished finally only in 1880, remains a supreme example of the Gothic spirit at its most indomitable.

*"I sincerely hope that Cologne will not lose an important component of its historical legacy."*

—Francesco Bandarin, Director of the World Heritage Center, 2004

Although much of the detailed stonework was completed in the 15th century, the cathedral's façade remained unfinished for 400 years.

# BAMBERG

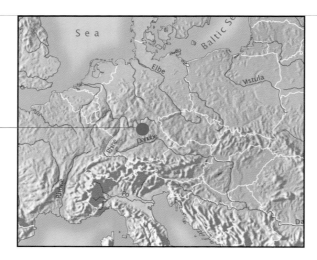

## Germany

**Period:**

From the 10th century

**Significance:**

Bamberg was a leading city in the early Holy Roman Empire.

*Bamberg Cathedral, the resting place of Pope Clement II, is notable as the only Papal burial site north of the Alps.*

B amberg, in Bavaria, in southern Germany, reflects the growing confidence and prosperity of Germany in the Middle Ages. As one of the leading cities of the burgeoning Holy Roman Empire, it not only grew prosperous on trade, it also developed an exact sense of its own self-worth. It became the center of the Enlightenment in late 18th-century Germany.

Today, it enjoys a reputation as one of the handful of Germany's most obviously historic cities that were not targeted and, in almost every other case,

destroyed by the Allied bombing campaign in the Second World War. Visitors today may be grateful to the Allied decision to spare the city.

Bamberg lays claim to another distinction: beer. True, in Bavaria, a region which has elevated the production and consumption of beer to something approaching not just a way of life but an art form, it has much in the way of competition. But sipping a foaming stein of the lustrous beers produced by the city's nine breweries remains a memorable experience.

*Bamberg's Old Town Hall, with its Bavarian timbered façade, borders the River Regnitz. The historic city escaped damage during World War II.*

# WARTBURG CASTLE

D eep in the heart of Thuringia, in central Germany, its encroaching forests and rocky outcrops etched in the German folk memory, Wartburg castle, dating originally from 1067, is the epitome of the grimly commanding, hilltop German fortress.

According to legend, the first castle here was built by a local ruler, Ludwig der Springer, who asserted his dubious claim to the site by transporting clay to it from his family territories to pretend that the imposing structure was being constructed on "his own land."

Greatly expanded, the castle achieved notoriety of a different kind in 1521–1522 when Martin Luther, newly excommunicated by Leo X in Rome, took refuge here, working on a German translation of the Bible, an act almost as subversive to the Roman Catholic Church as his nailing of his *95 Theses* to the door of the church at Wittenburg in 1517.

### Germany

**Period:**

11th century

**Significance:**

Wartburg is an iconic medieval German castle. It was here that Martin Luther took refuge after his excommunication from the Roman Catholic Church.

*Wartburg Castle rises 600 feet (180 m) above the forest of Thuringia. The name Wartburg is possibly derived from the German "wacht-burg" or watch-fort.*

*"Wait, mountain—you should become a castle for me!"*

*—According to legend, the words of Ludwig der Springer in 1067, when he first saw the hill upon which it was built*

*It was inside the walls of Wartburg Castle that Protestant reformer Martin Luther—or "Knight George"—translated the New Testament into German.*

# TOLEDO

## Spain

**Period:**

From the 11th century

**Significance:**

Toledo is arguably the most complete medieval city in Spain.

Successively a Roman settlement, the capital of the Visigothic kingdom, a fortress of the Emirate of Cordoba, an outpost of the Christian kingdoms fighting the Moors and, in the 16th century, the temporary seat of supreme power under Charles V, Toledo is the repository of more than 2,000 years of history. Famed for the production of swords, the city remains a center of the manufacture of knives and other steel implements.

Well-known for its religious tolerance during the Middle Ages, Toledo was home to large communities of Jews and Muslims until those groups were expelled from the country in 1492 and 1502 respectively. The city still offers great testimony to that era thanks to religious monuments such as the Synagogue of Santa María la Blanca, the Synagogue of El Transito, and the Mosque of Cristo de la Luz, all of which date from before the expulsion.

*"Rocky gravity, glory of Spain, and light of her cities."*

—Spanish author Miguel de Cervantes y Saavedra (1547–1616), describing Toledo

*Toledo, with its medieval flavor, rich cultural history, and striking topography, is considered one of Europe's premier cities.*

In addition to its man-made wall, Toledo possesses several natural defenses, including the moatlike Tagus River and a steep approach.

*A panoramic view of Toledo, similar to the one painted by El Greco, highlights the steepled Alcazar, site of a former Roman fortress.*

# SANTIAGO DE COMPOSTELA

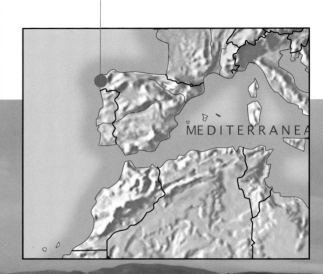

## Spain

### Period:

From the late 4th century though the Middle Ages

### Significance:

During the Middle Ages Santiago de Compostela—according to tradition the burial place of St. James the Apostle—was the third most visited pilgrimage site in the world.

Santiago de Compostela, in the inaccessible, rocky wastes of northwest Spain, is difficult to reach even today, Yet remarkably, for much of the Middle Ages, it was rivaled as a pilgrimage destination only by Jerusalem and Rome itself. Every year, thousands of dusty, foot-sore pilgrims from across Europe made their way to this lonely outpost. The rich rode; the overwhelming majority walked. The journey took months.

Its fame stemmed from the fact that it was here that St. James, one of Christ's 12 apostles, was said to have been buried. Commemorating this, an immense Romanesque cathedral was built, today still easily one of the most movingly impressive of Europe's medieval churches: gray, sober and overwhelming.

Today's pilgrims, following routes from across Europe that nonetheless converge on the Camino de Santiago, wending its way across northern Spain, have sparked a remarkable upsurge in interest in Santiago. In 1986, 2,491 made their way to Santiago. In 2006, the number was 100,377.

Anyone walking at least 60 or more miles to Santiago "and able to attest to their journey" has been eligible for a *Compostela*, a document issued by the diocese confirming that they are true modern pilgrims.

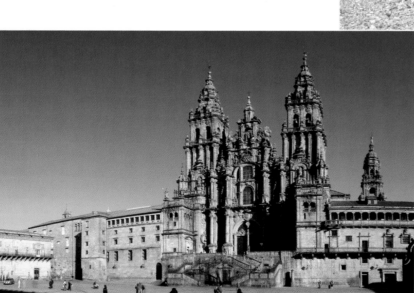

The Cathedral of Santiago de Compostela was purportedly built over the spot where a shepherd buried the bones of St. James the Apostle.

*"The body of Saint James was buried at a place where now stands the cathedral of Santiago de Compostela. Saint James appeared on earth and helped the Spanish Christian army win a decisive victory over the Moors."*

—Story of Saint James's appearance in 834

The Camiño de Santiago—or Way of St. James—represents the 1,000-year-old pilgramage to the shrine that is still undertaken by thousands annually.

*The 15th century Castillo de Belmonte, constructed in the Gothic-Mudejar style, reflects the Moorish heritage of Cuenca.*

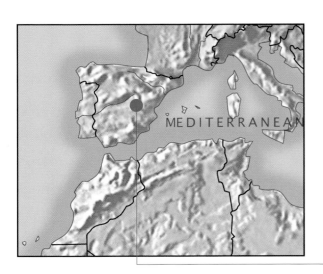

MEDITERRANEAN

Cuenca, high over the rocky gorges of the rivers Huécar and Júcar in central Spain, was first established by the Moors. All but impregnable, it was a natural site for the castle, or *alcazaba*, they established here. Nonetheless, it fell to the advancing Christian Castilians in the 12th century. Since the 18th century, its prime claim to fame are its hanging houses, or *casas colgados*, rising improbably above the river Huécar, rickety miniature skyscrapers before their day.

## Spain

**Period:**

12th century

**Significance:**

Cuenca is the site of Spain's first Gothic cathedral.

*Cuenca's cathedral, the Basilica of Our Lady of Grace, was consecrated in 1208, though the present facade was rebuilt in the 19th century.*

# A V I L A

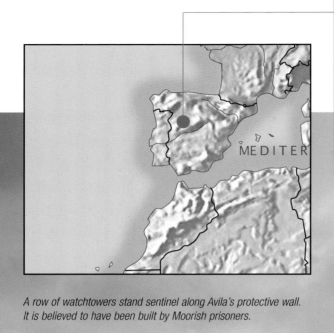

## Spain

### Period:

11th century

### Significance:

Avila is home to the best-preserved medieval city walls in Europe and was headquarters of the Spanish Inquisition.

*A row of watchtowers stand sentinel along Avila's protective wall. It is believed to have been built by Moorish prisoners.*

Avila, high on Spain's central plateau, is noteworthy for probably the best-preserved medieval city walls in Europe, their brown granite studded with 88 massive circular towers and pierced by nine stout gates. Built from 1090 onwards, the walls make clear the determination of the Christian rulers of Spain to defend those territories newly wrested from the Muslims.

The city's importance was underlined in the 15th century when Castille's joint rulers, Ferdinand and Isabella, persuaded the pope to make the city the head-quarters of the Spanish Inquisition. And it was in Avila, too, that the mystic St. Teresa was born, in 1515.

*Avila's 11th-century wall is a mile and half (2.4 km) long, more than 45 feet (14 m) high and in places as much as 10 feet (3 m) thick.*

## Spain

**Period:**

13th century

**Significance:**

Burgos was, until the 1500s, the most politically important city in Spain.

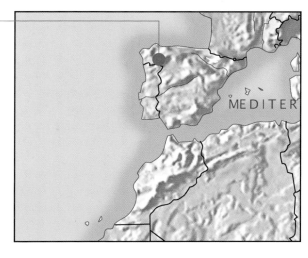

*A gilded cupola sheds light on the interior of Our Lady of Burgos. The city's name was taken from a Visigoth word meaning consolidated walled villages.*

*Eleventh-century warrior—and Spanish national hero—El Cid was born on the outskirts of Burgos in a small town that is now called Vivar del Cid.*

*In addition to its Gothic cathedral, Burgos is home to more ecclesiastical monuments than any city in Spain, including Toledo.*

U ntil the rise of Madrid in the 16th century, Burgos, capital of Castile since the 11th century, was politically the most important city in a rapidly expanding Catholic Spain, which in the Middle Ages increasingly meant a rapidly expanding Castile. It was a crusading society in every sense, one determined to extinguish Muslim rule, which in 1492 it would finally manage.

Hardly surprisingly, Burgos is a city of churches. The cathedral, for example, built from 1221, was an emphatic statement of the reality of Christian rule, a vast and soaring structure owing a debt to the parallel developments in Gothic church architecture in France. Its flying buttresses, at the time a properly radical development, could almost have come from any of the great cathedrals of 13th-century northern France. More characteristically Spanish is the later lantern spire, immense and ornate, over the crossing and a startlingly rich side-chapel at the east end of the building, the Capella del Condestable, alive with tracery and carved figures.

Outside the cathedral is a statue of one of the province's most famous sons, El Cid, the most celebrated of the Christian warriors who battled the Muslims and whose conquest of Valencia in 1094 ensured his legendary status in the *Reconquista*.

# LISBON

Portugal, initially no more than one of the handful of Christian Iberian states struggling to oust the Muslims from Iberia, but fully independent after 1143, played a key role in the great age of European discovery. Beginning with the voyages launched by Henry the Navigator in 1434 along the west coast of Africa, Portuguese navigators were the first not just to reach Newfoundland and Brazil but to round the Cape of Good Hope and cross the Indian Ocean.

These achievements are celebrated in Lisbon, the Portuguese capital, by two remarkable buildings, the Belém Tower and the Monastery of the Hieronymites, the former built in the river Tagus itself between 1515 and 1521, the latter between 1502 and 1550. Both remarkable buildings, largely financed on the profits of these voyages, are prime examples of the late-Gothic Manueline style, frothy, elaborate and highly decorative.

*Constructed on the Tagus estuary to defend Lisbon from attack, the Belém Tower was dedicated to St. Vicente, the city's patron saint.*

The entry mosaic at the Monument to the Discoveries, which shows a compass and map of the world, was a gift from South Africa.

## Portugal

**Period:**

16th century

**Significance:**

Lisbon played a key role in the age of European discovery during the 15th century.

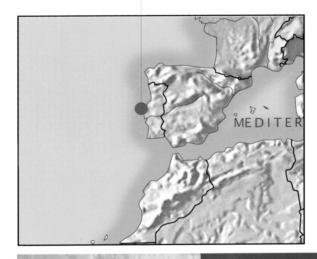

Once the Belém Tower was no longer needed to safeguard the city, it served as a customs office, a lighthouse and a telegraph station.

The Monument to the Discoveries, erected in 1960, commemorates the 500th anniversary of the death of Prince Henry the Navigator.

# OPORTO

## Portugal

**Period:**

From the 9th century

**Significance:**

Oporto was a vital maritime center during the Middle Ages; its shipyards were key to the Portuguese fleet.

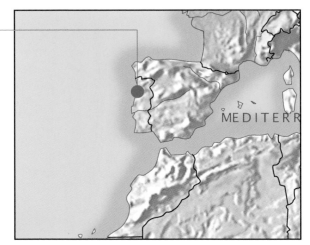

*With the exception of the waterfront, much of Oporto is literally carved into the granite cliffs at the outlet of the Douro River.*

*Although Oporto is known as the "Capital of the North," the city maintains an easy-going, working class attitude.*

Bustling Oporto on the river Douro in northern Portugal is not merely one of the oldest cities in the country but one of the most rewarding to visit; its historic heart is a microcosm of Portuguese history.

It was in Oporto, a great maritime center, that many of the ships used in the country's voyages of exploration were built. And it was in Oporto that the world's oldest military alliance, between England and Portugal, was forged, in 1387. The links between the two countries were forged in other ways, too, the most famous being the rich reinforced wine not merely produced here but named after the city: port.

And it was in Oporto that Britain and Portugal launched the titanic struggle that led to the eventual fall of Napoleon after the French emperor's invasion of Spain and Portugal in 1807. The strife spawned one great tragedy, however, when in March 1809 the citizens of Oporto fled across a pontoon bridge over the Douro. The bridge gave way under the great press of people and 6,000 were drowned.

*One of Portugal's most famous exports, port—a fortified wine from the Douro valley—was originally shipped from Oporto and so took its name.*

Built on the site of a Hieronymite monastery, the fanciful 19th-century Pena Palace retains the original 15th-century cloister and chapel.

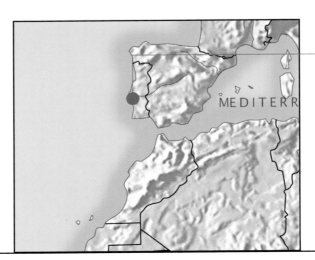

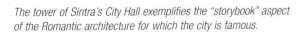

The tower of Sintra's City Hall exemplifies the "storybook" aspect of the Romantic architecture for which the city is famous.

*"In all the land of Portugal, the whole expanse of Europe, Sintra stands out as one of the loveliest, rarest places that Nature's prodigious hand has created."*

—Portuguese poet Afonso Lopes Vieira

There are few more bizarre buildings than Sintra's Palácio da Pena, poised dramatically above the city a few miles to the north of Lisbon. Built on the site of a ruined medieval monastery for Ferdinand II of Portugal, who acquired the site in 1838, it elevates whimsy, to say nothing of out-and-out eccentricity, in architecture to heights rarely scaled before or since.

Part Rhineland castle, part Moorish fantasy palace, the whole, intended as a summer home for the Portuguese royal family and completed in 1857, strikes an even more unexpected note by being clad in brilliant layers of red and yellow paint. The exotic theme is continued in the gardens, filled with rare plants from the Portuguese empire.

## Portugal

**Period:**

19th century

**Significance:**

Sintra, the site of the eccentric Palácio da Pena, was a center of European Romantic architecture.

# FLORENCE

By the early 15th century, Florence, financed by the Medici, had decisively emerged as the greatest of the Italian city-states. Yet it was not merely material riches that drove the questing, busy people of the Tuscan city. At much the same time, an intellectual revolution was forming that was nowhere more important than in Florence. There was a conscious desire to return to the glories of Rome, which, among other things, meant studying the ancient culture's physical remains—not just its buildings but statues, too. Likewise, there was an attempt to appraise the world rationally, to impose logical solutions on what could be verifiably observed and measured.

The revolutionary result was the Renaissance, literally "rebirth." It meant the deliberate revival of classical styles of architecture, in which no two figures were more important than the architect Brunelleschi and the theorist Alberti. Brunelleschi, architect of the first fully classical building of the Renaissance, the Foundling Hospital, also built the dome of Florence's magnificent cathedral.

The Renaissance also saw the development of perspective in painting and of convincingly naturalistic figures, both trends early epitomized by Masaccio in his heroically uncompromising frescos in the church Santa Maria del Carmine. Sculpture, too, chiefly in the works of Ghiberti, then of Donatello, was simi-

Spanning the Arno, the Ponte Vecchio links two districts of Florence. The city was originally the site of the Etruscan town of Fiesole.

Designed by Brunelleschi, the dome of the Basilica di Santa Maria del Fiore was, upon its construction, the largest dome in the world. The church itself was based on the cathedrals in Pisa and Siena.

*"When I returned to Florence, I found myself famous. The City Council asked me to carve a colossal David from a nineteen-foot block of marble—and damaged to boot! I locked myself away in a workshop behind the cathedral, hammered and chiseled at the towering block for three long years ..."*

—Renaissance sculptor, architect and painter, Michelangelo (1475–1564)

**SUCCESS STORY**

## Italy

### The Challenge:

Rising waters put Venice at risk of devastating floods.

### The Solution:

The government developed a plan to protect Venice lagoon with the use of pontoons.

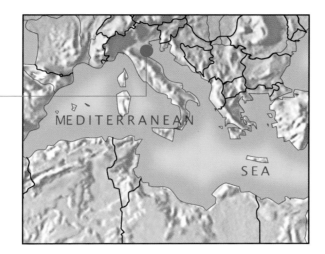

MEDITERRANEAN

SEA

*During the Middle Ages Venice served as an embarkation point for the Crusades. The city-state remained a major maritime power during the Renaissance.*

*The Piazza San Marco, the only true square in Venice, was named for one of the city's two patron saints and was once the vegetable garden of a monastery.*

# PIENZA

## Italy

**Period:**

15th century

**Significance:**

Pienza was the birthplace of Renaissance urban planning.

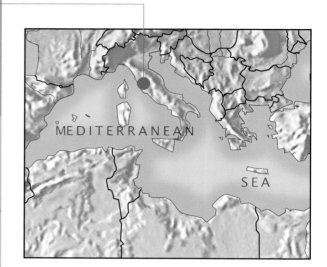

The elegant classicism of little Pienza's central piazza belies the fact that this was the first attempt at town-planning during the Renaissance. The notion of an "ideal city," centrally planned with buildings following the humanist classicism of the Florentine architect Alberti, was here transformed from theory into practice. The impetus was provided by Pope Pius II, born in the town, who in 1459 employed Bernardo Gambarelli to design the church, palace and town hall that make up the principal buildings of the square.

*The transformation of a pope's humble birthplace into a utopian Renaissance city was overseen by architect Bernardo Gambarelli, also known as Rossellino.*

*Today a preservation society protects the cultural heritage of the five towns in the Val d'Orcio: Pienza, Castiglion d'Orcia, Montalcino, San Quirico d'Orcia and Radicofani.*

PART II - HUMAN CULTURE

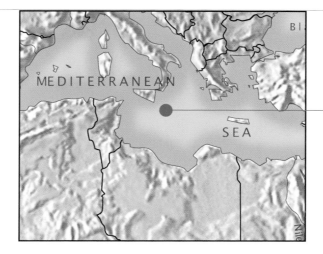

n 1530, the Knights of St. John, expelled by the Ottomans from their former island fortress of Rhodes in 1522, were given permission by the Habsburg emperor, Charles V, to settle on the little central Mediterranean island of Malta. This was more than a simple act of charity on the part of the emperor. The Knights of St. John were key actors in the Christian West's struggle to contain the aggressively expanding Muslim Ottomans, by this point the dominant power in the Near East. The threat was made real in the summer of 1565.

## Malta

**Period:**

16th century

**Significance:**

Valletta was the only Mediterranean city planned and built on a uniform grid.

*The skyline of Valletta displays a mix of Eastern and Western influences, the result of Malta's location at the crossroads of the Mediterranean.*

An Ottoman force, probably in excess of 40,000, laid siege to Malta, held by about 700 knights and perhaps 8,000 other soldiers. It was an epic and brutal struggle. But Malta held. An act of such conspicuous heroism guaranteed the gratitude of the West. Money and men were made available on an unprecedented scale.

The result was the construction in no more than 15 years of an entirely new, heavily fortified city, Valletta, named after the order's leader, Jean Parisot de la Valette, on the rocky spur of land, Sceberras Peninsula, that lies between the island's two great natural harbors, Marsamxett, to the north, and the aptly named Grand Harbor, to the south.

Valletta emerged not just as the only Mediterranean city planned and built on a uniform grid plan but as one of the most harmonious and elegant in Europe:

stately, grand and imposing, the whole enormously enhanced by the island's softly golden stone.

Highlights include the Grandmaster's Palace, still the seat of Malta's government; St. John's Co-Cathedral; and the Barrakka Gardens, with stunning views over the waters of the Grand Harbour.

*"I've heard the anchor fall and knew that we were in the harbor of Malta … Valletta and all those proud ships here under the world's strongest fortress were only the frame for it. The setting was beautiful, one of the most beautiful I have seen."*

—Danish author
Hans Christian Andersen, March 1841

*This powerful stone lion could easily symbolize Valletta's protective walls, considered the strongest medieval fortifications in the world.*

# VISBY

## Sweden

**Period:**

12th and 14th centuries

**Significance:**

Visby is the best-preserved medieval city in Scandinavia.

*Called the city of "roses and ruins," Visby has managed to preserve much of its medieval past intact.*

*Visby's one and a half mile (2.4 k) wall, or "ringmuren," was begun in the 1200s and built higher over the following century.*

The Little Swedish island of Gotland in the Baltic has only one city, Visby. Today's placid community belies a dramatic and often violent history. Its medieval remains, which lie above almost two miles of wall that encircle the old city, underline a long story of bloodshed. The city reached its peak during the 12th and 14th centuries as the Hanseatic League extended trade routes across much of northern and western Europe.

In 1361, Visby was conquered by Denmark and would remain Danish until retaken by Sweden in 1645. By the end of the 14th century, the city was repeatedly plundered by pirates, the Victual or Vitalian Brotherhood. After it fell to Pomerania in 1411, it became little more than a nest of pirates. Consequently, in 1470, lawless Visby was expelled from the Hanseatic League. In 1525, the island was attacked again, by Lübeck, who left it a smoking ruin. Slowly, Visby declined. By the 18th century it was little more than an obscure backwater making a meager living from subsistence farming and fishing.

*The name Visby possibly derives from the Old Norse vis, or sacrificial place, and baer, meaning farm; or from the Polish wyspa, which means "island."*

After failing to reclaim the Holy Land, many Crusaders sought battle with the pagan inhabitants of Latvia and Estonia, as shown in this reenactment.

## Latvia

**Period:**

13th century

**Significance:**

Riga was an important Baltic trade city during the Middle Ages.

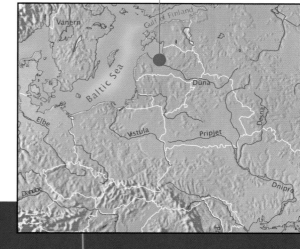

A statue of Roland, Charlemagne's nephew, faces the town hall. His raised sword was used as a starting point to measure distances between Riga and other cities.

Riga is the capital city of Latvia, which is one of the three so-called Baltic states with neighboring Estonia and Lithuania. It dates its founding to 1201 as German settlers and missionaries—later to be formed into the Livonian Brothers of the Sword, an off-shoot of the better-known Teutonic Knights—pushed eastward along the Baltic shores. Latvia's early prosperity as a member of the Hanseatic League subsequently gave way to a troubled history as a succession of foreign powers—Poland, Sweden and then Russia, which annexed the little country in 1721—bloodily struggled for dominion over the coastal region.

Riga, in fact, remained officially Russian until the end of the First World War in 1918. It was then briefly independent until, in September 1939, the Soviet Union forcibly reincorporated it within its communist empire. Nazi invasion and Soviet liberation both wreaked havoc. Only in 1991 did Latvia reemerge as an independent, democratic country.

Riga today is a handsome, spacious city of historic buildings. Chief among them are the 13th-century cathedral, under its distinctive bulbous spire, and a 14th-century castle. Unusually, the city also claims some of the most noteworthy Art Nouveau buildings in Europe.

# VILNIUS

*In the square outside Vilnius Cathedral is a tile marked "Miracle." The custom is to stand on it, make a wish, and spin three times.*

**V**ilnius, Lithuania's capital, was founded in the 13th century. The city's history and that of Lithuania have been exceptionally entangled. From 1386, Vilnius was in union with neighboring Poland, ruled by Lithuania's Grand Duke Jogaila. Lithuania engaged in breakneck territorial expansion that by 1440 saw it embrace Hungary, by 1466 reach the Black Sea and by 1526 take over Bohemia. Yet from 1582, Lithuania became in effect a Polish possession, a situation that lasted until the successive partitions of Poland at the end of the 18th century when what remained of Lithuania was absorbed by Russia.

Though a nominally independent and much smaller Lithuania emerged after the First World War, it was crushed, like its Baltic neighbors, by the Soviet takeover in 1939. The nation emerged at the end of the Second World War once more within the communist camp. The collapse of the Soviet Union finally renewed Lithuania's independence, which was internationally recognized in 1991.

Today, Vilnius is probably the most cosmopolitan of the historic cities of the Baltic.

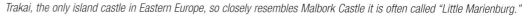

*Trakai, the only island castle in Eastern Europe, so closely resembles Malbork Castle it is often called "Little Marienburg."*

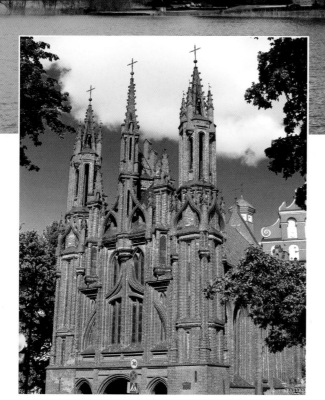

*It is said that when Napoleon saw the small, exquisite St. Anne's Church he wanted to bring it to France "in the palm of his hand."*

## Lithuania

**Period:**

13th century

**Significance:**

As the political center of the Grand Duchy of Lithuania from the 13th to the late 18th century, Vilnius profoundly influenced both the cultural and architectural development of much of Eastern Europe.

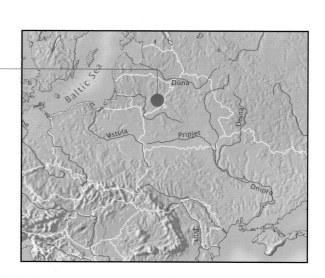

# THE KREMLIN AND RED SQUARE

The Cathedral of St. Basil the Blessed, with its distinctive onion domes, consists of nine separate chapels decorated with icons and medieval paintings.

## Russia

**Period:**

13th century

**Significance:**

The Kremlin has been linked to the majority of the important historical and political events in Russia since the 13th century.

The Kremlin is the very heart of Moscow. An immense fortress— the word *kremlin* means "castle"— the complex was begun in the 1320s as the first Russian state, Muscovy, began fitfully to expand. As Russia grew, so did the Kremlin grow with it, becoming progressively larger and grander. The walls, partly demolished by Napoleon after his disastrous invasion of Russia in 1812, were built between 1485 and 1495. The site includes four cathedrals, including the Cathedral of the Dormition (1479), where all Russia's tsars were crowned, and the Cathedral of the Archangel Michael (1508), where most of them were buried. There are also four palaces, the largest being the Grand Kremlin Palace, which is the most recent, and from 1851 the tsar's official home in Moscow. Perhaps the most remarkable building is the Ivan the Great Bell Tower, completed in 1508, and at 266 feet (81 m), still the highest building in the complex, its brilliant white towers topped by shimmering golden onion domes.

The mid-16th century St. Basil's Cathedral, which stands opposite the Kremlin in Red Square, consists of eight chapels surrounding a ninth central chapel. Each lies under a brick tower crowned by bulbous, brilliantly colored onion domes.

Prince Yuri Dolgurukiy's 12th-century hunting lodge was located above the the Moskva and Neglina Rivers, making it the ideal site for a fortified city, or kremlin.

*"Ilyich liked to stroll about the Kremlin, which commanded a sweeping view of the city. He liked best of all to walk along the pavement facing the Grand Palace, where there was plenty to fill the eye."*

—Nadezhda Konstantinovna Krupskaya, wife of the first premier of the Soviet Union, Vladimir Ilyich Lenin

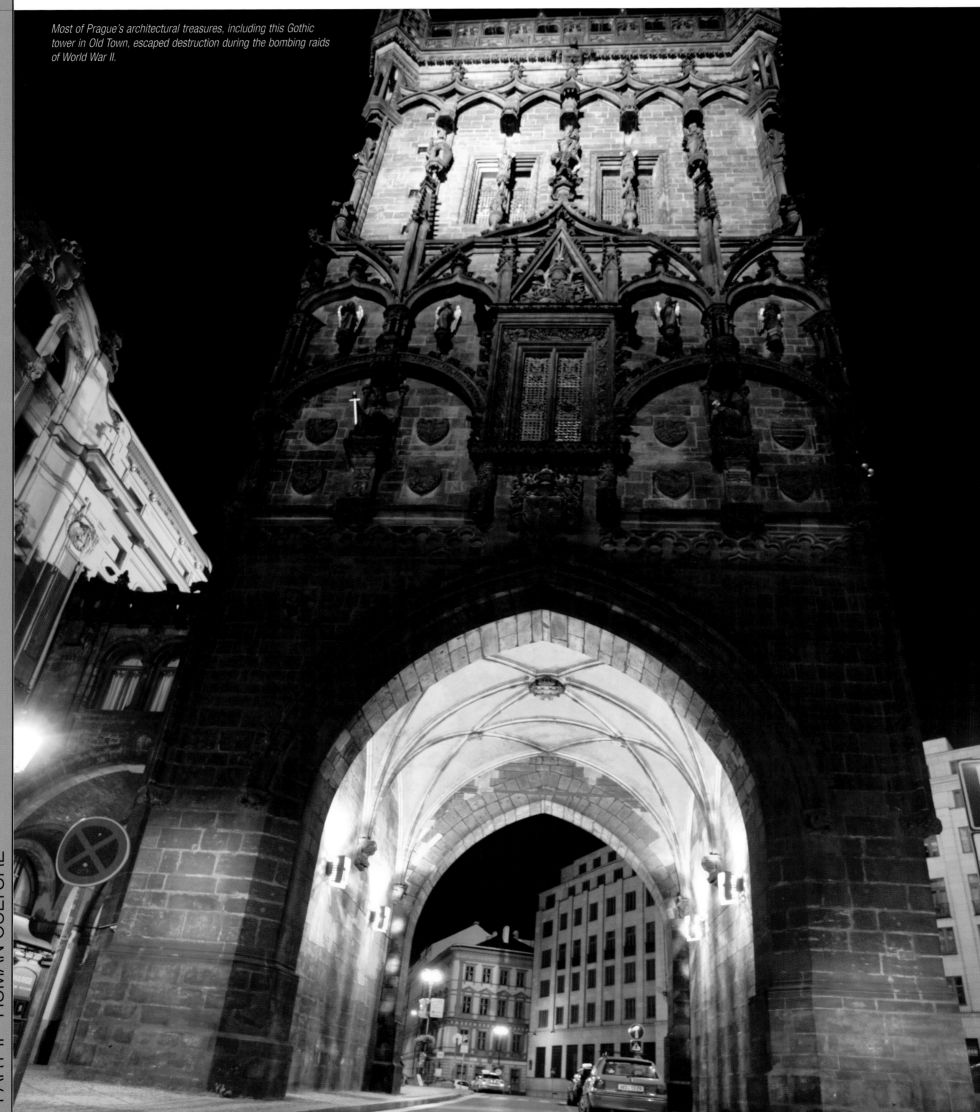

# PRAGUE

*Most of Prague's architectural treasures, including this Gothic tower in Old Town, escaped destruction during the bombing raids of World War II.*

*Prague's famous architecture exhibits centuries of varied influence.*

*The popular Astronomical Clock, or "Pragu Orloj," is mounted on the Old Town city hall and features an hourly "Walk of the Apostles."*

## Czech Republic

**Period:**

9th century

**Significance:**

Built between the 11th and 18th centuries, Prague speaks of the great architectural and cultural inspiration enjoyed here since the Middle Ages.

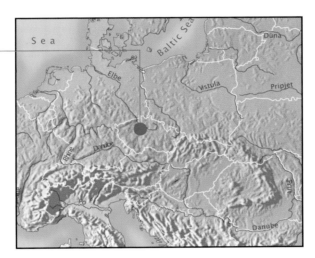

Prague is one of the most beautiful cities in Europe, despite the vicissitudes of its history and of the Czech Republic. It emerged, as Bohemia, in the 13th century. One hundred years later, under Charles IV, Prague acquired the earliest of the many historic buildings that distinguish the city today, including the Gothic cathedral, the Charles University and the Charles Bridge over the broad river Vltava that runs through the city.

By 1519, it had become a Habsburg possession and so it remained until the breakup of the Austro-Hungarian empire after the First World War. Czechoslovakia, as the new state was called, was the only country formed in central and Eastern Europe between the wars to remain fully democratic. In 1938 the city was abandoned by France and Britain to Hitler's Germany. When World War II ended, Nazi domination was followed by Soviet rule, which gave way in 1990. After a peaceful separation from Slovakia, the Czech Republic was formed in 1993.

Despite being the first democracy to fall to Hitler, the country, however oppressed and impoverished, suffered little or no physical destruction. The impressive historic city center with pastel-colored buildings under high pitched-roofs, remained intact. The city is home to many notable structures, among them the 15th-century astronomical clock in the Old Town Square; the impressive Hradcany Castle; the elaborate 18th-century church of St. Nicholas; and the Charles Bridge itself.

*The Charles Bridge, built to connect the Old Town to Mala Strana or "the lesser quarter," made Prague a valuable trade link between east and west Europe.*

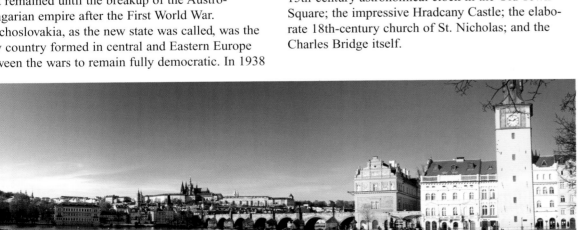

*The country's longest river, the Vltava (Moldau in German), inspired Czech composer Smetana's symphonic work of the same name.*

# MALBORK

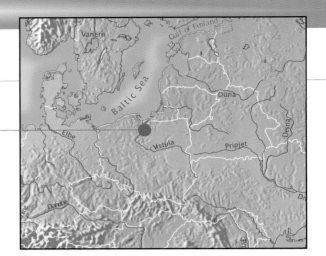

**M**albork in northern Poland, close to the Baltic, was the center of the Teutonic Knights, the religious order authorized by the pope in 1233, and backed by a succession of Holy Roman emperors, to bring about, at sword point if necessary, the conversion to Christianity of central and northern Europe. Built originally as a monastery, albeit fortified, in the later

## Poland

**Period:**

13th and 14th centuries

**Significance:**

The Castle of the Teutonic Order in Malbork is the largest medieval castle in Europe.

*The castle's location beside the River Nogat enabled the Teutonic Knights to exact tolls from merchant vessels leaving the Baltic Sea.*

*Originally known as St. Mary's Stronghold (Marienburg), Malbork was intended as a base for converting local inhabitants to Christianity.*

13th century, it was gradually extended after 1309, when it was made the principal residence of the Teutonic Grand Master. Eventually, it became the largest brick-built castle in Europe.

The site covers 80 acres (32.4 h) and is protected by massive walls studded with gates and towers under steep-pitched roofs. At its heart is the Palace of the Grand Master, a tiny-windowed, four-storied hulk of a building, itself also sheltering under vast expanses of tiled roofs and built between 1382 and 1399.

More miniature city than mere castle, the building was extensively damaged in the Second World War. It is the subject of a continuing program of restoration.

*"Next year we either conquer the Crossed Knights or we perish as a nation, and as individuals."*

—Wladislaus II Jagiello, Grand Prince of Lithuania and King of Poland, planning an attack against the Teutonic Knights in Malbork, August 1401

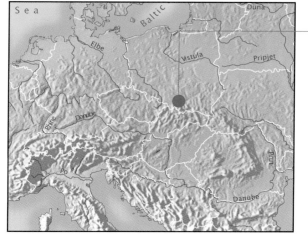

## Poland

**Period:**

13th and 14th centuries

**Significance:**

This 13th-century merchants' town boasts Europe's largest market square, as well as numerous historical houses, palaces and churches with magnificent interiors.

*Krakow attracts more than seven million visitors every year, many of them convening at the city's Main Market Square to sample traditional Polish food and handicrafts.*

*The official crest of Krakow features Poland's White Falcon, symbolizing the independence and strength for which the Poles are known.*

Krakow in southern Poland remains incontestably the most historic city in the country, and the "spiritual heart of Poland." It was the capital of an emerging Poland from as early as 1038, a role it retained until 1596.

Wawel Castle, part medieval, part Renaissance, is as compelling an attraction as the huge Market Square, the site of both the 14th-century brick-built St. Mary's Basilica—perhaps the most richly decorated Gothic church in Europe, its interior a darkly shimmering mass—and the hugely impressive 15th-century Sukiennice Cloth Hall.

# BUDAPEST

## Hungary

**Period:**

Late Middle Ages

**Significance:**

The Hungarian capital is one of Europe's most historic cities.

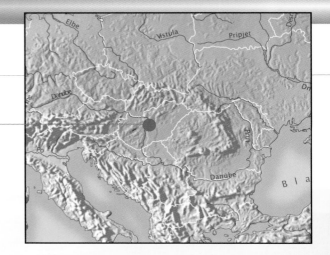

Almost as much as Prague, Budapest, capital of Hungary, is a city reborn. Its escape from communist rule in 1990 breathed new life into one of Europe's most historic cities. Situated on the river Danube, Budapest dominated much of central Europe before it fell, progressively, under partial Ottoman, then Habsburg domination. In 1918, the significantly shrunken city reemerged again briefly as an independent state. From 1939 it was a Nazi puppet state, and at the end of the Second World War it found itself a puppet state of Stalin's Soviet Union.

Properly speaking, it is two cities: Buda, on the west bank; Pest, on the east. Officially, they were united only in 1873. Buda itself is dominated by Buda Castle. A magnificently bombastic 19th-century structure, the castle stands on the site of a series of much earlier buildings, overlooking the Danube. It is the traditional home of Hungary's monarchs.

The high dome of Budapest's Parliament, which was erected over the site of timber depots, mills and barracks, is a striking landmark in the city.

Although Buda Castle was destroyed several times as a result of sieges and fires, portions of the 14th-century palace remain within the current opulent structure.

"The architectural heritage of Budapest is breathtaking, and no architect should miss visiting this fantastic city."

—Lewis Gilbert Koerner,
President of the American Institute of Architects–Europe Division, 2001

Designed by Britons William Tierney Clark and Adam Clark, the Széchenyi Chain Bridge over the Danube originally linked the two cities of Buda and Pest.

# WOODEN CHURCHES OF MARAMURES

### Romania

**Period:**

From the 16th to the 18th century

**Significance:**

The wooden churches of Maramures are among the most distinctive buildings in Europe.

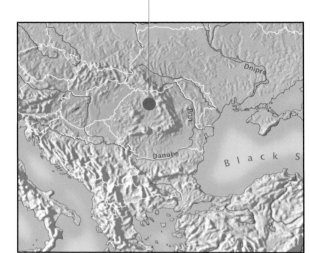

Romania's wooden churches, 42 of which survive, are among the most distinctive and improbable buildings in Europe. They are clustered in Transylvania, in the south of the country, and were built in the 17th and 18th centuries. Clearly reflecting a local tradition of building in wood, they nonetheless have no obvious counterparts anywhere else in Europe. Typically, they are simple rectangular structures made memorable by pairs of steeply pitched wooden roofs, dominated over the main, western, entrance by dizzyingly tall spires that rise to exactly precise points.

*To maintain authenticity, repairs and reconstruction at historic Barsana Monastery are done using traditional methods and tools.*

*The church at Barsana is one of 42 remaining wooden churches in Maramures, one third the total that existed there two centuries ago.*

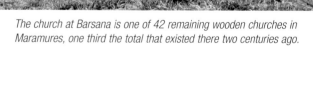

# SIGHIŞOARA

Sighişoara, deep in Romania's mountainous fertile heart, was one of Europe's most important medieval settlements. It was founded by the Saxons of Transylvania, German craftspeople and merchants who thrived commercially in the small fortified town for centuries. The town contains a mid-16th century clock tower and late-medieval buildings that are outstanding examples of Transylvanian Saxon architecture. Sighişoara today is a remarkable old city on the border of Central Europe, in a stunning landscape.

Sighişoara was also the home of the 15th-century Vlad Tepes, known as Vlad the Impaler, or Vald Dracula.

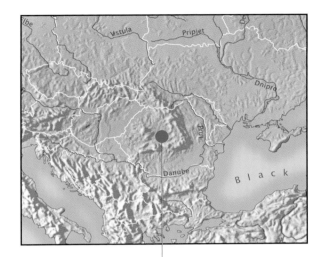

*Built in the 12th century on the site of a Roman fortress, Sighişoara's Citadel was then known as Castrum Sex, or Fort Six.*

## Romania

**Period:**

15th century

**Significance:**

A beautiful village in the heart of the Romanian mountains.

*"He was not very tall, but very stocky and strong, with a cruel and terrible appearance, a long straight nose, distended nostrils, a thin and reddish face in which the large wide-open green eyes were framed by bushy black eyebrows, which made them appear threatening …"*

—Vatican Ambassador Nicholas of Modrussa, reporting in a letter to Pope Pius II on the horrible acts of Vlad Tepes in 1464

*In addition to its medieval buildings and historic churches, hilly Sighişoara is also home to nine defense towers, each formerly manned by a craft guild.*

# DUBROVNIK

**SUCCESS STORY**

### Croatia

**The Challenge:**

In late 1991 the city was attacked by the Yugoslav People's Army.

**The Solution:**

The city is now the focus of a major restoration program coordinated by UNESCO.

C roatia's Adriatic coast is among the most beautiful in the world, a necklace of sun-drenched and rocky wooded islands. At its southernmost tip is the port city of Dubrovnik. It is a place of great history, twisting streets and elegant public spaces.

Tourism drives Dubrovnik today. Yet in the Middle Ages it was the hub of a maritime empire, the Republic of Ragusa, that rivaled Venice's. Napoleon, who conquered the Republic in 1806, brought it to a sudden halt. Thereafter, the city was ruled by Austria until, after the First World War, it was incorporated within the newly formed Yugoslavia.

Croatian independence in 1991 was won at great cost. Dubrovnik itself was bombarded and almost 70 percent of its buildings severely damaged. Today, restored and gleaming, it is once more the "Pearl of the Adriatic."

*The stone ramparts surrounding the Old Town open onto Dubrovnik's main street, the Stradun, which bisects the city.*

*Among Dubrovnik's many notable visitors was Irish playwright George Bernard Shaw, who declared the city "paradise on earth."*

*"You walk around the inner city, and there's nothing that reminds you of the war."*

—Dutch NATO official Bert Tiemes, about the city's recovery after the war with Serbia

*As an independent merchant republic, Dubrovnik established sea trade with Turkey, India, and Africa—and became a powerful rival of Venice.*

# ŠIBENIK

## Croatia

**Period:**

13th century

**Significance:**

The cathedral of Šibenik shows the considerable exchange in the field of monumental arts between northern Italy, Dalmatia and Tuscany in the 15th and 16th centuries.

The glory of the little Croatian coastal town of Šibenik is its cathedral, St. Jacob's. Šibenik itself, founded in 1066, passed under Venetian rule in 1412 until Napoleon's abrupt dissolution of the Venetian Republic in 1797. The brief period of direct French rule was succeeded by Austrian Habsurg hegemony before the creation of Yugoslavia. The city subsequently emerged as part of an independent Croatia in 1991, but heavy fighting against Serbian-backed forces in September of that year inflicted substantial damage, all since restored.

It is above all the Venetian connection that explains the Cathedral of St. Jacob. Work on the building lasted for more than 100 years, from 1431 to 1535. In other words, begun in a period when the Gothic still dominated, it was completed when the classicism of the High Renaissance was rapidly spreading across the Mediterranean world. It is these classical elements that predominate, for all the lingering influences of the Gothic. The dome over the crossing, for example, set on a tall, arcaded lantern, is fully classical. The lacy carvings that surround the main entrance are strongly Gothic in overall effect if not individual detail.

*A stone sculpture of St. James (Jacob) greets visitors at the portal. The cathedral was built of limestone and marble quarried on the Croatian island of Brac.*

*One of the most original churches of the Middle Ages, the Cathedral of St. Jacob was the masterwork of local architect Juraj of Dalmatia and Niccolo of Florence.*

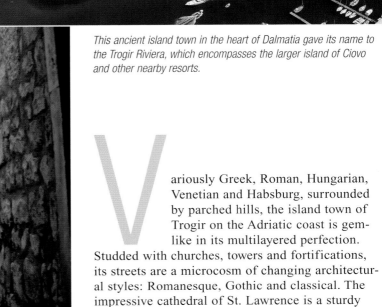

*This ancient island town in the heart of Dalmatia gave its name to the Trogir Riviera, which encompasses the larger island of Ciovo and other nearby resorts.*

Variously Greek, Roman, Hungarian, Venetian and Habsburg, surrounded by parched hills, the island town of Trogir on the Adriatic coast is gem-like in its multilayered perfection. Studded with churches, towers and fortifications, its streets are a microcosm of changing architectural styles: Romanesque, Gothic and classical. The impressive cathedral of St. Lawrence is a sturdy late-Romanesque building with a soaring square tower that dominates the historic center. The Venetian-built fortress of Kamerlengo, built to resist Ottoman designs on the Adriatic coast is itself a massive fortification.

*Quaint cobbled streets belie Trogir's turbulent past, which includes Saracen conquest, Venetian and Hapsburg rule and French occupation.*

## Croatia

**Period:**

13th century

**Significance:**

Trogir's Romanesque-Gothic buildings are the best-preserved in Central Europe.

# KOTOR

## Montenegro

**Period:**

Since the 6th century

**Significance:**

In the Middle Ages, this natural harbor on the Adriatic coast in Montenegro was an important artistic and commercial center.

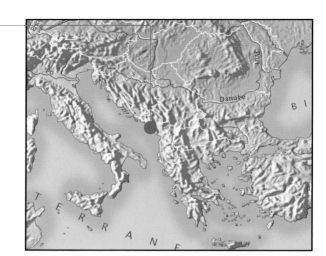

Located on fjordlike Gulf of Kotor, one of the best natural harbors in the Adriatic (until the First World War it was the main base for the Austro-Hungarian navy), Kotor bears witness to more than 2,000 years of history. Originally Roman, then Byzantine, Venetian between 1420 and 1797, subsequently Habsburg and then Yugoslavian, today it is part of Montenegro, declared legally independent only in June 2006.

Other than the view of the city from the surrounding hills, which slope steeply into the gulf, Kotor's most impressive feature is its fortified walls, built by the Venetians in the face of repeated Ottoman attempts to take the town. Over 2.5 miles (4 km) of the original walls remain today, in places 60 feet (20 m) high and almost 50 feet (16 m) thick.

The cathedral, dedicated to the town's patron saint, St. Tryphon, is a sturdy Romanesque structure, begun in 1166, though the exterior was later extensively remodeled. An earthquake in 1979 caused serious damage, all since repaired.

*Kotor harbor, viewed from the military fortress "San Giovanni," is one of Europe's finest ports and lies on the largest fjord in the Mediterranean Sea.*

*In addition to its dramatic topography, Kotor is known for its medieval buildings, churches and other cultural monuments.*

## Greece

**Period:**

11th to 16th century

**Significance:**

The site is the second largest and most important complex of monasteries in Greece, just after Mount Athos.

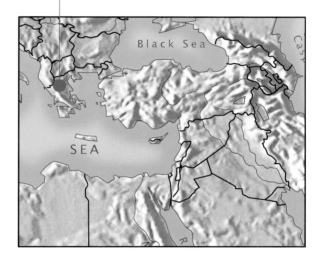

The Meteora are a group of six Greek orthodox monasteries in Kalambaka, in central Greece, built on high and almost entirely inaccessible sandstone pillars. They are all that remain of what were once 20 such monasteries, built from the 14th century onward in an attempt to protect the monks from the occupying Ottomans. These extraordinary survivals constitute some of the most remarkable religious structures in the world.

*Devoted to a life of simple contemplation, as reflected by this spare cloister, the monks of Meteora were lowered by nets to till their fields.*

*Tucked behind the sandstone expanse of the Rock of the Holy Spirit—yet precariously exposed—sits the Monastery of Rousnaou.*

# QIN'S TERRACOTTA ARMY

Lying at the center of this extraordinary necropolis is the tomb of the ruler of the Qin Dynasty, the first emperor to rule over a unified China, Qin Shi Huang (260–210 BC). A brutal and ambitious ruler, Qin was extravagant even in death, and ordered the creation of a terracotta army of some 7,000 warriors to stand guard over his tomb. Perhaps the most remarkable aspect of this site is the realism and artistry of the terracotta warriors, where each life-sized figure is portrayed as an individual.

Grouped according to rank and skill, the warriors are accompanied by horses, chariots and weaponry, rendered with equal realism and accuracy of detail. Traces of purple paint can still be seen on many of the figures. Construction began in 246 BC; contemporary historian Sima Qian stated that it would have taken 700,000 laborers and craftspeople 36 years to complete. The layout of the site mirrored the urban plan of the capital, Xianyan. It was first discovered in the 1920s during the digging of irrigation wells on farmland near Xi'an in the Shaanxi Province.

## China

**Period:**

246 BC to 210 BC

**Significance:**

The army is a remarkable collection of 7,000 life-sized terracotta figures created for Emperor Qin's tomb.

The terracotta army was created to serve Emperor Qin Shi Huang in the afterlife. Layers of colorful paint once enhanced the warriors' lifelike appearances.

*"Emperor Qin believed that the life under the ground was a continuation of it in the world; he ordered such a huge mausoleum to be constructed 2,200 years ago. At the same time, he left his highly developed civilization to people today."*

—Emperor Qin's Terracotta Museum

It is estimated that the terracotta army consists of more than 7,000 soldiers, 150 cavalry horses, and 130 chariots drawn by 520 draft horses.

The faces of the statues were cast in molds, after which artisans carved unique facial features.

Though the ancient Chinese historian Sima Qian stated that the army required some 700,000 artisans working 36 years, at least one modern historian believes the task would have taken 16,000 men roughly two years.

# CAIRO

*The Mosque of Muhammad Ali sits atop the Saladin Citadel of Cairo. Its namesake ruled Egypt for more than 40 years and modernized and industrialized the economy.*

Cairo is one of the oldest Islamic cities. Once a Byzantine stronghold, it surrendered to the Muslim armies commanded by the Arabian general Amr ibn al-A'as in 640 AD. By the 10th century, Cairo was the new center of the Islamic world. The city flourished, reaching its golden age in the 14th century. Replete with celebrated mosques, madrasas and beautiful hammams and fountains, today Cairo is Egypt's foremost city and the largest in Africa. The Citadel in Cairo is named after

*Cairo became Egypt's capital in 1169. It has since become one of the great cities of the world, with a metropolitan population of 17 million.*

Saladin (1137–1193), 12th century Kurdish Sultan of Egypt and great leader of the Muslim world, who recaptured Jerusalem from the Crusaders in 1187. Within the citadel is the spectacular Mosque of Muhammad Ali Pasha, built between 1830 and 1848.

Cairo is also home to the greatest Islamic center for learning, Al-Azhar University. Its school of theology dates to 988 AD, making it one of the world's oldest continuously operating universities. The university is connected to the beautiful Al-Azhar Mosque, built in 971 AD over a period of just two years.

## Egypt

**Period:**

From the 7th century

**Significance:**

Cairo is one of the world's oldest Islamic cities.

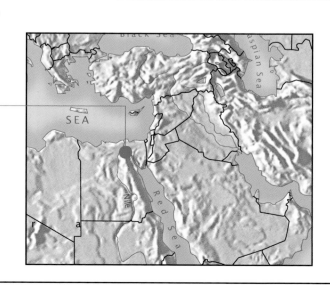

## Jordan

**Period:**

3rd century BC

**Significance:**

Petra was a vital crossroads between Arabia, Egypt and Syria-Phoenicia.

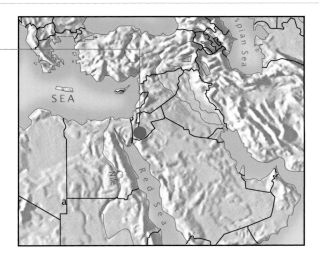

Petra was the capital of the Nabateans, an ancient Arab trading people who controlled a series of oases. Petra became an important stop for the trading caravans that traveled the region.

The ruins of Petra lie in a hollow among the mountains, accessible only through narrow gorges. In 1812 the Swiss explorer Johann Ludwig Burckhardt walked through a small canyon and first encountered the grand carved entrance to Al Khazneh ("the Treasury"). The combination of raw sandstone rock and the elaborate man-made structure embedded within is as startling today as when it was first revealed to Western eyes in 1812. Although no clear date is known for when the city of Petra was first established, the site was inhabited since prehistoric times. By 312 BC Petra was the Nebataeans' capital city, an ancient trading caravan city and important crossroads between Arabia, Egypt and Syria-Phoenicia.

The Treasury was constructed between 100 BC and 200 AD as a royal tomb; its name derives from a legend that told of riches stolen by bandits and hidden inside a stone urn high on the edifice. The structure suffered damage as a result. Stories abound about Bedouins shooting at the urns in the hope of releasing the hidden treasure.

Al Khazneh stands at the end of a 1-mile (1.6 km) fault through the rock, called al-Siq ("the shaft"). A natural defense for the city, al-Siq was easily guarded by the Nabateans.

# SHIBAM

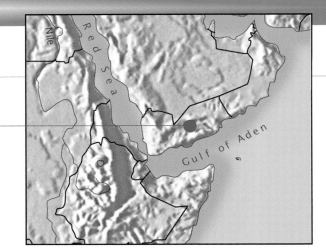

## Yemen

**Period:**

16th century

**Significance:**

Shibam is one of the world's earliest examples of "high-rise" architecture.

*Rebuilt many times over the centuries, the mud-brick towers of Shibam require constant maintenance. Their tops are whitewashed to guard against rain and erosion.*

At first glance, Yemen's fortified city of Shibam might be mistaken for a modern metropolis, and as such it has earned the nickname "Manhattan of the Desert." Yet these densely packed desert skyscrapers—some rising as high as nine stories—are built entirely of mud and brick. They date to the 16th-century, when the tiny city was a trade hub on the Incense Road. A superb early example of urban "high-rise" planning and architectural skill that has endured for half a millennium, this ancient city is now home to 7,000 inhabitants.

*Situated in the Wadi Hadramawt, a large oasis in southern Yemen, Shibam was an important stop for spice traders leading caravans through the region.*

# S A N A ' A

Constructed of stone, brick, and mud blocks, the old houses generally rise several stories, with their best rooms situated on the buildings' highest floors.

Entrance to the city of Sana'a is through the 700 year-old "Yemen Gate"— into the heart of ancient South Arabia. It was from this mountain valley, 7,217 feet (2,200 m) above sea level, that the 6th-century Sabaean Dynasty ruled over the spice trade. Later, in the 7th and 8th centuries, Sana'a became the seat of the powerful Himyarite Kingdom and an important center for the dissemination of Islam throughout the region.

Inhabited for more than 2,500 years, the city of Sana'a is filled with reminders of its long and rich history. Its 103 mosques, 14 hammams (bathhouses) and over 6,000 houses all pre-date the 11th century.

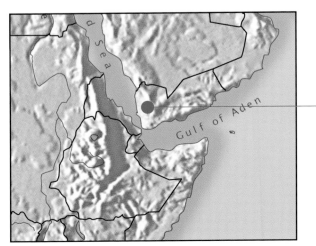

The houses of Sana'a's old quarter cluster against one another to create labyrinthine alleyways and a striking collage of spectacularly decorated façades.

## Yemen

**Period:**

Since the 1st century

**Significance:**

Sana'a was the heart of ancient South Arabia.

The ancient clay walls protecting Sana'a's old quarter reach nearly 30 feet (9 m) high in places. The city itself predates the rise of Islam in the region.

# ESFAHAN

The residents of Esfahan live, work and worship amid spectacular architecture, representative of many periods of design, and stretching back to pre-Islamic motifs.

The variety of Islamic architectural sites and historical monuments that can be found today in Esfahan is proof of its turbulent past. This 2,500 year-old city—once the large and thriving capital of Persia (1598–1722)—was almost destroyed and was rebuilt several times over the course of its long history. In the 13th century Esfahan fell to the Mongols, and its inhabitants were massacred. By the 16th century however, the city flourished as the capital of the Safavid Dynasty, the greatest of the Iranian empires. Esfahan suffered another collapse in 1722 after being raided by the Afghans, who left the city in ruins.

First built in the 8th century, The Jamé Mosque of Esfahan was rebuilt 300 years later. Remodeled many times, it exhibits a variety of architectural styles.

## Iran

**Period:**

Since the 11th century

**Significance:**

The 2,500-year-old Esfahan was once the capital of Persia.

Persian architecture is unique for its inventiveness and decoration, and many consider Esfahan's Shah Mosque, which dates back to the 17th century, to be Iran's masterpiece.

The white marble walls of the Taj Mahal are ornately decorated with inlays of jasper, jade, and yellow marble. Some decorations depict floral motifs, others, Islamic calligraphy.

The most iconic view of the Taj Mahal is the sight of it over the reflecting pool, which placidly mirrors its white marble flanks.

Nearly perfectly symmetrical, the mausoleum radiates from the cenotaph, or false sarcophagus, of Mumtaz Mahal, which occupies the central point inside the tomb.

# MAHABALIPURAM

*Mahabalipuram's Shore Temple rises some 60 feet (18 m) above the ground. Of its three shrines, two are dedicated to Shiva and the third to Vishnu.*

### India

**Period:**

7th and 8th centuries

**Significance:**

Mahabalipuram is notable for its pioneering examples of Dravidian architecture and of Pallava art in general.

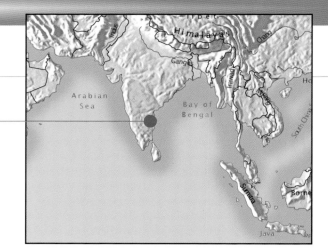

Mahabalipuram is nicknamed the "Seven Pagodas," for a British traveler's account of the area along the ancient seaport in the 18th century. The site was established in the 7th century during the reign of King Mahendravarman I, ruler of the powerful Pallava Kingdom in South India, and continued by his son and successor Mamallan (Mahabalipuram means "city of Mamallan").

The site's excellent examples of Dravidian architecture, and Pallava art in general, are Mahabalipuram's claim to fame. The temples are especially notable for their distinctive pyramidal roofs, and the site contains many sculptures, Madapas (cave sanctuaries), exquisite bas-relief carvings and Rathas—monolithic stone temples carved in the form of chariots.

*The Descent of the Ganges is a monumental bas-relief carved from an enormous rock. It depicts the legendary lowering of the river Ganges from heaven to earth.*

## India

**Period:**

14th to 16th centuries

**Significance:**

Hampi is a masterpiece of Dravidian architectural achievement.

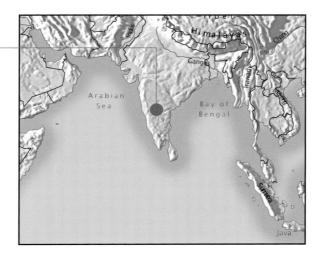

*Common to Dravidian architecture, statues depicting the Hindu pantheon stand among the stonework of Hampi. Later Muslim occupiers of the site disapproved of such idolatry.*

The ancient Dravidian culture comprises a diverse group of linguistically related peoples of southern India believed to have been the country's first original settlers. The approximately 9-square-mile (23.3 sq km) area of Hampi is a masterpiece of Dravidian architectural achievement. Most notable is the celebrated 16th-century Vittala Temple, but the site is replete with superb monuments, sculptures, and Hindu temples, and it still functions as a religious center today.

Hampi occupies just a portion of the last great Hindu Kingdom of Vijayanagar. Sanskrit for "City of Victory," Vijayanagar was founded during the Sangama Dynasty by princes Harihara I and Bukka Raya I in 1336. It reached the height of its power during the early 16th century and was destroyed by the confederacy of Deccan Sultanates in 1565.

*The Stone Chariot at Hampi's Vittala Temple is a shrine to Vishnu built from numerous blocks of carved granite. Its elaborate designs were at one time painted.*

# ITCHAN KALA

The fortified oasis town of Khiva, a small city in the Xorazm province, contains another, smaller, walled city within its boundary, Itchan Kala, whose brick wall foundations were laid as early as the 10th century. The crenelated inner walls preserved at the site today, constructed mostly in the 10th century, reach a height of 30 feet (10 m). Similarly, while the Djuma Mosque inside Itchan Kala dates to the 10th century, the majority of mosques, madrasas and palaces at the site date from the 17th century onward. The jewel in the city is arguably the Islam Koja Minaret, whose blue-glazed tiles sparkle in the desert sun.

The oasis town was important as a stopping point along the ancient caravan trade route, the Great Silk Road, and the last point in the arid region for caravans traveling from Russia and the Caucasus to rest and replenish supplies before continuing across the desert into Iran. Today it is one of the foremost historical Muslim centers in Uzbekistan.

## Uzbekistan

**Period:**

10th century

**Significance:**

This walled city was an important stopping point along the Great Silk Road.

*Constructed in the 10th century, Itchan Kala's Djuma Mosque is still used today. Its interior contains a hypostyle hall supported by 212 carved wooden pillars.*

*Itchan Kala lies in the heart of Khiva. Its minarets and fortifications testify to the Islamic culture that lived and fought there centuries ago.*

*Djuma Mosque's beautiful blue-green Kalta-Minor minaret was never completed. It rises to only 85 feet (26 m), but it was originally planned to scrape the sky at 263 feet (80 m).*

# MAUSOLEUM OF KHOJA AHMED YASAVI

## Kazakhstan

**Period:**

14th and 15th centuries

**Significance:**

The mausoleum—which boasts the largest dome ever constructed in Central Asia—commemorates the great Sufi poet and religious scholar, Khoja Ahmed Yasavi.

*The Mausoleum of Khoja Ahmed Yasavi remains unfinished. Also visible on the site is Yasavi's underground house, where he spent the end of his life in darkness.*

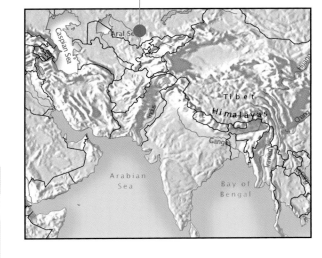

B uilt by Tamerlane (1370–1405), ruler of the Timurid Dynasty, the mausoleum of Khoja Ahmed Yasavi (1103–1166) in the town of Yasi commemorates the great Sufi poet and religious scholar. Construction of the mausoleum began in 1389 and continued until the death of Tamerlane in 1405, when it remained unfinished.

Khoja Ahmed Yasavi is a revered figure in Kazakhstan, commonly referred to as the "father of the Turks" for his role in the conversion of Turkish speaking Kazakh people to Islam. Built over the site of an earlier 12th-century shrine to the Sufi master, the huge mausoleum boasts the largest dome ever constructed in Central Asia. Embellished with radiant blue and green glazed tiles the dome measures 92 feet (28 m) in height with a 59 foot (18 m) diameter. It remains one of the largest and best-preserved examples of Timurid architecture.

*The dome topping the mausoleum is 92 feet (28 m) high and 59 feet (18 m) in diameter, making it the largest dome ever built in the region.*

# THE GREAT WALL OF CHINA

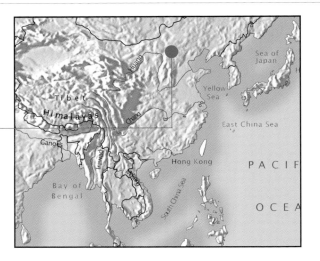

## China

**Period:**

From the 3rd century BC

**Significance:**

The Great Wall is the largest man-made structure on earth.

The Great Wall used materials native to the construction sites: quarried stone in the mountains and packed soils on the prairie.

During the Ming Dynasty (1368–1644), the Great Wall was rebuilt using brick and stone. Owing to its great length, the wall required nearly continuous repairs to guard against the constant threat of Mongol and Manchurian raids and invasions.

Originally built to defend China from attack from the north by Mongolian nomadic tribes, the earliest sections of the Great Wall date from more than 2,000 years ago to around 700 BC. Built by countless laborers during the Qin Dynasty (221–206 BC), the Great Wall is the largest man-made structure on earth and remains an extraordinary achievement. Approximately 400,000 laborers are thought to have perished in the construction of the Great Wall, earning it the less illustrious reputation as "the longest cemetery on earth."

The earliest construction of the wall was of simple earth and stones packed into wood frames; the fortified walls and watchtowers preserved today were largely built and extended during the Ming Dynasty (1338–1644). The wall is not a continuous structure, but rather a series of structures snaking across 1500 miles (2400 km) of mountainous terrain. The scale of the battlements is such that it required a communication system of watchtowers in which fires would be lit to signal enemy activity along the border.

Although largely well-preserved as a historic monument, public and governmental attention is focused mainly on the portion of the wall north of Beijing. Unfortunately, more remote sections have fallen into disrepair as stones have been removed for use in building local roads and houses.

*"A young woman by the name of Ming Jiangnu came to the Great Wall looking for her husband. Hearing the sad news of the death of her beloved, she sat down at the foot of the Wall and started crying. She cried day and night, and her wailing made the wall fall. She finally saw her husband's bones under the wall."*

—The Legend of Ming Jiangnu's Bitter Weeping

More than one million men may have guarded the wall during the Ming Dynasty. Hundreds of thousands died building it over the centuries.

The Great Wall meanders roughly 4,000 miles (6,400 km) east to west across China.

# CHINESE IMPERIAL PALACE

*This gilded lion guards the Palace of Tranquil Longevity, which sits in the inner court of the Forbidden City.*

## China

**Period:**

17th and 18th centuries

**Significance:**

The Chinese Imperial Palace is an important artifact from the Ming and Qing dynasties.

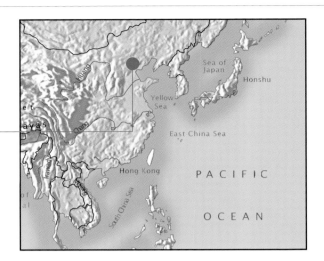

*Tiananmen, or the Gate of Heavenly Peace, sits at the north edge of Tiananmen Square. One must pass through it to reach the Meridian Gate, which guards the Forbidden City, now a historic tourist attraction but once the heart of the mighty Chinese empire.*

The Forbidden City in Beijing, the center of imperial power from 1416 to 1911, is a spectacular monument to symmetry and beauty. The architecture of the palace and layout of the Imperial city are filled with symbolic meaning, from the orientation of the palace itself to the colors of the building materials used in its construction. The Imperial Palace of the Qing Dynasty in Shenyang was built between 1625 and 1783. A huge complex of 114 buildings, it now functions as a museum, notable for having the largest collection of wooden structures to have survived from antiquity. The palace today contains outstanding artifacts of the Ming and Qing dynasties.

*"Without seeing the magnificence of the royal palace, one can never sense the dignity of the Emperor."*

—Line from a Tang Dynasty poem

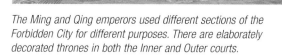

*The Ming and Qing emperors used different sections of the Forbidden City for different purposes. There are elaborately decorated thrones in both the Inner and Outer courts.*

PART II - HUMAN CULTURE

# THE SUMMER PALACE

## China

**Period:**

18th and 19th centuries

**Significance:**

The Summer Palace has the largest classical garden in China.

*"The Garden of Health and Harmony (Yi He Yuan)."*

—Empress Dowager Cixi, renaming the Palace in 1888

As the Imperial Palace of the Forbidden City exemplifies Chinese Palatial architecture, the Summer Palace is the masterpiece of the Chinese Imperial garden. First built in 1750, the palace was largely destroyed by the Anglo-French alliance during the war of 1860. The Empress Dowager Cixi rebuilt the palace in 1888 during the reign of Emperor Guangxu (1875–1898) at immense cost, with silver intended for the Chinese Navy.

The Summer Palace has the largest classical garden in China, occupying a site of 717 acres (290 h), three quarters of which is taken up by a lake. The many elegant architectural features of the garden, including the 17-arch bridge, the famous marble boat and numerous towers (all extravagantly decorated), were designed to harmonize with the natural features of the landscape, achieving an aesthetic balance of beauty and serenity befitting a summer retreat.

On the southern slope of Longevity Hill stands the Tower of Buddhist Incense, which rises 135 feet (41 m) above Kunming Lake.

*"Two robbers broke into this museum, devastating, looting and burning, and left laughing hand in hand with their bags full of treasures; one of the robbers is called France and the other Britain."*

—French writer Victor Hugo, describing the destruction of the old Summer Palace

The Summer Palace was carefully designed to harmonize with the landscape which surrounds it—this arched bridge echoes the rise of Longevity Hill and the ripples of Kunming Lake.

# POTALA PALACE

The site of this high-altitude complex, perched 12,140 feet (3,700 m) above sea level on the side of Marpo Ri (Red Hill) in the Lhasa Valley, has long been a sacred place for Tibetans. King Songtsen Gampo, first emperor of unified Tibet, established a palace at Marpo Ri in 637 as a gift for his Chinese bride, Princess Wen Cheng of the Tang Dynasty. The vast structure at the site today,

the Potala Palace, was built by the fifth Dalai Lama, Lozang Gyatso, in the 17th century and became the residence of successive Tibetan rulers until 1959, when Tibet failed in an uprising against China, and the 14th Dalai Lama fled to India.

At 13 stories high and containing more than 1,000 rooms, the massive complex covers an area of more than 3,875,039 square feet (360,000 sq m) and is the

greatest monumental structure in Tibet. The White Palace is traditionally the residential quarters of the Dalai Lama, while the Red Palace is devoted to prayer and Buddhist training. For centuries the Potala Palace was the traditional seat of the Tibetan government. Today, under the control of the Chinese government, it is a spectacular museum.

The Potala Palace is now administered as a museum, visited by thousands of people every day.

Potala Palace, and its city, Lhasa, has been a seat of Tibetan Buddhism for centuries. Lhasa means "place of the gods."

*"The majestic, brilliant, magnificent and uninhibited Potala Palace has a strong artistic appeal and is an architectural art treasure that can be shown off to the world."*

—Ministry of Culture of the People's Republic of China

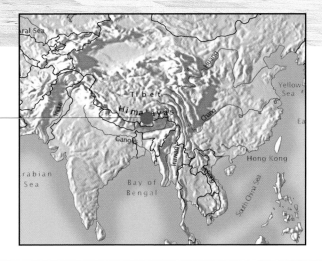

The current Dalai Lama, Tenzin Gyatso, first took up residence at the Potala Palace as a 4-year-old child. He was appointed Dalai Lama at age 15, but was forced to flee the palace in 1959, at age 25.

## China

### Period:

17th century

### Significance

Potala Palace is the greatest monumental structure in Tibet.

# KYOTO

## Japan

**Period:**

794 AD

**Significance:**

Kyoto is foremost among Japanese cities in preserving the country's traditional arts and known for its celebrated wooden architecture.

*The top two stories of Kyoto's Golden Pavilion, first built in the late 14th century and recently rebuilt, are clad in gold leaf.*

A s the center of Japanese culture for 1,200 years the ancient city of Kyoto is foremost among Japanese cities in preserving the country's traditional arts. Known for its celebrated wooden architecture, the city dates to 794 AD, the Heian period, when it was built according to the ancient Chinese model of urban design and architecture. It flourished as Japan's capital city until the middle of the 19th century. The height of Kyoto's power, however, was in the middle ages, until the 11-year-long civil wars of Onin and Bunmei (1467–1477). This had a devastating impact on the city, which never regained its former prosperity. The finest examples of the art of the classical Japanese garden can be found in Kyoto, their simplicity and serenity reflecting Shinto reverence for the natural world of trees, water and rocks.

*This torii marks the entrance to a Shinto shrine in Kyoto. Torii are sacred gates; they sanctify those who walk beneath them.*

*Built in 1895, the Heian Jingu is a three-quarters-scale replica of the Kyoto Imperial Palace. The shrine's construction commemorated the 1,100-year anniversary of Kyoto's founding.*

# N A R A

## Japan

**Period:**

8th century

**Significance:**

Nara was once Japan's capital and the cultural, economic, and political heart of the country.

Older than the ancient city of Kyoto, Nara enjoyed the position as Japan's capital for just 74 years, from 710 to 784, when it prospered as the cultural, economic, and political heart of Japan. At its height the city boasted a population of 100,000 people, making it the largest city in ancient Japan. Heavily influenced by Chinese Tang Dynasty architecture, the wooden temples and buildings of the Nara period exerted a major influence on subsequent Japanese architecture. Buddhism became established as the dominant religion during this period, one of great cultural change for Japan.

*"When the Sun Goddess dispatched her grandson to Earth, he landed on the island of Kyushu, and was enthroned as the first ruler of Yamato [present-day Nara]."*

—Nara's origins according to Japanese mythology

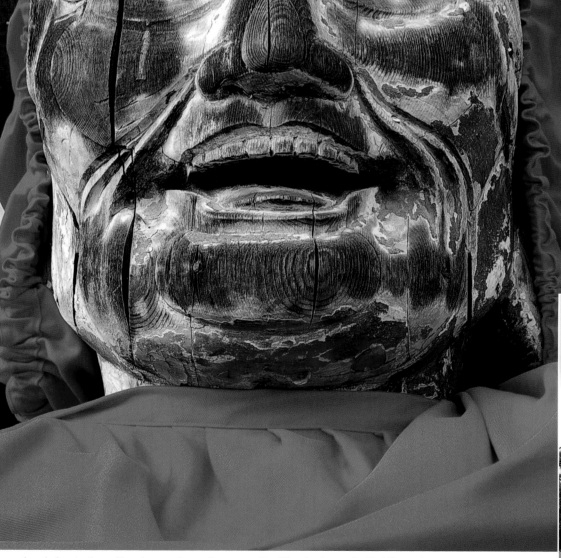

*A god of protection, with red garments warding away evil spirits, stands guard at Todaiji temple.*

*Nara boasts the largest wooden temple in Japan.*

# HWASEONG FORTRESS

## Korea

**Period:**

late 18th century

**Significance:**

Hwaseong is one of the greatest fortresses in the Korean peninsula.

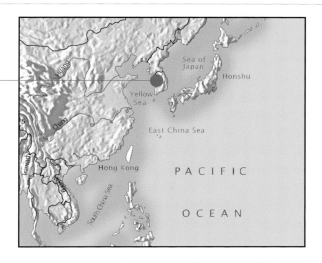

*At the northwestern corner of the fortress stands Seobuk Gongsimdon, an observation tower equipped with cannons.*

One of the greatest fortresses in the Korean peninsula, Hwaseong—or *brilliant fortress*—was constructed between 1794 and 1796 by King Jeongjo (r. 1776–1800) during the Joseon Dynasty (1392–1910). It is said that 700,000 workers labored for two years to built the massive structure, comprising four main gates, many towers and observation decks, and two large floodgates.

Designed by the Confucian Silhak scholar Jeong Yakyong (1762–1836) the fortress contained features that were unprecedented in Korean architecture, and was constructed using innovative and modern techniques. The fortress was built to honor and restore the reputation of Jeongjo's father, Prince Sado who had been murdered in 1776 at the age of 27 by his own father, the reigning King Joseon, and to assert Jeongjo's own royal authority in the Korean courts. Originally enclosing the entire city of Suwon, the walls of the elaborate fortress today fall within the boundaries of the sprawling modern city.

*"I will then be able to fulfill my greatest wishes. I will retire to Hwaseong with Your Ladyship…"*

—King Jeongjo, founder of Hwaseong, to his mother Lady Hyegyeong

*Demonstrations of historic weapons and strategies are presented during the tourist season, providing insight to a bygone era.*

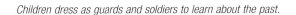

*Children dress as guards and soldiers to learn about the past.*

# ANGKOR

Now a major archeological site, Angkor was the living heart of the powerful Khmer civilization in Cambodia from the 9th to the 15th century. Religious temples are all that remain of what was once a vast network of houses, public buildings, and palaces. Secular buildings were built of wood, whereas stone was reserved for sacred structures; therefore all but the temples have perished. These temples and shrines number more than a thousand, making Angkor the largest religious complex of antiquity in the world. The biggest and most magnificent temple, Angkor Wat, was built by King Suryavarman II in the first half of the

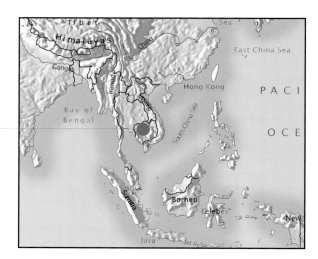

## SUCCESS STORY

### Cambodia

**The Challenge:**

The temples at Angkor Wat were under threat from looters and the detonation of land mines.

**The Solution:**

A multinational conservation plan was put into place.

12th century and dedicated to the God Vishnu (although it was later converted for Buddhist worship and remains Buddhist today).

Abandoned and forgotten in the 15th century, Angkor deteriorated and was subsumed by tropical growth. It was not until the French explorer Henri Mouhot rediscovered the site in 1860 that it became widely known and appreciated for its scale and splendor. French archeologists began a sustained period of renovation beginning in 1907, which was interrupted for five years during the Cambodian Civil War (1970–1975), but resumed after the war ended. Angkor was placed on the World Heritage in Danger list in 1992, instigating a multinational conservation effort to save the site from looting and destruction from land mine explosions. The effort proved a great success, leading to the removal of Angkor from the endangered list. Conservation continues at Angkor today.

*"It is grander than anything left us by Greece and Rome."*

—French naturalist Henri Mouhot, who rediscovered Angkor in 1860

*Breaking with predecessors, King Suryavarman II devoted Angkor Wat to Vishnu, aligning himself with a more monotheistic form of Hinduism.*

*Angkor Thom, the empire's final capital, centers on the Bayon Temple. Its beatific faces may represent King Jayavarman VII or the bodhisattva Avalokiteshvara, a Buddhist divinity of compassion of particular popularity in Southeast Asia.*

*Abandoned in 1431, Angkor was reclaimed by the forest until discovered nearly six centuries later. Conservationists are currently working to halt the processes of decay and reclaim Angkor from the wild.*

# P O L O N N A R U W A

Buddha stands at the entrances to Ran Kot Vereha, the largest shrine of Buddhist relics in Polonnaruwa.

The medieval city of Polonnaruwa is the second oldest in Sri Lanka. Established as the capital by King Wijayabahu I in 1070, it replaced the former capital Anuradhapura. Polonnaruwa flourished during the reign of Wijayabahu's grandson King Parakramabahu I (1153–1186), the last great king of Sri Lanka. The foremost examples of Sinhalese rock carvings—four great monolithic sculptures of the Buddha at Gal Vihara in Polonnaruwa—were created during Parakramabahu's reign.

Ancient Sri Lankans considered rain a prized and precious commodity and tapped every source of water. King Parakramabahu I believed that not one drop should be wasted and, as a result, Sri Lanka has a network of irrigation systems, including the famous Parakrama Samudra (Sea of Parakrama), a 29-square-mile (75-sq-km) reservoir that is, remarkably, still in use today.

*This monument stands to Ananda Thera, cousin and personal priest to the Buddha, who successfully argued for the ordination of women.*

## Sri Lanka

**Period:**

From the late 11th century

**Significance:**

The medieval city of Polonnaruwa is the second oldest in Sri Lanka.

# DAMBULLA

Five caves were transformed into temples filled with statues and paintings depicting the life and teachings of Buddha.

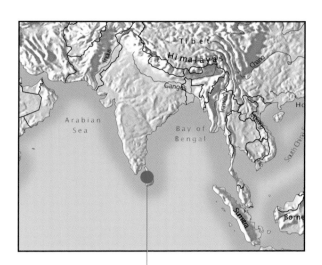

**W**hen King Valagambahu of Sri Lanka was forced into exile in the 1st century, he found refuge and protection among Buddhist monks inside a vast cave complex beneath a gigantic overhanging rock rising 525 feet (160 m) above the ground. After his return to the throne at Anuradapura 14 years later, the grateful king created a magnificent rock temple to Buddha at the site in a princely gesture of gratitude to the monks.

The five large cave sanctuaries are filled with devotional statues and the wall paintings depict scenes from the life of Buddha and illustrate his sermons. Although the earliest paintings at the site date to the 1st century, they were extensively restored in the 11th, 12th, and 18th centuries, making it the best-preserved ancient edifice in Sri Lanka.

## Sri Lanka

**Period:**

late 18th century

**Significance:**

This rock temple to Buddha is the best-preserved ancient edifice in Sri Lanka.

Buddha meditates at the center of the Medirigiriya Vatadage, among the oldest shrines in Sri Lanka.

Paintings in Dambulla depict Buddha and bodhisattvas among gods and goddesses.

# LUMBINI

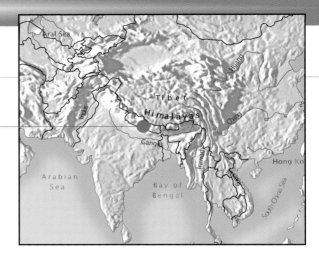

## Nepal

**Period:**

7th century BC

**Significance:**

Lumbini is the birthplace of Buddha.

*"Oh, Maharaj! Here the Blessed One was born."*
—Emperor Ashoka the Great (294–232 BC)

Colorful prayer flags—panels of hanging bright fabrics—mark the visits of pilgrims. The flags are unique to Himalayan Buddhism.

Monasteries and temples at Lumbini represent styles of various Buddhist cultures, including the golden Burmese Lokamani Cula Pagoda.

On the Terai Plains at the foothills of the Himalyas in Southern Nepal is the birthplace of the Shaka Dynasty Prince, Siddhartha Gautama, Lord Buddha, founder of Buddhism. The beautiful gardens at Lumbini (in Sanskrit "The Lovely") where he was born in 623 BC are marked with a stone pillar commemorating his birth and draw pilgrims from around the world.

At the age of 29 Siddartha turned his back on the life of ease and splendor he had always known. He left his wife and child and departed from the royal residence to live the austere life of an ascetic and develop the Buddhist philosophy. In addition to ruins of ancient monasteries and other sacred relics at Lumbini, modern temples devoted to the Lord Buddha surround the site and receive a constant flow of worshippers and pilgrims.

A centuries-old pillar marks the purported birthplace of Siddhartha Gautama, who would become Buddha.

# KATHMANDU

*A Buddhist monk meditates as he circles a stupa. This "walking" meditation is a common activity in some Buddhist traditions.*

## Nepal

**Period:**

late 17th century

**Significance:**

Kathmandu—the capital of Nepal—is one of the most historic and culturally rich cities in the country.

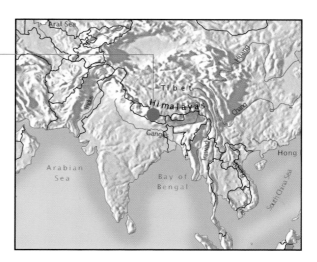

Kathmandu is part of a trio of great royal Nepalese cities: Kathmandu, Patan, and Bhaktapur. These three cities represent the highest achievement of Nepalese art and culture.

The largest and most developed city in Nepal is Kathmandu; the capital of the country spreads across an elevated valley at the foot of the Himalayas. As the region is prone to earthquakes, many of the buildings in the old quarter of the Kathmandu city—temples and shrines built in the 17th century—have been damaged, but the biggest threat comes from the march of modern urban development. There is a danger that the value of Kathmandu's rich heritage may be forgotten in the desire for progress. The entire valley was added to the World Heritage in Danger list in 2003.

*Kathmandu streets are home to ascetic yogis of various sects, such as this naga sadhu, or "sky-clad" yogi.*

*Turning a prayer wheel adds significance to a spoken mantra.*

# BOROBUDUR

## SUCCESS STORY

### Indonesia

**The Challenge:**

This Hindu/Buddhist temple—the largest in the world—was abandoned in the 10th century.

**The Solution:**

An international campaign launched in 1972 saved the temple from further deterioration. By 1983, the temple had been completely restored.

The famous 8th- and 9th-century Mahayana Buddhist temple on the volcanic Island of Java is the largest Hindu/Buddhist temple in the world. At 592,020 square feet (55,000 sq m) the massive pyramid structure dominates the landscape. This astonishing structure was built with lava rock over a period of 75 years during the reign of Samarattunga. It was begun by Hindu builders around 775; then, as the Hindu dynasty in Java weakened, it was completed by Buddhist workers in 835. The temple is embellished with 2,672 bas-relief carvings and more than 500 statues of Buddha, and is crowned with a monumental stupa (traditional dome-shaped Buddhist reliquary). Pathways direct pilgrims ever upward, leading symbolically toward Nirvana. The stupa at the summit is empty, asserting the perfection of enlightenment. It seems remarkable that during the 10th century the temple was abandoned and left for the jungle to take it over; it was not rediscovered until 1814, by Sir Thomas Raffles. In 1972 an international campaign was launched to save it from further deterioration, and restoration was completed in 1983.

*Seventy-two bell-shaped stupa, each containing a statue of Buddha, adorn the top of the enormous Borobudur temple.*

*Although weathered, the finely-carved statues of Buddha at Borobudur have largely withstood the test of time.*

# PRAMBANAN TEMPLE

*Although damaged by an earthquake in 2006, the elaborately decorated Prambanan temple was soon reopened to visitors.*

## Indonesia

**Period:**

10th century

**Significance:**

The Hindu Prambanan temple in central Java is the most beautiful and largest of all Hindu temples in Indonesia.

The 9th century Hindu Prambanan temple in central Java is dedicated to the Gods Shiva "the Destroyer," Vishnu "the Keeper," and Brahma "the Creator." Prambanan is held to be the most beautiful of all the Hindu temples in Indonesia, and it is certainly the largest. The elevated inner area of the compound comprises three tall, slender, pointed shrines, each dedicated to one of the primary Hindu Gods, and the outer section of the compound contains numerous smaller shrines.

The shrine to Shiva located at the center of the temple is the biggest, standing at 130 feet (39.6 m), and it houses a further five chambers. One of these is dedicated to Shiva's consort, the fierce and beautiful Goddess Durga, mother of Ganesha, among others, and the chamber contains a magnificent statue of her. The shrine is also known locally as the Lara Jonggrang Temple, Javanese for "Slender Virgin," after a Javanese princess forced to marry against her will. Eventually however she capitulated, under the condition that her prospective groom build a temple for her filled with a thousand statues.

Prambanan Temple was abandoned not long after its construction. It underwent restoration in the first half of the 20th century but was badly damaged by an earthquake in 2006.

*Hundreds of shrines were built on the ascending platforms to the three main shrines devoted to Brahma, Vishnu and Shiva.*

# MACHU PICCHU

The Incas used dry-stone construction to build Machu Picchu. The stone walls possess no mortar; Incan builders, with outstanding skill, carefully carved the stones to fit against each other.

## Peru

**Period:**

15th century

**Significance:**

Machu Picchu was likely a religious mountain retreat for the Inca Emperor Pachacuti Inca (1438–1471) 100 years after the collapse of the Inca Empire.

Architecture was perhaps the greatest Incan art. Isolated high in the Andes, Machu Picchu is one of the few places where Incan architecture is still relatively intact.

PART II - HUMAN CULTURE

Cradled between two mountains on the Eastern slopes of the Andes, the Lost City of the Incas is named for the bigger of the two mountains rising above it. Machu Picchu means "old mountain." The other peak is Wuayna Picchu, which translates as "young mountain."

A breathtaking site of great natural beauty, Machu Picchu remained unknown to the outside world for four centuries—hence its nickname "the Lost City"—until it was discovered in 1911 by American

*Many Incan architectural techniques were learned from earlier Mesoamerican cultures, in particular from the people of Tiwanaku, in Bolivia.*

archeologist Hiram Bingham. Its remote, isolated location 7,972 feet (2,430 m) above sea level in tropical mountainous terrain, suggests that Machu Picchu did not play a significant role in the ancient Peruvian administration but rather was a religious mountain retreat for the Inca Emperor Pachacuti Inca (1438–1471), one hundred years after the collapse of the Inca Empire.

The Spanish Conquistadors never discovered the Inca city, and the site and its artifacts remained untouched until Bingham's arrival. Bingham removed as many

as 500 artifacts from Machu Picchu to Yale University, where he was a professor. The modern Peruvian government fought hard for the return of these artifacts and in 2007 Yale finally agreed to return them.

*"It fairly took my breath away. What could this place be? Why had no one given us any idea of it?"*

—Explorer Hiram Bingham III, who rediscovered the Inca settlement in 1911

*Well-adapted to Peru's mountainous terrain, llamas have served generations of Andean peoples as pack animals, and as a source of milk, meat and fibers for yarn. They remain as integral a part of the landscape today as when the Incans built Machu Picchu centuries ago.*

# SGANG GWAII

*"Our culture, our heritage is the child of respect and intimacy with the land and sea. Like the forests, the roots of our people are intertwined such that the greatest troubles cannot overcome us."*

—Extract of the Haida constitution

## Canada

**Period:**

From the 2nd through the 19th centuries

**Significance:**

The Haida people, First Nations of British Columbia.

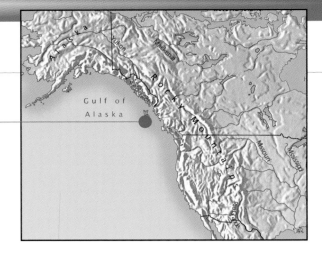

The Haida tribe of SGang Gwaii, off the West Coast of British Columbia, is famous for its elaborately carved totem poles, and for their magnificent dugout canoes. Master woodworkers, the Haida people were especially skilled at boat making, carving vessels from the single trunk of a red cedar tree. These lightweight canoes reached lengths of over 60 feet (18 m) and could hold as many as 60 people. Operated by paddles, they were also capable of traveling over great distances.

The Haida were the first to occupy the Haida Gwaii archipelago (commonly known as the Queen Charlotte Islands) comprising 150 islands. The once thriving population was decimated by small pox, measles, and other diseases introduced by Europeans in the early 19th century, and descendants of the tribe survive today only in two villages. The small, remote island of SGang Gwaii is now a National Heritage Park Reserve containing the remains of a traditional village.

*Though carved from cedar logs, which are abundant and weather resistant, totem poles rarely last more than a few decades in the damp environment of northwest North America.*

*It is believed that the Haida people initiated totem pole carving on the Queen Charlotte Islands; the art soon spread to other Pacific Northwest cultures. Totem poles serve several functions, often tell a story and usually refer to a specific individual or family.*

# CAHOKIA MOUNDS

## United States

**Period:**

650 to 1400

**Significance:**

The mounds of Cahokia were an amazing achievement—to construct them, 55 million cubic feet (1.6 million cu m) of earth was moved in woven baskets.

The people of Cahokia occupied different districts of the city according to social class. The chief lived atop the largest mound.

The largest mound in Cahokia, Monk's Mound is composed entirely of soil. Rising and sinking groundwater levels in recent years have undermined the core of the mound, causing some slumping of the structure.

The pre-Columbian city of Cahokia occupied this six square-mile (15.5 sq m) area in modern day Missouri from approximately 650 to 1400. Its inhabitants, Indians of the Late Woodland culture, began building mounds at the site around 1050. Monk's Mound is the largest at 1,037 by 790 feet (316 x 241 m) at the base and 100 feet (30.5 m) high. Considering the sheer labor involved—55 million cubic feet (1.6m cu m) of earth moved in woven baskets—the mounds are an amazing achievement. Furthermore, there is archeological evidence of a large building atop Monk's Mound, and ruins of other structures. Cahokia reached its peak between 1050 and 1150 AD when its population exceeded any other city in the United States. The population declined throughout the 13th century and the site was abandoned by 1400 AD.

The people of Cahokia were skilled potters. Since they did not develop a writing system, artifacts such as this human-faced pot are the chief testimonials of their developed culture.

# MESA VERDE

## United States

**Period:**

550 to 1300

**Significance:**

This national park is famous for having the highest number of well-preserved archeological sites in the United States.

ncestral home of the ancient Pueblo Indians, Mesa Verde (green table) in Southwest Colorado has been un-inhabited for more than 700 years. This spectacular ancient site was occupied from approximately 550 to 1300 and contains more than 600 cliff dwellings—ranging from the earliest primitive cave sites to the sophisticated multi-level Cliff Palace, spread out under the massive overhang of sandstone rock. The extensive chambers (numbering almost 150), sunken kivas (ceremonial rooms) and towers make the Cliff Palace the largest of its kind in North America. The

Ancestral Puebloans, as they are now known, were called the Anasazi, "ancient," by the Navajo. They are also known as the Basket Makers because of their skill and sophistication in the craft.

The first white American to lay eyes on Mesa Verde was a prospector called John Moss, who came across a few cliff dwellings in 1874. The following year he returned with the photographer William Henry Jackson in tow, who first documented the site. It is now a cele-brated national park famous for having many of the best-preserved archeological sites in the United States.

*Cliff Palace contains roughly 150 rooms, though it is thought that fewer than a third of them were living spaces, while others were used for storage or as yet unknown purposes. The sunken round rooms are kivas, used for religious or spiritual ceremonies.*

*"The falling snowflakes sprinkling the piñons gave it a special kind of solemnity. It was more like sculpture than anything else ... preserved ... like a fly in amber."*

—Richard Wetherill, cowboy who discovered the major ruins of Mesa Verde in 1888

The Square Tower House sat a short distance above a natural spring, and not far beneath fields growing on cliffs above.

In the late 19th century, Cliff Palace was regularly looted and vandalized by curio seekers. Today the National Park Service diligently cares for and watches over the delicate archaeological site.

Most Puebloan rooms featured doors cut out of their wooden ceilings. Occupants used removable ladders to enter and exit the rooms.

The four-story Square Tower House is the tallest building in Mesa Verde. It was not always a monolithic tower—it is believed that the surrounding pueblo once rose to an equal height, but has since crumbled, suffering from time and weather.

# PUEBLO DE TAOS

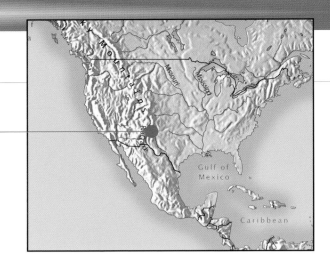

*Today the rooms of the Pueblo de Taos utilize front doors, but for centuries, they were accessible only by ladders, which could be removed if the pueblo were threatened by wars or raids.*

## United States

### Period:
1000 and 1450

### Significance:
Pueblo de Taos is a superb example of pre-hispanic architecture of the Pueblo Indians of Arizona and New Mexico.

*About 150 people live traditionally in Taos Pueblo, without electricity or indoor plumbing. The Red Willow Creek, which crosses the pueblo, is the chief source of water.*

Constructed entirely of adobe—a compound of mud and straw mixed with water—the Pueblo de Taos ancient village just outside the modern city of Taos is a superb example of pre-hispanic architecture of the Pueblo Indians of Arizona and New Mexico. The adobe dwellings

in the village are supported by large wooden beams and include simple houses to multi-storied ceremonial buildings. The site gives rare insight into the lifestyle and practices of the ancient communities that lived here between 1000 and 1450, despite being still inhabited today.

Pueblo de Taos is situated on land that was seized by the U.S. government in 1906. The confiscated land also contained the Blue Lake, an important site sacred to the Pueblo people. About 44,000 acres (17,807 ha) of land were returned to the Pueblo people in 1970, and they now control the area.

Palenque is a ruined Mayan royal city abandoned during the 8th century and hidden in the dense jungle of Mexico for hundreds of years. Spanish explorers discovered it in the 16th century and gave it the name Palenque, a Spanish translation of the Mayan word Otolum "land with strong houses."

Archeological evidence dates Palenque as early as 100 BC, but most of the buildings were constructed from the 7th century onward during the reign of the greatest Mayan ruler Pacal II. The site contains a palace and several temples, providing outstanding examples of Mayan bas-relief stone carvings, sculpture and architecture.

Numerous artistic flourishes, some of them hinting at ancient religious rituals, grace the limestone architecture of Palenque.

## Mexico

**Period:**

100 BC to the 8th century AD

**Significance:**

Palenque provides outstanding examples of Mayan bas-relief stone carvings, sculpture and architecture.

The Temple of the Sun is one of three main temples at Palenque. The temple itself contains an antechamber with three sanctums behind it, as well as "holy portals" which channeled the underworld.

# TEOTIHUACAN

## Mexico

### Period:

1st century AD to the 7th century

### Significance:

The Aztec city of Teotihuacan is notable for the massive scale of its monuments, honoring such powerful Aztec deities as Quetzalcoatl.

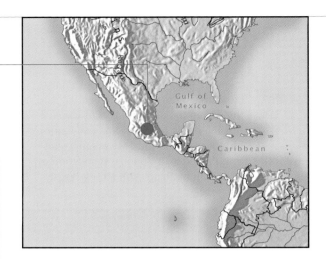

The Aztecs called this place in the Mexican highlands "the place where the gods were created." The site is extraordinary for the massive scale of its monuments, honoring such powerful Aztec deities as Quetzalcoatl. Two pyramid temples dominate the horizon; one dedicated to the sun, the other to the moon.

Construction of Teotihuacan began during the 1st and 2nd centuries. The city grew to great power in the 4th century. At the peak of Teotihuacan's political and cultural influence, it was the largest pre-Columbian city in the Americas, with a population of more than 150,000 citizens. Exactly why the city went into sudden decline in the 7th century, its population decimated and its influence vanished, is one of the ancient world's mysteries. It is known that a great fire swept the city around 700, possibly set by invading forces, but no written documents have survived to give clues about the decline of the city.

*"In Teotihuacan, here were created the sun, the moon and the universe."*

—Aztec mythology

Teotihuacan's Temple of Quetzalcoatl honored the creator god Quetzalcoatl—the feathered serpent—who later entered the Aztec pantheon.

As seen from atop the Pyramid of the Moon, Teotihuacan's Avenue of the Dead traversed much of the ancient city, meticulously laid out on a grid. The gargantuan Pyramid of the Sun stands at left.

The Pyramid of the Magician, as it is commonly known, dominates the center of Uxmal and is the tallest structure at the site. Built in the Puuc style of Mayan architecture—distinctive for its austere simplicity at the base and ornamentation at the top—the pyramid temple is also unique because of its rounded sides and oval-shaped base.

Uxmal was founded in 500 AD and flourished during the 7th through the 10th centuries. An important religious and urban center in Western Yucatán, at its peak Uxmal dominated the Northern Mayan areas but eventually fell into decline after the Spanish conquest of Yucatán.

*The House of Turtles, named for its frieze of turtles along its cornice, stands alongside the Governor's Palace, raised above the city.*

*The Governor's Palace is a long, low, intricately decorated building seated on a stone platform above the city. It was among the last structures built at Uxmal.*

## Mexico

### Period:

The 6th through the 10th centuries

### Significance:

An important religious and urban center in Western Yucatán, at its peak Uxmal dominated the Northern Mayan areas.

Caribbean

*Uxmal's Pyramid of the Magician, the tallest structure in the city, was built over four centuries. It is unique among Mayan architecture for its eliptical base and rounded sides.*

# TIKAL

Tikal is arranged around five towering pyramids, each carefully aligned with the others. Temple V, as seen here, is the second-tallest structure in the city, at 189 feet (58 m).

## Guatemala

**Period:**

The 6th century BC through the 10th century AD

**Significance:**

Tikal boasts a wealth of architectural remains and is the largest excavated site in the Americas.

A city of great significance to the ancient Mayans, Tikal had a ceremonial center and over 3,000 buildings. Inhabited from the 6th century BC to the 10th century AD, the site boasts a wealth of architectural remains and is the largest excavated site in the Americas.

Tikal's grand temples, palaces and public squares, surrounded by the lush Guatemalan jungle, are testimony to its importance.

*"Many people recognize the magic of Tikal. And yes, there is great magic. We are not creating experiences. We are given experiences as a gift…"*

—Mercedes Barrios Longfellow, Mayan Shaman and Priestess from the highlands of Guatemala

*Temple I, the Temple of the Grand Jaguar, rises to 143 feet (44 m). Like all Mayan pyramids, it was built without use of wheels, ropes or pulleys; details of design and construction remain unclear.*

# SAN AUGUSTIN

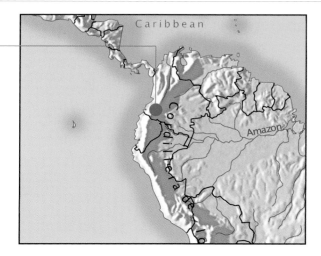

## Colombia

**Period:**

From around 4000 BC

**Significance:**

San Augustin is the site of some of the Andean culture's earliest sculptures and rock carvings.

*The chinas, as the statues of San Agustin are called, were pain-stakingly sculpted from large blocks of volcanic rock, and can weigh several tons. Some still bear traces of ancient paint.*

Not a great deal is known about Columbia's mysterious ancient Andean culture. Archeologists estimate that an archaic mountain culture existed in San Augustin as early as 3,300 BC; some of its earliest sculptures are thought to be as old as 6,000 years. The monolithic sculptures and rock carvings of gods and mythological figures probably served a ceremonial purpose and they number in the hundreds, suggesting a developed religion.

*The culture that occupied San Agustin remains mysterious, though the chinas, which can reach more than 20 feet (6 m) high, tell a story of shamans, animal gods and ritual practices.*

# TIWANAKU

P re-dating the great Inca Empire, the cultural center of the prehistoric people of ancient Bolivia was established high in the Andes in 200 BC. Archeological data suggests that at its peak between 500 and 900 AD, the city of Tiwanaku held as many as one million inhabitants, and this powerful civilization left behind monumental remains.

## Bolivia

**Period:**

From 200 BC

**Significance:**

The prehistoric city of Tiwanaku was home to as many as 1 million of the people of ancient Bolivia.

*Builders accomplished the distinctive mammoth stonework at Tiwanaku using rock quarried from some 25 miles (40 km) away from the city—no easy distance in the mountainous Andes.*

*"Although dozens of national and international projects began to unlock Tiwanaku's secrets during the last century, we are only recently beginning to piece together the puzzle..."*

—The University of Pennsylvania Museum of Archaeology and Anthropology

*For many years, looters ravaged Tiwanaku as easy prey, but in recent years the site has been cared for and somewhat restored.*

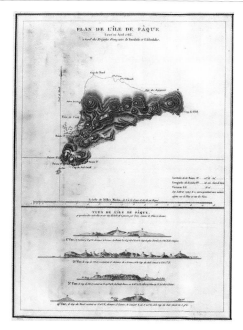

*This 1786 map of Rapa Nui (Easter Island) shows the island 64 years after Dutch explorer Jacob Roggeveen became the first European to encounter it, on Easter Sunday.*

Giant monolithic heads grace the slopes of Rapa Nui, a remote volcanic Island on the South Pacific Ocean. Rapa Nui, more commonly known by its European name, Easter Island, was settled by a people of Polynesian origin early in the 4th century, and its remote location—2,184 miles (3,515 km) off the Chilean coast—helped to preserve the culture's unique identity.

The Easter Islanders developed a distinctive tradition of monumental sculptures called Moai. These stylized human heads are scattered across the land.

Cut off from the outside world, Easter Island suffered from overuse. Denuded of trees, and its bird species hunted out of existence, the island's natural ecosystem was irreparably damaged. The population went into steady decline, reduced by famines, civil wars in the 1600 and 1700s, slave raids in the 1800s, and by European-introduced diseases. By the end of the 19th century the population numbered only in the hundreds.

*"The stone images at first caused us to be struck with astonishment, because we could not comprehend how it was possible that these people…had been able to erect such images."*

—Dutch explorer Jacob Roggeveen, first European to visit the island, 1722

## Chile

### Period:

The 4th through the 19th centuries

### Significance:

The giant monolithic heads of Rapa Nui are the last traces of the population of Easter Island.

*The Moai were mostly carved from volcanic rock, and represent godlike ancestors. The tallest Moai stood 33 feet (10 m) high.*

# QUÉBEC CITY

Québec City is unique as North America's only fortified walled city. It was founded in 1608 by French Explorer Samuel de Champlain, who established the region's distinctly French identity. The vast Québec region was originally referred to as New France and is one of the few truly bilingual areas in North America. The majority of Québec's population speaks French. The region's French identity was hard won however, and Québec City was the focus of a number of important battles between French and English troops as they vied for control of the colony of New France.

The British captured Québec City from the French in the famous Battle of the Plains of Abraham in 1759. Both military commanders—Marquis de Montcalm on the side of the French, and James Wolfe on the side of the British—perished in the battle, which signaled the end of French rule. In 1763 the whole of Canada was finally ceded to the British. Later in the century, during the American Revolutionary War, the fortified city of Québec came under attack again, from American colonial forces, who sought to enlist Canadian support against the British, but this attempt also ended in failure.

The Québec region was first populated by the Iroquois tribe and by the Eskimo-Aleut and nomadic Algonquin Indians. The Iroquoian name for the place on which Québec City now stands was "where the

river narrows." Champlain—the "Father of New France"—selected the location for its potential as an excellent location from which to control the fur trade.

Québec City, one of North America's oldest cities, is situated in a broad valley. Its distinctive skyline—dominated by the massive Château Frontenac Hotel—rises above the great Saint Lawrence River. The hotel was built in 1893 and named after Louis de Buade, Count of Frontenac, governor of New France in the second half of the 17th century.

Québec City is divided into upper and lower districts. The upper district, lying within the historic ramparts, is known as Old Québec, or Vieux Québec. Filled with narrow, winding, cobbled streets, lending it an unusual "Old World" air, this beautifully preserved historic city attracts thousands of visitors a year.

## Canada

**Period:**

Since 1608

**Significance:**

Canada's Québec City is North America's most complete fortified colonial city.

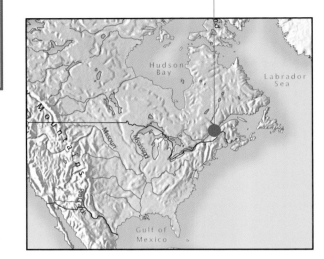

*"I am glad of it…I am happy that I shall not live to see the surrender of Québec"*

—Marquis de Montcalm, mortally wounded

*The rows of dormers lining these roofs are characteristic of French colonial architecture, which is common in the city of Québec.*

*"Now, God be praised, I will die in peace."*

—General James Wolfe a few hours later, just before he died on the Plains of Abraham, learning from one of his soldiers that the French troops ran away

*The Porte Saint-Louis gate was constructed as part of Québec's original fortifications and has been rebuilt several times over the centuries.*

*The Fairmont Le Château Frontenac (top in photo) is a historic hotel in Old Québec. Dating to the late 1800s, it boasts architecture recalling the Middle Ages and the Renaissance.*

# ZANZIBAR

**Z**anzibar City's old quarter, known as Stone Town, remains almost unchanged in appearance from its early history as an Arab trading town. Situated on a peninsula in the Zanzibar Archipelago in the Indian Ocean, Zanzibar City was well positioned as a trading post and transit hub between Arabia, India and Africa, and was an early cultural melting pot for disparate elements from Africa, Arabia, India and Europe.

In the 16th and 17th centuries Zanzibar was under Portuguese colonial rule, but was returned to Arab control by Omani forces in 1698. In its heyday, Zanzibar City drew merchant ships from around the world. Its economy prospered from the sale of spices and from the ivory and slave trade.

For much of the 19th and 20th century, Zanzibar was under British rule, until it was granted independence in 1964. Unfortunately, this ushered in a turbulent and violent period in Zanzibar's history, leading to an uprising and the overthrow of the newly formed government by communist rebel forces during the Zanzibar Revolution. Two years later, Zanzibar joined with mainland Tanganyika and formed the United Republic of Tanzania.

Today, Zanzibar City offers a glimpse into the trading towns of East Africa during the age of exploration.

*Ornately carved wooden doors are hallmarks of Zanzibar's buildings, many of which have been standing for 200 years.*

## Tanzania

**Period:**

From the 9th century

**Significance:**

Zanzibar provides a glimpse of an East African trading town that has been influenced by African, Arab, Indian and European culture.

*Houses in Zanzibar are often a combination of Arab, Indian and British colonial architecture, and feature central courtyards, street-side stone benches called* barazas *and carved balconies.*

# LUANG PRABANG

The city of Luang Prabang in North Central Laos can be traced to the 7th century, when it was founded by the warlord prince, Khun Lo. At that time the city was known as Muang Sawa. The ancient capital of the Lan Xang Kingdom, the city was renamed in the 14th century after the golden Buddha, the Prabang, a gift from Cambodia.

In 1893, French Colonial forces seized power in the area, which was then under control of the Kingdom of Siam, now Thailand. The country remained under French control until 1954, which it gained full independence.

Today, Luang Prabang exemplifies the fusion of Asian and European traditions of architecture, a legacy of the Colonial era. Its rich cultural heritage, natural surroundings and beautiful monasteries makes it the foremost city in Laos.

*A monarchy ruled Luang Prabang for hundreds of years, ending in the 1970s. The city retains its centuries-old flavor, however, and Buddhist temples still stand throughout the city.*

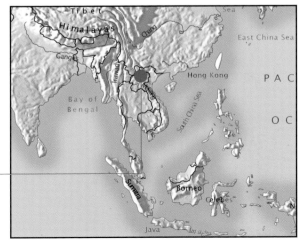

*Wat Mai Suwannaphumaham is one of a large number of temples in the ancient royal city of Luang Prabang. This temple is known for its gold-leafed wall and door carvings.*

## Laos

**Period:**

From the 7th century

**Significance:**

Luang Prabang exemplifies the fusion of Asian and European traditions of architecture, a legacy of the Colonial era.

# MACAO

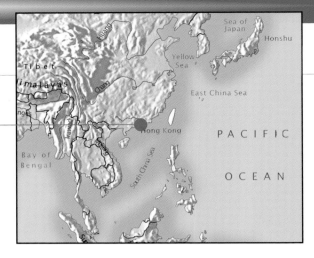

n the 16th century, Portuguese Colonial impact across the globe was broad and far-reaching. It was during this time that Macao became the first European settlement in China and the Far East. Portuguese explorers first entered the Pearl River Delta bordering the Guandong province in 1513 and established a trading post there in 1557. The trade port of Macao became the economic hub of the region and prospered under Portuguese control, reaching its peak between 1580 and 1640.

During the 19th century, Macao's importance waned and Hong Kong, 40 miles (64 km) east, became pre-eminent. Although China never relinquished sovereignty, the region has been under Portuguese administration since 1887.

Among the most celebrated historic buildings in Macao is St. Paul's Basilica, a Roman Catholic cathedral built in the Italian Renaissance style in 1635. A fire in 1835 destroyed most of the building and only the façade remains today, a fascinating hybrid of European architectural style and Chinese design.

## China

### Period:

Since the 16th century

### Significance:

Macao provides an example of the confluence of Eastern and Western cultures, architecture and technology.

Built in the late 1500s, all that now remains of the Cathedral of St. Paul in Macau is a stone façade. The remainder of the building succumbed to a fire in the 1800s.

*Much of the architecture of downtown Macau reflects its Portuguese heritage. The city remained a Portuguese colony until 1999, when it reverted to Chinese rule.*

## Philippines

**Period:**

Since the 16th century

**Significance:**

Vigan is an excellent example of a planned Spanish colonial town in Asia.

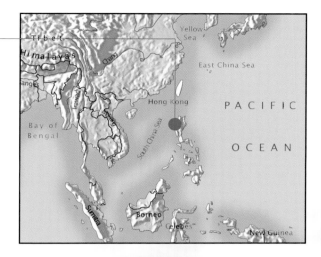

Founded by a young Spanish Conquistador, Juan de Salcedo, in the 16th century, Vigan is the oldest surviving Spanish colonial city in the Philippines. Located on the West Coast of the Island of Luzon approximately 248 miles (400 km) from Manila, it was originally conceived as a military base. The town's name derives from the native plants, biga'a, that Salcedo found growing there.

From its humble beginnings, the town grew and in 1758 became the seat of the Roman Catholic Church in the Philippines. Vigan's narrow streets and well-preserved urban character—a unique blend of Philippino traditional construction and European design—are reminders of its colonial beginnings. Modern Vigan's rich architectural heritage reflects the confluence of styles from the Philippines, China, and Europe.

*Historians believe the original inhabitants of Vigan were of Malay origin. Spanish conquistadors arrived in the late 1500s and Catholic missionaries followed. Some of the resulting churches remain.*

*Bell towers and other structures beckon travelers to Vigan today, but at one time it was the gold mines that drew visiting merchants from Japan and China.*

# SANTO DOMINGO

Santo Domingo de Guzman can be considered a city of firsts. Its cobblestone street, the Calle de las Damas in the old district—the Zona Colonial—is the oldest in the Americas, dating to 1502, and the city itself is the oldest colonial city in the New World. Christopher Columbus first arrived at Santo Domingo in 1492, but the city was officially founded by his brother, Bartholomew Columbus, six years later. It became the site of the first Catholic cathedral, hospital, customs house and university in the Americas. The austere and impressive stone fortress, Fortaleza Ozama, named for the Ozama River at the site, is the oldest in America.

Sea-faring explorers such as the Columbus brothers used the stars and the curvature of the earth for navigation; in honor of this, Bartholomew named the settlement after Saint Dominic, the patron saint of astronomy.

The dawn of the 16th century heralded bloody and difficult years for the native people of Santo Domingo. In 1502 Nicolás de Ovando, the newly appointed governor of Hispaniola, arrived with some 2,500 colonists from Spain. Large numbers of the population were subjugated and forced into slave labor in the gold mines. Rebellions and draconian counter-suppression ensued, decimating the native population from its pre-Columbian numbers of 200,000 to a mere 60,000.

*"First City of the Indies"*

—Coat of arms and emblem given to the city by King Ferdinand II of Aragon in 1508

Built in the early 1500s, the Fortress of Santo Domingo has a medieval style. The stone fortress, also known as Fortaleza Ozama, is among the New World's oldest military outposts.

The Museo de las Casas Reales stands on Calle de las Damas, the first European-built street in North America. Once a government palace, it is now an art gallery.

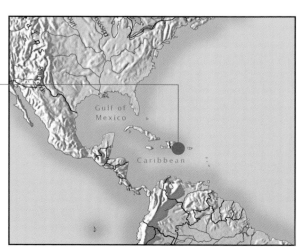

## Dominican Republic

**Period:**

From the late 15th to the early 16th century

**Significance:**

Santo Domingo was the first colonial city in the New World.

# CIUDAD DE MÉXICO

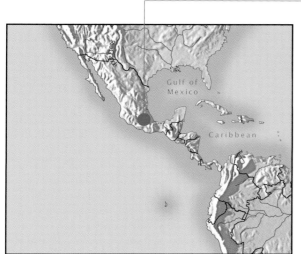

**Mexico**

**Period:**

Since the 16th century

**Significance:**

This modern metropolis stands on the ruins of the ancient Aztec capital of Tenochtitlan.

*Over the years, the Metropolitan Cathedral developed a serious tilt, but engineers have partially remedied it and now monitor the structure to ensure its safety.*

Mexico City stands on the site of the great Aztec city Tenochtitlan. In 1519, Tenochtitlan's population was more than 200,000. It was then that Hernán Cortés and the conquistadors arrived and attempted to conquer the city. The Aztecs managed to resist the overthrow. Thwarted, Cortés returned in 1521 with Spanish forces and their Indian allies. They besieged the city, which was forced to surrender within months, and Tenochtitlan was all but destroyed.

Five Aztec temples survive in Mexico City, today a modern metropolis and one of the largest cities in the world. It boasts the continent's largest Roman Catholic cathedral—a magnificent Spanish Baroque structure with two large Neo-classical towers. Just yards away from the cathedral are the ruins of an Aztec temple, and all over the city one can find splendid examples of 19th and 20th century architecture.

*The Metropolitan Cathedral, also known as the Mexico City Cathedral, includes gilded altars, domes and 14 chapels, and is filled with priceless statues and other artwork.*

# LA ANTIGUA GUATEMALA

## Guatemala

### Period:

From the mid-16th to the late 18th centuries

### Significance:

La Antigua Guatemala is preserved as a living historic site—rich with Spanish baroque architecture and monuments.

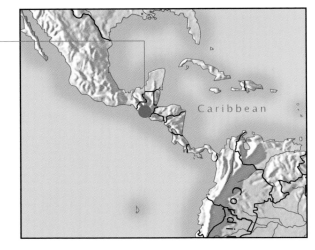

*Most Antiguans are Christian. For much of their history, most of these churches were branches of institutions based in England. The Antiguans have made their mark, particularly in church music, which often has gospel, calypso and reggae overtones.*

A highland city built 4,920 feet (1,500 m) above sea level and flanked by three majestic volcanoes, Antigua was established by Conquistadors in 1543, who gave it the name Santiago de los Caballeros. After a 1773 earthquake largely destroyed the city, the Spanish crown ordered the removal of the capital to a safer location, one that would be less vulnerable to the earthquakes that affect the region. The city was reestablished in a low-lying valley known as the Valley of the Shrine. The citizens of Antigua were ordered to move to the new location; however, some residents stayed behind and began to refer to the old city as La Antigua Guatemala—Old Guatemala.

Today, the old highland city is preserved as a living historic site, rich with Spanish baroque architecture, monuments and ruined churches. The small, wonderfully preserved town now provides a fascinating and unusual window into Guatemala's colonial past.

*The island nation of Antigua is a unique blend of European, West African and Amerindian cultural traditions, and also shows the influence of several nearby Caribbean island cultures.*

*This cannon is a reminder of the importance of the Spanish port settlement of Campeche on an inlet of the Gulf of Mexico. Today, Campeche is best known for its numerous Mayan ruins.*

## Mexico

**Period:**

Since the 16th century

**Significance:**

Campeche provides an excellent example of a Spanish colonial town in the New World.

*A lovely tourist attraction today, the 17th-century fortifications at Campeche once protected against the repeated incursions of opportunistic pirates.*

The Caribbean harbor town of Colonial Campeche dates to the mid-16th century, when it was founded by Spanish conquistadors. Prior to that, the area was occupied by Mayans since the 3rd century.

After colonization in 1541, Campeche became a trade hub and one of the most important ports in the country. The port was fortified early on to defend against marauding pirates, who were attracted by the city's immense wealth. However, the town's original fortifications proved a poor match against determined and frequent attacks. More extensive defenses were required to protect the port and in 1686, by order of the Spanish government, construction began on the fortifications preserved at the site today. The system of outer walls, laid out in a roughly hexagonal shape around the main port, together with its watchtowers, drawbridges and moat provide a superb example of European military architectural design of the 17th and 18th centuries.

# HAVANA

## Cuba

**Period:**

From the 16th century

**Significance:**

Today a city of 2 million, Havana was an important trade center between the Old and New Worlds in the 17th century.

Spanish conquistadors arrived in Cuba in 1510 and established the current location of La Cuidad de la Habana in 1519. Valued primarily for its advantageous location in a natural bay, the harbor city became one of the world's earliest great trade centers, and by the 17th century, Havana functioned as a vital conduit for the Old and New Worlds. The 17th century saw the rapid expansion of Havana's economy and it was during this period of prosperity that many of its grand buildings were constructed, including monuments, religious institutions and governmental buildings—most notably the El Moro Castle.

*In its colonial period, Havana was a busy port, military post and administrative center. It was during this period that many of its most attractive buildings were constructed.*

Invading British forces of more than 10,000 besieged Havana in 1762 and seized control of the city. New trade routes were quickly established under the new government as the British established new commercial links to other British colonies in North America and the Caribbean. British rule was short-lived however, and under the Treaty of Paris one year later Havana was returned to Spain. At this time Spain greatly reinforced its military defenses and today Havana remains the most heavily fortified city in the Americas.

Havana's trade relationship with North America, initiated under British rule, continued after Spain's return to power and into the next century. By the middle of the 18th century Havana had grown larger than either New York or Boston and had became a prosperous and highly fashionable city, known in its heyday as the "Paris of Antilles."

*"In Habana Vieja, we are preserving the values of the architecture of another century…"*

—Cuban President Fidel Castro

*The culture of Havana is a highly social one. Residents spend many hours mingling on the bustling and crowded streets with fellow Cubans.*

Vintage American automobiles are still common on Cuba's roads. A trade embargo outlawed the export of U.S. goods, including automobiles, to the country after Cuba's 1959 revolution.

# LIMA

Until the mid-18th century, Peru's capital city of Lima enjoyed importance as the foremost city on the South American continent. Known as La Ciudad de los Reyes—the City of Kings—Lima was founded in 1532 by the Spanish Conquistador Francisco Pizarro in an area of great natural beauty on the Peruvian plains. Under Colonial rule, Lima flourished as a trade center serving the Americas, Europe and the Far East. It grew into a sophisticated city, one that in later generations could boast the oldest officially established university and the first printing press.

Although Lima today is a modern city of steel and concrete, its downtown quarter has a high concentration of historic monuments and magnificent public buildings from the colonial era. Lima has also been called the city of balconies because of the distinctive architectural feature adopted by the Spanish from the Arabic style. There are estimated to be as many as 1,600 distinctive enclosed "box" balconies concentrated in the old city, to stunning effect.

The 17th and 18th centuries brought catastrophe to the prosperous city of Lima. Two earthquakes in the mid-1600s, just three years apart, caused considerable damage to the city. A subsequent earthquake, which struck in 1746, crushed Lima's Port Callao and nearly destroyed the city.

*San Francisco de Asís (St. Francis of Assisi) Church in Lima dates to the period following the arrival of the Spanish conquistadors in Peru. The Spanish structures were not the first here, however; the indigenous Inca population had long previously erected entire urban centers.*

*"Peru is from this moment free and independent by the wish of the people and the justness of the cause which God defends."*

—José de San Martín, Protector del Peru, proclaiming the country's independence

## Peru

**Period:**

Since the 16th century

**Significance:**

Lima was the capital city of the Spanish empire in South America.

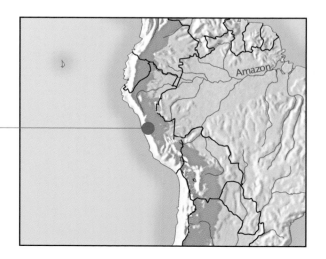

# CARTAGENA

Caribbean

## Colombia

**Period:**

Since the 16th century

**Significance:**

Cartagena's colonial defensive system is the most extensive in South America.

*Stone walls and cannons protected Cartagena during the 17th and 18th centuries, when pirates cruised the Caribbean waters attacking ships carrying goods between this port city and Spain.*

*A typical street in the Caribbean port city of Cartagena is lined with cheerfully painted colonial-style buildings standing two or more stories tall. Some tourists visit the city simply to view these unusually vibrant original buildings, with their distinctive "New World" atmosphere.*

The wealthiest cities of the colonial era in South America were fortified against raids from pirates and other invaders. Cartagena's position as one of the chief ports for the Spanish treasure fleet made its defense system the most extensive in South America.

The city's founder, Don Pedro de Heredia, chose the site in 1533 because of its large deep-water bay and potential as a trading port. Within a few years, construction of fortifications was underway; eminent European military engineers were enlisted to design the fortifications, and they created an impressive complex of battlements, watchtowers and underground tunnels. In the end, massive walls encircled the city for a distance of 7 miles (11 km). Work on the defenses continued over a period of 108 years.

Cartagena's battlements faced a serious test from invading British forces during the Battle of Cartagena de Indias in 1741. Greatly outnumbered in both troops and weapons, the Spanish and native Cartagena troops fought off the British attack for three months, and against all odds won victory for Spain.

The fortifications, including the Castle of San Felipe de Barajas and the walls enclosing the Old City are still intact today, providing an austere contrast to the picturesque downtown quarter of Cartagena the historic center of the city.

# SALVADOR DE BAHIA

Portuguese settlers sailed into the natural harbor of All Saints Bay in 1749 and established the first capital city of Brazil. Colonial Salvador de Bahia became a city of great wealth, as evidenced by the large number of landmark buildings preserved there today. The city's golden age, which lasted from the beginning of the 16th century to the middle of the 19th, is reflected in its many outstanding Renaissance buildings and colorful stuccoed houses.

Salvador was the New World's first slave market, operating as early as 1558 and dealing in slaves from Africa destined for work on the sugar plantations. The large majority of Salvador's population is of African origin, and its cultural heritage a fusion of Afro/Brazilian traditions. Today Salvador city is a popular tourist destination, an immensely appealing combination of natural beauty, historical interest and a famously joyful atmosphere.

## Brazil

**Period:**

From the mid-16th century

**Significance:**

Salvador de Bahia was the first capital of Brazil and the locale of the first New World slave market.

*With its cobblestone streets, Pelourinho is the historic center of Salvador de Bahia. Today, "Pelo," as the natives often call it, is also a popular hub for dining, cultural pursuits and nightlife.*

*Many of the colonial Portuguese buildings in Salvador have arched windows that are set off against light blues, creamy yellows, pinks and other pastel colors.*

# VALPARAISO

*Valparaiso is home to a number of historical monuments and statues. This statue of a sailor is particularly appropriate for the city, which is the major harbor for the country of Chile.*

Once a small 16th-century Colonial village in Central Chile, Valparaiso grew in the 19th century into an important seaport. The city was colonized in 1536 by Diego de Almagro, who sailed there from Peru in a ship captained by Juan de Saavedra. (The captain chose the name Valparaiso, after his hometown of Valparaíso de Arriba in Spain.)

The natural horseshoe-shaped bay in the Pacific Ocean was an ideal stopover point for ships traveling between the Atlantic and Pacific oceans. Valparaiso was at the height of its importance in the second half of the 19th century, after the independence of Chile from Spanish colonial rule. The flood of immigrants from all over Europe at this time made a significant impact on the evolution of Valparaiso's cultural heritage, and this is reflected in its institutions, traditions, and most visibly in its historic architecture.

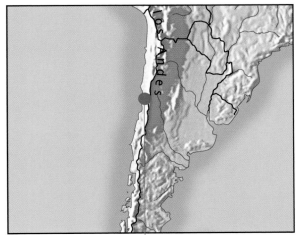

## Chile

**Period:**

19th century

**Significance:**

Valparaiso offers an excellent insight into the development of globalization in the late 19th century.

*With about 800,000 residents, Valparaiso is one Chile's largest cities. Its popular historic harbor is still important for shipping industries.*

# WILLEMSTAD

*The port town of Willemstad has a decidedly tropical feel with its peach, aqua and pink buildings set off against their vivid orange roofs.*

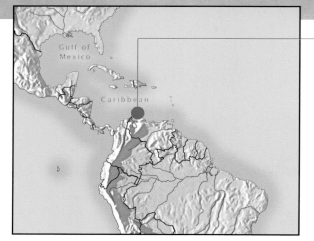

## Netherlands Antilles

**Period:**
Since the 17th century

**Significance:**
Willemstad offers an excellent example of European colonial influence in the Caribbean.

**W**illemstad, a harbor town on the Island of Curaçao, was settled as a trading post by the Dutch in 1634. The island's capital, the city grew steadily over the next two centuries, supported in part by the slave trade.

The town is divided in halves connected by a bridge over the St. Anna Bay. The buildings in the beautiful historic section—on the Punda side of the bridge— vividly reflect the city's multicultural origins.

*The Dutch took possession of the so-called "ABC islands"—Aruba, Bonaire and Curaçao—in the 1600s. The architecture of many of Curaçao's brightly colored buildings, including those in Willemstad, reflects the island's old Dutch heritage.*

San Juan, founded in 1521 by the Spanish Conquistador Juan Ponce de León, is the capital of Puerto Rico. The city's great El Castillo San Felipe del Morro fortress was built to defend the colonial city from the scourge of pirates and attack by invading nations. Named after King Philip II of Spain, the fortress was begun in 1540, after the port city had already grown to prominence. With its 18-feet-deep (5.5-m) walls, maze of underground tunnels and dungeons, watchtowers and barracks, the stronghold withstood repeated attack in the 16th, 17th and 18th centuries. These attacks were led mainly by the rival colonial powers of Britain and Holland.

American forces conquered San Juan during the Spanish-American War in 1898; the treaty of Paris was drawn up the same year and control of Puerto Rico (along with Guam and the Philippines) was transferred from Spain to the United States.

*The Spanish spent considerable effort defending the island of Puerto Rico from invasion by other Europeans who saw it as a strategic shipping location. One of their defensive strategies was to wall off the city of San Juan, and to set up armaments along on the coast.*

*The Castillo de San Felipe del Morro (lower left) is the well-known historic fortress that once protected San Juan against enemies from the sea. Today, the castle is a popular tourist destination.*

## United States

**Period:**

Since the 16th century

**Significance:**

San Juan is the oldest city of Colonial origin in the United States and the second oldest city in the Americas.

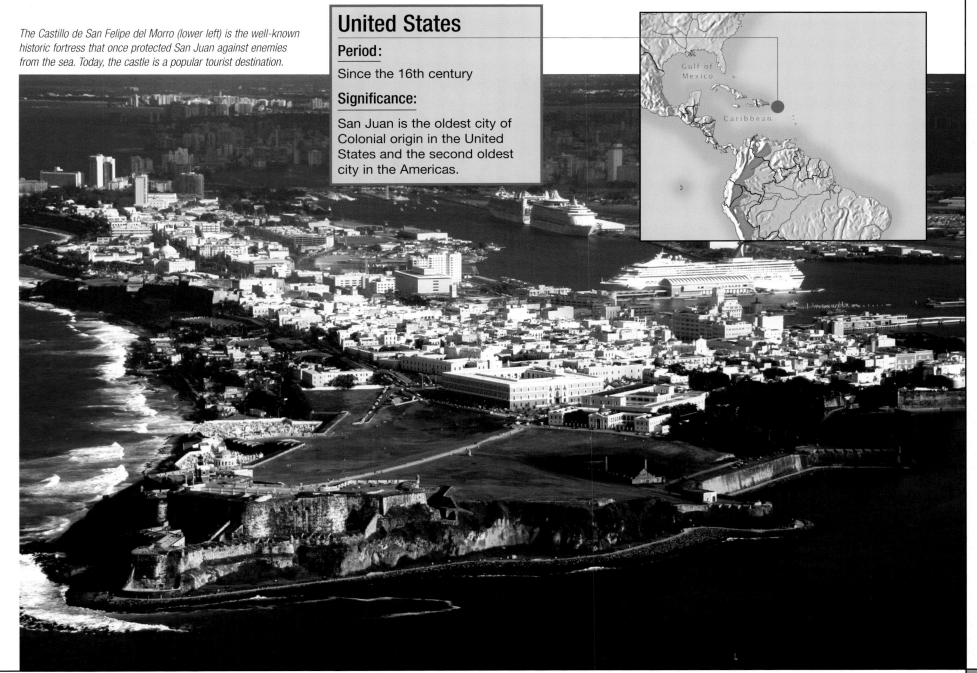

# INDEPENDENCE HALL

Independence Hall is an historic building of enormous political significance to the United States. Two documents fundamental to the founding of constitutional democracy in the United States were signed here—the Declaration of Independence in 1776 and the Constitution of the United States in 1787—the former justifying, and the latter organizing, free government by the people.

Flanked on either side by the Old City Hall and the Congress Hall, Independence Hall was originally Pennsylvania's State House. It was designed and built in the Georgian style by the architect Edmund Woolley in collaboration with the amateur architect and Philadelphia lawyer Andrew Hamilton between 1732 and 1753.

The U.S. Constitution begins with a noble statement of purposes, commonly known as the Preamble: "We the People of the United States, in order to form a more perfect union, establish justice, insure domestic tranquility, provide for the common defense, promote the general welfare, and secure the blessings of liberty to ourselves and our posterity, do ordain and establish this Constitution for the United States of America."

*"Proclaim liberty throughout all the land unto all the inhabitants thereof—Lev. XXV, x. By order of the Assembly of the Province of Pennsylvania for the State House in Philada [Philadelphia]"*

—Inscription on the Liberty Bell

The red-brick Independence Hall, where the U.S. Constitution and the Declaration of Independence were signed, is near other historic sites, including the Liberty Bell, Carpenters' Hall, and George Washington's home during his tenure as the first U.S. president (1789-1797).

The Liberty Bell is mainly composed of copper and tin. The original bell, which was made in 1752, weighed more than a ton.

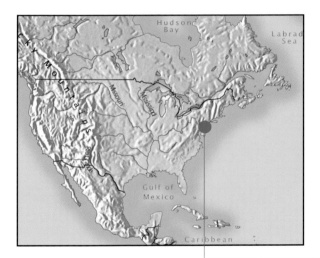

The Assembly Room in Independence Hall, where representatives of the thirteen North American colonies of Great Britain met to declare independence and, later, in the brutally hot summer of 1787, to debate the principles and structure of a new form of government.

## United States

**Period:**

1732–1787

**Significance:**

Two of the most important documents in American History were signed at Independence Hall.

The spire atop Independence Hall, in the heart of Philadelphia's historic district, was added during a renovation in 1828.

The most noticeable signature on the Declaration of Independence is that of John Hancock. He was the first to sign the document.

# PART III - THE MODERN WORLD

The past 200 years of world history have been marked by great and rapid change. The industrial revolution, abolition of the slave trade, the immigration boom to the United States, two world wars, and revolutions all have had a lasting impact on the way we live. World Heritage sites around the world testify to these changes and achievements. The darker times in history are also commemorated in sites across the globe, serving as reminders of the struggle for liberty, freedom, and justice throughout time.

*The iconic Golden Gate Bridge, spanning the opening of San Francisco Harbor, was the world's longest suspension bridge when completed in 1937, a distinction it would hold for nearly three decades.*

# STATUE OF LIBERTY

Icon of freedom and democracy, the Statue of Liberty stands on a small 12-acre (5-ha) fortification in the busy waters of New York Harbor. Liberty Island, as it is known, is adjacent to Ellis Island, the clearinghouse and gateway for millions of immigrants entering the United States from 1892 to 1954. For many immigrants seeking better lives, the Statue of Liberty symbolized the freedom America promised, although a small percentage were denied entry because of disease or criminal records.

The Statue of Liberty was a gift to the United States from France, in recognition of the friendship formed between the two countries during the Revolutionary War, and it commemorated the 100th anniversary of the signing of the Declaration of Independence. It was designed by the French sculptor Frederic Auguste Bartholdi, who collaborated on the project with architect Gustave Eiffel, who—as the builder of the Eiffel Tower—had expertise in the construction of large-scale monuments. In order to transport, the copper statue was taken apart and shipped to New York in 350 separate parts packed into 214 crates.

When placed on the massive pedestal that was designed and constructed in the United States, the statue reached a height of 305 feet (93 m).

The imposing robed figure of the Statue of Liberty is based on the Roman goddess Libertas. The flaming torch in her right hand signifies enlightenment; she crushes shackles underfoot. The stone tablet held in her left hand bears the date of the signing of the Declaration of Independence, and her spiked crown represents the seven seas and the seven continents.

*The complete statue was disassembled into 350 separate pieces for shipping by sea to New York Harbor, where it arrived in June of 1885. There, the statue was reassembled over the next several months and dedicated on Oct. 28, 1886. Since then it has become iconic not just for New York City, but for the United States of America as well.*

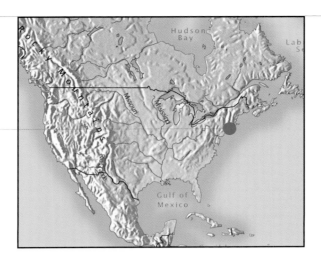

## United States

**Period:**

1886

**Significance:**

The Statue of Liberty represents the famous promises of America, freedom and democracy.

*"Not like the brazen giant of Greek fame,
With conquering limbs astride from land to land;
Here at our sea-washed, sunset gates shall stand
A mighty woman with a torch, whose flame
Is the imprisoned lightning, and her name
Mother of Exiles"*

—Excerpt of Emma Lazarus' poem "The New Colossus," written for the statue in 1883

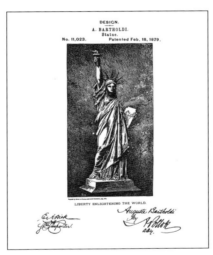

*For the site of the Statue of Liberty (the 1879 design patent is shown here), sculptor Frederic Auguste Bartholdi chose the country's main entry point at the time: New York Harbor.*

*From the base of the pedestal to the top of the torch, the Statue of Liberty stands more than 305 feet (about 93 meters) tall.*

*Mainly active between 1892 and 1924, Ellis Island welcomed some 17 million immigrants to America, most of them from Europe and Russia. For many, the sea voyage was rough and long, and the Statue of Liberty a glorious sight after so many months.*

# D. F. WOUDA STEAM PUMPING STATION

## Netherlands

**Period:**

From 1920

**Significance:**

This steam-powered pumping station is the largest ever built; it is still in operation.

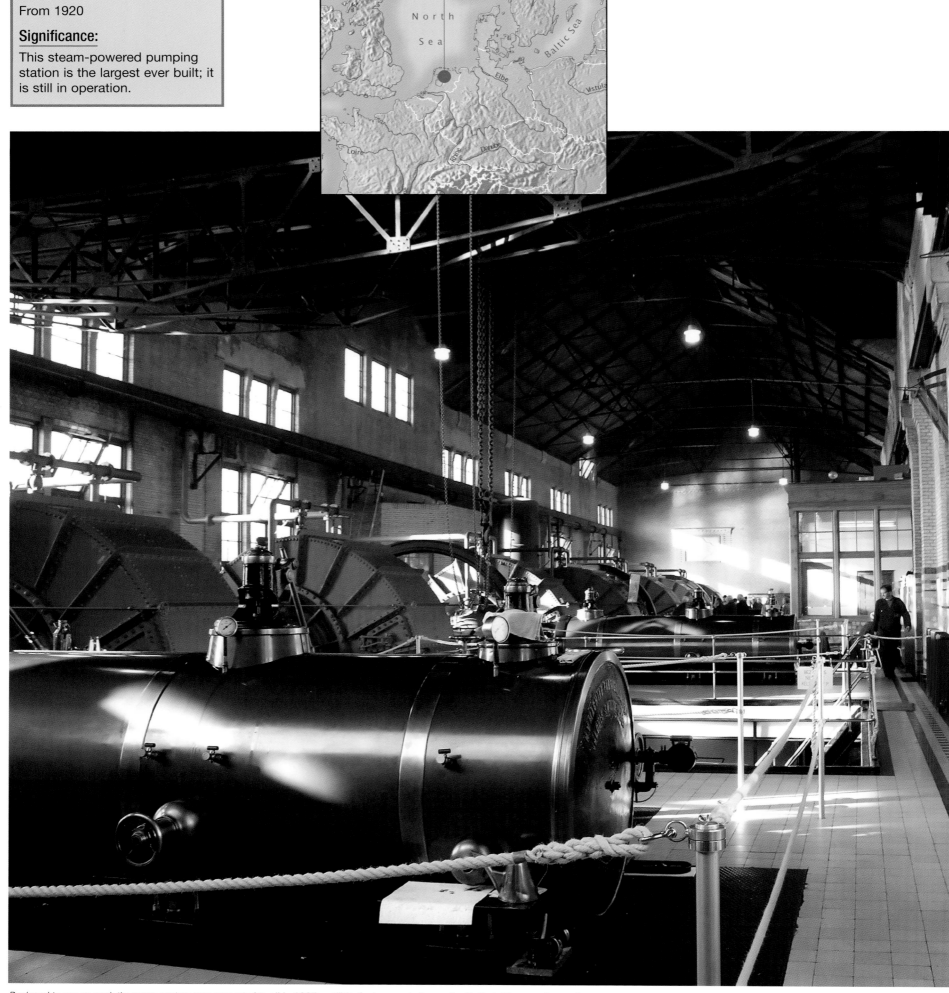

*Designed to run on coal, the pump system was converted to oil in 1967—still its fuel source today—after its first 47 years of operation.*

*Maintained in pristine working order, the pumps are dormant in summer months and activated for a few weeks in winter.*

The steam-powered pumping station in the town of Lemmer in the Northern Netherlands is the largest ever built and a masterpiece of engineering. The massive complex is named after its designer and chief engineer Dirk Frederik Wouda, whose brilliant design provided an efficient way to control the problem of the region's high water levels in its low-lying provinces.

The station went into operation in 1920 and is still running today. The massive pump engines are capable of moving vast quantities of water, pumping and discharging 1,056,688 gallons (4,000,000 l) every minute. A more modern electric pumping station was built in 1967, which is responsible for much of the drainage in Friesland today. The D.F. Wouda Steam Pumping Station is now an excellently maintained and pristine site, kept in a constant state of readiness for operation whenever it is needed.

*Unlike modern electrical systems that work with the flip of a switch, the steam pumps require six hours to warm up.*

# IRONBRIDGE

*Ironbridge is unusual not just for being the first of its kind; also, its individual pieces were fitted together without using bolts or welds.*

## United Kingdom

**Period:**

From 1779

**Significance:**

Ironbridge is home to the world's first iron bridge, which was constructed using woodworking techniques.

**B**irthplace of the Industrial Revolution, this is where Abraham Darby perfected the technique of smelting iron with coke. It revolutionized the industry because it made the production of iron much cheaper. In 1779, his grandson Abraham Darby III built the famous iron bridge—the first of its kind in the world and a monument to the Industrial Revolution—over the River Severn. It took 379 tons of iron to build it. The bridge had a considerable influence on developments in technology and architecture. The Iron Bridge became an 18th-century tourist attraction. As a result, a new town grew up around it. It became simply known as Ironbridge.

*"After the Bridge survived the great floods of 1795, cast iron was used widely and imaginatively in construction of bridges, buildings and aqueducts."*

—Ironbridge Gorge Museums

*The 100.5-foot (31m) spans the River Severn, near Coalbrookdale, England. Today, the bridge is a British national monument.*

# LIVERPOOL

A monument to iron, brick, and stone, the great Albert Dock in Liverpool's historic docklands was the height of modern industrial design in the 19th century. The Maritime Mercantile City of Liverpool was a major trade center and vital arm of the British Empire during the Industrial Revolution. Liverpool's prosperity was due in large part to the slave trade and the booming textile industry. By the early 19th century Liverpool had replaced the capital city of London as the foremost importer of cotton. The city

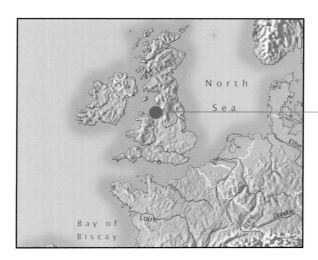

### United Kingdom

**Period:**

19th century

**Significance:**

The maritime city of Liverpool pioneered modern industrial technologies.

*A trio of landmark buildings dubbed "the three graces" rise from the Pier Head of Liverpool's waterfront.*

pioneered new and innovative technology and when the landmark Albert Dock opened in 1846, its buildings, which were constructed entirely without wood, constituted the world's first fireproof warehouse system. Similarly, Liverpool's mammoth Stanley Dock Tobacco Warehouse was the largest brick warehouse of its time in the world, built 14 stories high with 27 million bricks, 8,000 tons (8,128 t) of steel and 30,000 panes of glass. Liverpool was officially designated a city in 1800, by which time it was the second most prosperous city in England after London, with a bustling population of 611,000.

*Cast iron is a prominent feature of the docks, from the massive architectural facades of its warehouses to their ubiquitous moorings.*

# NEW LANARK

## United Kingdom

**Period:**

From 1784

**Significance:**

New Lanark is the site of a model industrial community created by noted philanthropist and social reformer Robert Owen.

*Tidy sandstone buildings included dye works, mills and a school for workers' children, sited attractively along the River Clyde.*

Scotland's powerful River Clyde is fed by waterfalls. That is why Scottish mill owner David Dale established a large cotton mill there in 1784. Dale included in the mill's construction purpose-built houses for its workers. His son-in-law Robert Owen took over management of the mill in 1800 and ran it for 25 years.

A forward-thinking social reformer, Owens continued Dale's philosophy of industrial philanthropy that defied contemporary industrial values. He was particularly sensitive to the living conditions of children,

and under his management child labor and corporal punishment were banned, and working families were provided with a clean healthy environment, free education and health care. Owens is also credited with opening the first preschool in Britain, in 1816. Despite the company's success, Owens' business partners chafed at the extra costs incurred by his philanthropy and so Owen bought them out.

New Lanark still operates today, producing organic woolen yarns and merchandise, with proceeds going to maintain the historic town.

*Bridged walkways connect buildings over a canal in Robert Owen's utopian village, unusual in both design and intent.*

# SALTAIRE

The Victorian industrial village of Saltaire in the north of England is preserved in its entirety at this World Heritage Site. Its founder, Sir Titus Salt, was a visionary industrialist with a philanthropic mission to improve the day-to-day conditions of the common worker. His textile mills and workers' accommodations were purpose-built to high architectural and aesthetic standards, and were intended to harmonize with the rural surroundings—in marked contrast to the notorious "dark satanic mills" of the heavily industrialized midlands. Such considerations were unusual in the context of the Industrial Revolutionary period, which championed rapid growth and technological development above all else.

## United Kingdom

**Period:**

1784 to 1825

**Significance:**

Saltaire is a classic example of a well-preserved 19th-century industrial village.

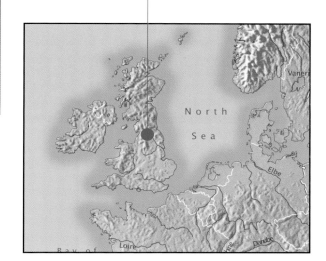

*An attractive towpath, once employed to move barges along the canal, is now a popular tree-lined promenade.*

*"…that would enjoy the beauties of the neighborhood, and who would be a well fed, contented, and happy body of operatives … nothing should be spared to render the dwellings of the operatives a pattern to the country."*

—Sir Titus Salt (1803–1876), about building a model village

*The mills, which operated until 1986, today house shops, restaurants, residences and a gallery devoted to the work of artist David Hockney.*

# CANAL DU CENTRE

The Industrial Revolution in Europe was largely defined by ambitious innovations in engineering, and the 18th and 19th century was a period of rapid technological advancement. In 1888, the first of four boatlifts was placed on Belgium's Canal du Centre to solve the problem of significantly varying water levels over a stretch of the canal. Modeled on an English prototype, the hydraulic elevators were designed to raise or lower boats up to 55 ft (17 m) depending on the water level at each lock. Three more boatlifts were installed in 1917. Today the lifts are no longer used by commercial traffic, which is diverted through the gigantic modern boatlift at Strépy-Thieu.

A roadway at boatlift number four in Thieu, which is located near the modern lift, and a massive reminder of an older era.

The canal's elevators operate by counterbalancing weights: the vessel is raised or lowered by the movement of mobile caissons.

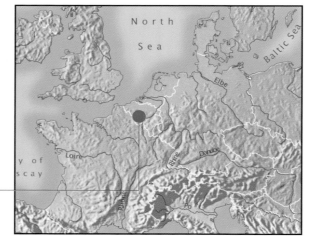

## Belgium

### Period:

From the late 19th to the early 20th centuries

### Significance:

The boatlifts of Canal du Centre are outstanding examples of 19th-century advances in hydraulic engineering.

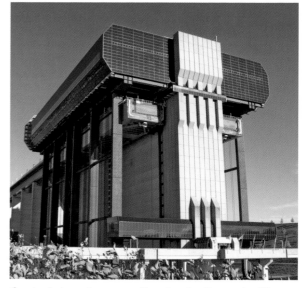

Constructed over the course of two decades, the new boatlift utilizes counterweighted caissons, just like its older counterparts.

# CANAL RIDEAU

The extensive Canal Rideau system in Canada's Thousand Island region was built for military purposes in the early 19th century, born of the archipelago's vulnerability to attack from the bordering United States. The war between British Colonial Canada and the United States of America in 1812 was the catalyst for a decisive solution to the problem.

Canal Rideau opened in 1832, providing a safe route between Kingston, Ontario, and the nation's capital Ottawa, and creating a continuous stretch of navigable waterways over a distance of 125 miles (202 km). Connecting natural rivers and lakes, the system also added 12 miles (19 km) of manmade waterways.

There are a total of 47 unique, mostly hand-operated, locks and 24 stations along the historic waterway—the oldest continuously operated canal in North America.

In the winter months the canal freezes solid, and a 5-mile (8-km) section in Ottawa is transformed into the world's longest skating rink.

## Canada

**Period:**

From 1832

**Significance:**

The Rideau Canal is the only example of an early 19th-century slackwater canal that is still in operation.

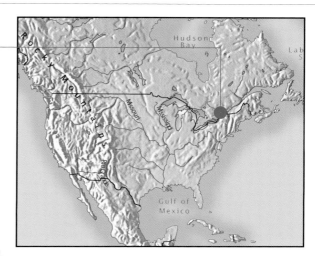

*Each winter, some one million visitors use the world's largest ice rink.*

*The canal is part of the Rideau Heritage Route, site of regular events commemorating the region's rich and varied history.*

# ESSEN

**Period:**

From 1847 to 1986

**Significance:**

The Zollverein mining complex is considered the preeminent example of German industrial architectural design of the 19th and 20th centuries.

*Designed by architects Fritz Schupp and Martin Kremmer, the winding tower of Shaft 12 became emblematic of Essen.*

In continuous operation from 1847 to 1986, the coal mine at Essen was once the largest and most advanced in the world, both technically and architecturally. Architects Fritz Schupp and Martin Kremmer built the Zollverein mine complex between 1928 and 1932. Pit number 12 is especially notable. Built in the Bauhaus style, it has earned Zollverein the title of "most beautiful coal mine in the world."

Work ceased at the mine in 1986 when coal supplies were finally exhausted; Zollverein was the last mine in Essen to close. Today the Zollverein mining complex is considered the preeminent example of German industrial architectural and engineering design of the 19th and 20th centuries.

*"Zollverein has kept its distinctive character with its famous 'Dopplebock' double rack, even if the facilities inside have fallen silent."*

—Museum Zeche Zollverein

*A compressor and leaded glass are installed side-by-side in an Essen machinery building.*

*Industry and avant-garde design combined in Essen with utilitarian architecture showing modernist elements.*

# VÖLKLINGEN IRONWORKS

Massive machinery and vast workstations constitute the core of the ironworks facility, now operated as a museum.

At its height of production in postwar Germany, the Völklingen Ironworks employed more than 17,000 workers. Julius Buch established the vast ironworks in 1873 on a 15-acre (6-ha) area in the city of Völklingen, Saarland. Carl Röchling succeeded him in 1881 and under his management the iron and steel works grew to dominate the industry across the whole of Europe. The central point of the plant is the group of 148-feet (45-m) high blast furnaces surrounded by 104 coke ovens, and machinery of gargantuan scale.

The ironworks ceased operation in 1986 and the huge industrial complex at Völklingen is a hugely important historical site and research center, the only intact surviving example of an 19th century ironworks in Europe and North America.

## Germany

**Period:**

From 1873 to 1986

**Significance:**

Völklingen is the only surviving example in Europe and North America of an intact 19th-century ironworks .

Pipes, machinery and walkways, silent after more than 100 years of use, extend over the ironworks' 15 acres (6 ha).

Enormous pipes, once central to the production of steel, now shape the contours of an industrial landscape.

# DARJEELING HIMALAYAN RAILWAY

## India

**Period:**

From 1881

**Significance:**

The Darjeeling Himalayan Railway is one of the boldest engineering achievements in the world.

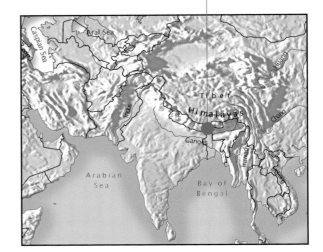

*Passengers take in views of the Himalayas from narrow cars.*

*Of the thirty-four steam engines built for the railway between 1889 and 1925, twenty-four are still in use.*

Nicknamed the "Toy Train," the Darjeeling Himalayan Railway carries passengers along precipitous slopes and hairpin loops of a 53-mile (86-km) stretch of mountain terrain in the Himalayas. The railway was first operational in 1881. The railway is powered by steam along extremely narrow-gauge tracks only 2 feet (610-mm) wide—half the standard gauge—which earned the railway its appealing nickname.

The Darjeeling Himalayan Railway is the first of its kind, and it is still fully operational today. Establishing an effective rail link across such difficult terrain—it rises from 302 feet (100 m) at Siliguri at the base to 7,220 feet (2,200 m) at Darjeeling at the top on the slopes of the Himalayas—it represents one of the boldest engineering achievements in the world.

*"The most enjoyable day I've spent on earth is a mixed ecstasy of deadly fright and unimaginable joy."*

—Mark Twain, after his ride on the "Toy Train," 1895

*A steam-powered engine stops to take water in Darjeeling.*

PART III - THE MODERN WORLD

# VARBERG RADIO STATION

## Sweden

**Period:**

1922 to 1924

**Significance:**

Varberg contains the original Alexanderson machine transmitter, and is the only surviving example of pre-electronic transmitting technology in the world.

The need for long-distance telecommunication after World War I initiated the creation of the Varberg Radio Station in Grimeton, Sweden. The station was built between 1922 and 1924 and enabled secure and reliable transatlantic wireless communication between Europe and the United States. More transmitting towers were erected later, opening international communication.

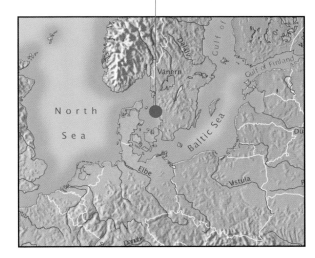

The well-preserved facility at Varberg contains the original Alexanderson machine transmitter, and is the only surviving example of pre-electronic transmitting technology in the world.

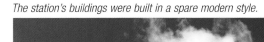

*The station's buildings were built in a spare modern style.*

*When constructed, the station's six radio towers were the tallest structures in Sweden.*

# MOSTAR

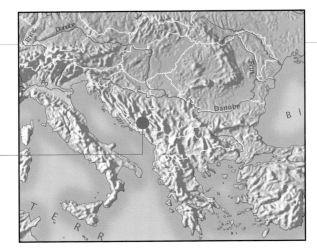

## SUCCESS STORY

### Bosnia and Herzegovina

**The Challenge:**

Mostar's historic bridge was destroyed in the Bosnian War.

**The Solution:**

The bridge was rebuilt; control of the city is now shared.

S pread across both banks of the Neretva River, the beautiful ancient city of Mostar in Bosnia-Herzegovina (part of the former Yugoslavia) was for three centuries the foremost town of the Ottoman Empire, until it became part of Yugoslavia after World War I. Mostar's ethnic groups coexisted throughout its long history until a disastrous and bloody civil war erupted in 1992.

The city was long famed for its Old Bridge, the Stari Most, designed in the 16th century by the great Ottoman architect Mimar Hayruddin and completed in 1566. The bridge—which spanned the Neretva River in a single, graceful arc—was the town's defining feature and symbol of identity for its inhabitants. It became a strategic target in the Bosnian War that ravaged the country from 1992 to 1995. In 1993 it was obliterated by Croatian forces.

*Opened under tight security in 2004, the reconstructed Old Bridge was funded by a coalition of nations, including those who had sent peacekeepers during the conflict.*

*Bombardments during the 1992–1996 war destroyed much of Mostar, including many significant historic and cultural sites.*

The destruction of their beloved historic bridge was a devastating blow to the people of Mostar, and in the postwar reconstruction of the devastated city, they insisted on exactly replicating the Old Bridge. Original stone was salvaged from the river wherever possible and incorporated into the rebuilding. The bridge reopened in 2004, and is a symbol of peace and ethnic unity for the people of Mostar. Today control of Mostar is shared between its two main ethic groups, with the Croats administering the west bank and the Bosnians the east.

*"Many people were killed during the war, but it was when the bridge was destroyed that Mostarians spontaneously declared a day of mourning."*

—Emir Balic, Muslim resident of Mostar

*The formerly neglected historic district around the Old Bridge is now protected as a World Heritage Site.*

# ISLAND OF GORÉE

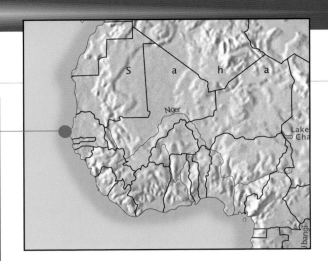

Gorée's reputation as the largest slave-trading center on the African coast makes it an enduring symbol of oppression. The tiny island off the Senegal Coast was largely uninhabitable because of the scarcity of drinking water and was not settled before the arrival of Europeans in the 15th century. The Portuguese arrived first in 1444, and from then until the 19th century Gorée was ruled by a succession of colonial powers. The busy slave industry on the island was French owned and operated from 1677 onward (until Gorée's achieved independence in the 20th century).

The French government under Napoléon Bonaparte abolished the slave trade in France in 1815, but it was not until the middle of the century that trading on the colony fully ceased.

*A mid 18th-century map of the island includes buildings, fortifications and gardens that remain today.*

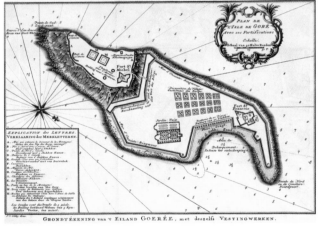

## Senegal

### Period:

From the 15th through the mid-19th century

### Significance:

Gorée's reputation as the largest slave-trading center on the African Coast makes it an enduring symbol of oppression.

The stark contrast between the historic buildings on Gorée today—grand colonial residences and squalid slave buildings— exemplifies the profound inequality intrinsic to the island's history. The most famous building is the House of Slaves, erected on the island sometime between 1780 and 1784. Today it is a museum that has preserved the cells, weighing room, traders' quarters and grisly artifacts used in the slave trade.

*"My hope is that this site contributes to making more people visit our museum and that the pilgrimage to the Island of Gorée provides an impetus to an enhanced brotherhood able to exorcise the demons of the past."*

—Abdoulaye Wade, president of the Republic of Senegal, 2005

*Under French colonial rule, a circular fort was built on a point at the island's harbor.*

*Chains are broken and raised in a recently installed statue commemorating the liberation of African slaves.*

# S A N S   S O U C I

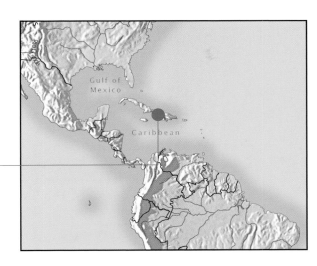

## Haiti

**Period:**

Early 19th century

**Significance:**

Enduring symbols of freedom, the citadel and palace remains of Sans Souci were constructed by free black slaves.

Haiti declared independence from French colonial rule in 1804, after the slave uprising and Haitian Revolution in 1803. As a precaution against future attack from France, Henri Christophe, at that time a general in the Haitian army, ordered the construction of a fortress on the northern part of the island. The citadel covers 108,000 square feet (10,033 sq m) at the top of Bonnet a L'Eveque Mountain, 3,000 feet (915 m) above sea level. It was built with the forced labor of up to 20,000 former Haitian slaves. The gargantuan and heavily stockpiled fortress survived earthquakes intact, but it was never tested by military action, because a counter-attack by the French never came.

Sans Souci Palace, which is located approximately 3 miles (5 k) from the citadel, was the official residence of Henri Christophe, who had declared himself King in 1811. The palace, whose name translates as "without a care" is in ruins today, destroyed by an earthquake in 1842. Henri Christophe committed suicide in the palace after he suffered a stroke; his body was entombed there.

Built atop Bonnet a L'Eveque mountain, the imposing Citadelle Laferrière looks out over the island to the Caribbean Sea. The massive structure was constructed to keep Haiti safe from French incursions; it is the largest fortress in the western hemisphere.

In the event of attack, Haitians were directed to retreat to the citadel. Storage areas were built to stow food and water to supply 5,000 people for up to one year.

# AAPRAVASI GHAT

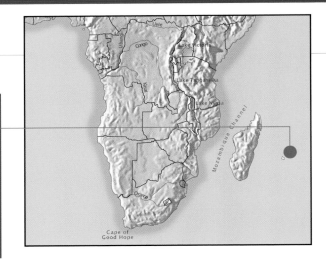

**Mauritius**

**Period:**

1834 to 1920

**Significance:**

It was here at Aapravasi Ghat that the concept of indentured servitude was first put into practice.

During the early 1800s, the island of Mauritius was the site of "the Great Experiment" initiated by the British government after abolition of slavery in 1807. From 1834 onward over a period of 86 years, Britain shipped almost half a million indentured laborers from India to Mauritius to work on the sugar plantations. The plan was to replace the preexisting slave labor force with a "free" labor system of indentured workers. These workers were contracted to work in exchange for food, land and accommodation alone.

The Great Experiment was responsible for the migration of enormous numbers of people. Many workers arriving in Mauritius would then be sent on farther, to Australia, Africa and the Caribbean. The Aapravasi Ghat site, preserved today in Port Louis, is an extensive complex that was built as a processing facility for incoming workers. Many of these migrant workers put down roots, where they worked and stayed for life. Today descendants of Indian indentured workers make up more than half the population of Mauritius.

*"Indentured labor made the immigrant forget his home and his people. He came to Mauritius to settle for life and often reindentured. He passed a life of great difficulty and he worked hard…"*

—Kunwar Maharaj, Officer of the United Province Civil Service in India, Observing immigration in Mauritania for the British Government of India, 1925

*Indentured servants were registered with names, photographs and assigned numbers. Number 4983 came from Bombay.*

*Indentured servants arrived in Mauritius to work the sugar cane fields of its plantations.*

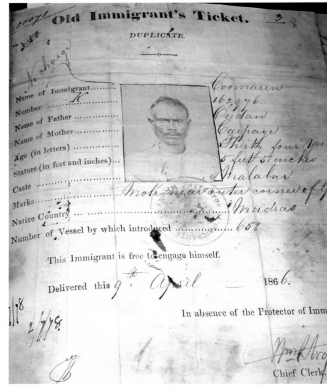

*This immigration ticket, dated April 9, 1886, is for a 34-year-old man who was contracted from Madras.*

## South Africa

**Period:**

From the 17th through the 20th centuries

**Significance:**

Robben Island—once a maximum security prison for political prisoners—is now a reminder of the death of apartheid.

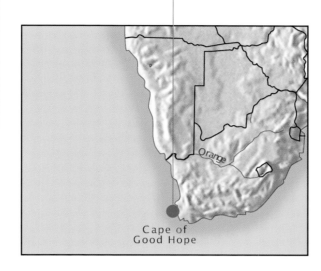

ust a few miles off the Coast of Cape Town, tiny, barren Robben Island served as a prison and a place of exile from the 17th century onward. It was a military training base during World War II and the repository for all kinds of undesirable elements banished from the mainland. Its notoriety, however, is derived from its role as a maximum-security prison for South Africa's political prisoners —and for its most famous inmate, Nelson Mandela. The anti-apartheid activist, leader of the African National Congress and eventual president of South Africa, spent 18 of his 27 years imprisoned by the South African government at Robben Island. Mandela was released in 1990, and fellow political prisoners followed a year later. The prison on Robben Island closed in 1996 and is now a museum.

*"There is no easy walk to freedom anywhere, and many of us will have to pass through the valley of the shadow of death again and again before we reach the mountaintop of our desires."*

—Nelson Mandela, first democratically elected president of South Africa

*Nelson Mandela's cell contained a mat and a small container in lieu of a toilet. At night, Mandela recalled, warders patrolled "to make sure we were not reading or writing."*

*Despite its proximity to the mainland, Robben Island is isolated by the Atlantic's vigorous surf. The island's sparse vegetation is due in part to its lack of fresh water.*

# SCHÖNBRUNN

The elaborate gardens of the Great Parterre lead from the palace to the Gloriette, which is situated on a hill. Its hillside location affords views of the palace and Vienna.

## Austria

**Period:**

From the 17th century

**Significance:**

The palace is one of the most important cultural monuments in all of Vienna.

The Royal Palace of Schönbrunn was the heart of the Austro-Hungarian Empire and the seat of the Hapsburg Dynasty. Built to rival the grand Palace of Versailles in France, Schönbrunn is a magnificent Baroque palace that has served as the summer residence for generations of the imperial Hapsburg family. It was built between 1696 and 1749; two architects worked on the palace and formal gardens, zoological gardens and deer park, beginning with Johann Bernhard Fischer von Erlach and ending with Nicolaus Pacassi, who introduced lighter Rococo elements. The stunning palace is one of the most important cultural monuments in Vienna.

Schönbrunn has a long and eventful political history. In the 20th century it was at the center of political upheaval, which led ultimately to the outbreak of World War I. The catalyst was the assassination in 1914 of Archduke Franz Ferdinand, heir to the Austria-Hungary throne. Austria had annexed Bosnia and Herzegovina in 1908, greatly angering the Bosnian people. The assassination was carried out on Serbian soil, in the capital, Sarajevo, when Archduke Ferdinand was on an official visit with his family to inspect troops. Both Ferdinand and his pregnant wife, Sophia, were killed, and in retaliation Austria-Hungary declared war on Serbia. Within a month nearly all of Europe was at war.

Banquets and festivals were held inside the Gloriette, which was also a favored breakfast room of Franz Joseph I.

Schönbrunn Palace was intended to rival Versailles in splendor. Built as the summer residence of the Hapsburgs, the palace and grounds were designed in the Rococo style at the behest of Maria Theresa.

The great city of Istanbul dates to the Byzantine era. Founded by Greek settlers in the 7th century, it was then known as Byzantium, the city's earliest known name. When Roman emperor Constantine established a government there in 324 AD, it became the capital of the Roman empire and was eventually renamed Constantinople.

Later in the 15th century the city would become the seat of the Ottoman Empire. At its height the Ottoman era was one of the great artistic and cultural centers of the world; many of the city's important buildings were erected during this time, and the famously cosmopolitan city flourished.

At the end of World War I in 1918, the allied armies occupied the city. It was reclaimed in the Turkish War of Independence in 1922, and in 1923 the Republic of Turkey, founded by the visionary leader Mustafa Kemal Atatürk, was established, replacing the sovereign tradition of the Ottoman Empire and removing the capital from the ancient city of Istanbul to Ankara. In 1930 the Republic proclaimed that the city should be known hereafter only as Istanbul.

*Incorporating elements of Ottoman mosque and Byzantine church architecture, the majestic Sultan Ahmed Mosque is also known as the "Blue Mosque" in reference to the colored tiles of the interior.*

*The current church of Hagia Sophia was dedicated in 537. Originally constructed as the bishop's seat of Constantinople, the building was converted to a mosque in 1453. In 1934 Hagia Sophia was secularized and became a museum.*

## Turkey

### Period:
From the 7th century

### Significance:
The cosmopolitan city of Istanbul has been a center of politics, religion, and art for more than 2,000 years.

*The Bosphorus Bridge, completed in 1973, connects Asia to Europe. More than a billion vehicles crossed the suspension bridge in its first quarter century.*

*The crescent, star and red field of the national flag give it the names Al Yildiz ("moon star") or Alsancak ("red banner").*

# SAINT PETERSBURG

*Built in the mid-18th century as a winter residence for the Tsars, the Winter Palace is now part of the Hermitage, housing the word's largest collection of art.*

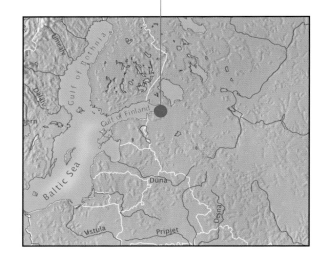

Tsar Peter the Great founded Saint Petersburg as the capital city of Russia in 1703. The city was designed with a distinct European feel, an effect its founder intended for his "Window to the West." The city remained the capital of the country until the repressive and ineffective Romanov Dynasty collapsed toward the end of the First World War. In 1917 Tsar Nicholas II and his entire family were placed under house arrest and murdered the following year. After the Revolution of 1917 Bolshevik forces led by Vladimir Lenin took control of the government and after three years of civil war between the Bolsheviks and monarchist supporters, the Bolsheviks emerged as victors, and the Soviet Union was born.

Despite its association with the revolution, Saint Petersburg is still known as a city of palaces; it is the site of the famed Winter Palace of the tsars and the Marble Palace, among others. The city's low-slung skyline is dominated by the Peter and Paul Cathedral, which sits on Zayachy Island along the right bank of the Neva river. With its many canals that wind

## Russia

**Period:**

From 1703

**Significance:**

Politically, culturally, and historically, St. Petersburg is one of the world's most important cities.

through the city and the 400 bridges that cross them, Saint Petersburg has also been called the "Venice of the North." Nevsky Prospekt, on the left bank of the Neva, is the city's main boulevard.

Having survived uprisings, civil conflicts and two world wars, the architectural character of Saint Petersburg is today under threat from urban development. There are plans to construct a giant tower in the heart of the city. If built, the 72- story torqued-glass skyscraper will dominate the historically low skyline of Saint Petersburg; it is the object of fierce resistance by conservationists.

*Vladimir Lenin orates in perpetuity outside the Smolny Institute, headquarters of the Bolsheviks during the October Revolution. After his death in 1924, Saint Petersburg was renamed Leningrad in his honor. In 1991, the city readopted it orginal name.*

*Saint Nicholas' Naval Cathedral was consecrated in 1760 to serve the area's sailors. Considered a great example of late Baroque architecture, it was one of the city's few cathedrals to remain open under the Soviets.*

## Germany

**Period:**

From 1730

**Significance:**

The palace was the site of the Potsdam Conference, during which allied leaders discussed the future of post-war Europe.

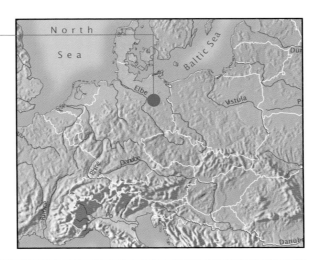

The garden façade of Sanssouci was built as the summer palace of Frederick the Great. Its name, meaning "no worries" in French, refers to the King's desire that the palace be a retreat from the work of governing.

Potsdam in Brandenburg was adopted as the residence of the Prussian kings from the 17th century until 1918. Frederick the Great II built his grand summer residence, Sanssouci Palace, there between 1745 and 1747; the French name of the palace, which translates as "without a care," reflects its function as a retreat.

Built largely between 1730 and 1916, Potsdam is a city of considerable natural beauty. Distinguished for its many lakes and rivers and its 1,235-acre (500-ha) complex of parks and 150 historic buildings, Potsdam constitutes the largest World Heritage site in Germany.

In 1945, directly after the end of World War II in Europe, Winston Churchill, Harry S Truman, and Joseph Stalin famously convened at Potsdam to decide the future of postwar Germany. The Potsdam Conference, as it was known, was also when the "big three" allied nations of Britain, the United States and the Soviet Union, together with China, issued an ultimatum to Japan to surrender and end the war.

Winston Churchill, Harry S Truman and Joseph Stalin posed for this historic photograph from the Potsdam Conference.

*"We, the President of the United States, the President of the National Government of the Republic of China, and the Prime Minister of Great Britain, representing the hundreds of millions of our countrymen, have conferred and agree that Japan shall be given an opportunity to end this war."*

—From the Declaration of Potsdam, July 26, 1945

# AUSCHWITZ

## Poland

**Period:**

1940 to 1945

**Significance:**

Auschwitz—the largest of the Nazi death camps—stands as a reminder of the horrors of the holocaust.

*"Auschwitz. What a sorrow. What a monstrosity. And still a hope for mankind."*

—General Charles de Gaulle

One of the most chilling places on earth today is the Nazi concentration and execution camp at Auschwitz-Birkenau in southern Poland. Auschwitz was the largest death camp built by the Nazi regime of the Third Reich. It is estimated that as many as 1.5 million people, mainly Jews, from all over Europe were sent to Auschwitz, where they were systematically starved, tortured and murdered in the camp's gas chambers.

Auschwitz was built in 1940, within a year of the outbreak of World War II, and it was operated by the Nazi elite special forces, the Schutzstaffel (SS). It comprised three separate compounds, each with a

specific purpose: Auschwitz I was a concentration camp and administrative center; Auschwitz II at Birkenau was the extermination camp where prisoners were gassed to death in chambers designed to look like communal showers; and Auschwitz III served as a labor camp.

In 1945, close to the end of World War II, Soviet troops advanced on Auschwitz. In an attempt to conceal the true purpose of the Birkenau camp, the SS destroyed the four gas chambers before the Soviet troops reached the Auschwitz complex. The Nazis abandoned Auschwitz 10 days before the Soviet Red Army reached the site. Retreating westward, the Germans forced 58,000 prisoners with them on what was essentially a death march.

*These rails led into the extermination camp, Auschwitz II-Birkenau, also referred to as the "death gate."*

*Approximately 700 prisoners attempted to escape from the Auschwitz camps. As many as 300 succeeded. As deterrence, the SS arrested the escapees' families and killed their block mates.*

*Each of the barracks at Aushwitz housed as many as 1,000 inmates.*

*Watch towers and barbed wire fences surround the camp.*

The monument to the heroes of the Warsaw uprising depicts insurgents emerging from walls crushed by monumental blank slabs.

n 1944, during the last months of the Second World War, Soviet allied forces advanced across German-occupied Poland toward Warsaw. In anticipation of Soviet liberation, the Polish Home Army staged an uprising against the German occupying forces, which failed after 63 days. The Soviet army was diverted from Warsaw, leaving its citizens at the mercy of Germany; Hitler retaliated by ordering the total annihilation of the city. German soldiers moved from house to house, block after block, setting fire to everything in their path. It is estimated that 650,000 people died and more than 85 percent of the historic city of Warsaw was obliterated. In just three months 700 years of Polish history and architectural heritage were gone.

The postwar reconstruction of Warsaw was and is an outstanding achievement. The Old Town center was completely restored, resurrecting the city's churches, palaces, libraries and ancient marketplace, and manifesting Warsaw's motto, *Semper invicta*: Always invincible.

## Poland

**Period:**

From the 13th century

**Significance:**

The reconstruction of Warsaw after its destruction by Nazi forces is a testament to the will and spirit of the Polish people.

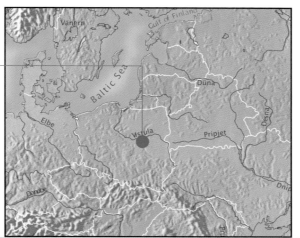

*"The city must completely disappear from the surface of the earth and serve only as a transport station for the Wehrmacht. No stone can remain standing. Every building must be razed to its foundation."*

—SS chief Heinrich Himmler, 1944

*The Royal Castle, at right, is located at the entrance to the Old Town, Warsaw's oldest historic district. The city's oldest monument, the Zygmunt Pillar, commemorates the king who moved Poland's capital from Krakow to Warsaw.*

# HIROSHIMA

The American B-29 bomber *Enola Gay* dropped the first nuclear weapon on Hiroshima at 8:15 on August 6, 1945. This act was the fulfillment of an ultimatum delivered to Japan by the allied nations just one month earlier at the Potsdam Conference in Germany. More than 70,000 people, roughly half the city's population, are thought to have died from the initial blast; an estimated 30,000 more died within a year from radiation poisoning and related illnesses.

Remarkably, one important building close to the site of the explosion survived. Everyone inside the grand Prefectural Industrial Promotion Hall was killed instantly; everything within a 1-mile (1.6 m) radius was annihilated. The skeletal remains of the Exhibition Hall with its eerily delicate dome is preserved today exactly as it was immediately after the impact, memorializing the victims of the atomic bomb and standing as a profoundly sad monument to the horror of nuclear war.

*"This horrible weapon brought about a "Revolution of Thought," which has convinced us of the necessity and the value of lasting peace."*

—First line of the first Peace Declaration read by Hiroshima Mayor Shinzo Hamai on August 6, 1947

*Named the "City of Peace" in 1949, Hiroshima is the site of international conferences and vigils on peace and social justice.*

## Japan

**Period:**

1945

**Significance:**

What is now the Hiroshima Peace Memorial was the only building within a 1-mile radius of where the nuclear bomb was dropped to survive its blast.

*This watch, at the Hiroshima Peace Memorial Museum, stopped at 8:15 A.M., the precise moment of the bombing.*

*The Peace Bell in the park was donated by the government of Greece. Visitors can ring the bell for world peace.*

*The mushroom cloud that formed after the bomb was dropped rose higher than 30,000 feet into the air.*

*The skeletal dome of the Hiroshima Peace Memorial—formerly the Prefectural Industrial Promotion Hall—offers mute testimony to the devastation of the atomic bombing.*

# BARCELONA

The distinctive Art Nouveau character of the city of Barcelona ranks it among the most beautiful in the world. Its modernist architectural heritage is the legacy of two great Spanish architects: Antoni Gaudí (1852–1926) and Luis Domènech y Montaner (1849–1923), whose startlingly innovative, often strangely beautiful buildings can be seen throughout the city. These two men developed an architectural style that replaced formal geometry and austerity with fluid, organic forms inspired by nature. They applied this imaginative style to private, public and religious buildings alike, such as Montaner's Hospital de Sant Pau and Palau de la Música Catalana, as well as one of the world's most beautiful gardens, Park Güell, designed by Gaudi.

The most famous landmark building of Barcelona is Gaudí's La Sagrada Familia cathedral, a notable combination of grandeur and whimsy. Construction of the cathedral began in 1882 and continues today. Only a small number of the 18 spires included in the original design have been erected so far. The current estimated completion date is 2026.

*In his design for the Guardian Houses at the entrance plaza to the Park Güell, Gaudí added fairy-tale elements to a projected housing development built between 1900 and 1914.*

*A colonnaded walkway under a road at Park Güell brings modern engineering concerns to stone construction by angling the outside columns to absorb weight.*

*To date, eight towers of the Sagrada Família have been completed. Eighteen are planned, representing the twelve Apostles, four Evangelists, the Virgin Mary and Jesus Christ.*

*"The temple grows slowly, but this has been the case with everything destined to have a long life. Hundred-year-old oak trees take many years to grow tall; on the other hand, reeds grow quickly, but in autumn the wind knocks them down and there is no more to be said."*

—Catalan architect Antoni Gaudí (1852–1926)

## Spain

**Period:**

1882 to 1926

**Significance:**

Barcelona is a showcase of the architecture of two great Spanish architects: Antoni Gaudí and Luis Doménech y Montaner.

*In restoring Casa Batlló, a middle-class residence, Gaudí and Josep Maria Jujol eschewed straight lines in favor of a highly decorative façade.*

# MONTICELLO

*"Palladio is the Bible. You should get it and stick to it."*

—Thomas Jefferson, speaking of Palladio's *I Quattro Libri dell'Architettura* (*The Four Books of Architecture*)

## United States

**Period:**

1768

**Significance:**

Thomas Jefferson, the third president of the United States, was also a gifted architect. He designed Monticello, his plantation home.

Thomas Jefferson did not conceive of Monticello as having a front entrance. Rather, the building was designed and built with east and west fronts, the former used primarily by guests.

The Palladian-style villa that appears on the United States 5-cent coin was designed by Thomas Jefferson (1743–1826), third president of the American Republic and chief author of the Declaration of Independence. Jefferson built the classical structure as his private home. Construction began in 1768; Jefferson moved into the completed South Pavilion two years later.

The house was built on a 5,000-acre (2,000 ha) plantation in the highlands of the Southwest Mountains of Virginia. The competed house features a dome room, library and innovations such as a dumbwaiter from the dining room to the kitchens. The grounds contain pavilions to the north and south of the main house, as well as gardens and small outlying farms. Approximately 150 slaves tended the lands and the Jefferson household.

After Jefferson's death, his daughter sold the house to settle his debt, but it was preserved as a monument to Jefferson by subsequent owners. The Thomas Jefferson Foundation acquired the site in 1923, turning it into a museum and educational center.

Americans can often find Monticello in their pockets; an image of its west front is minted on the back of the nickel coin.

# ROYAL SALTWORKS OF ARC-ET-SENANS

## France

**Period:**

1775 to 1779

**Significance:**

The design of the Royal Saltworks of Arc-et-Senans reflects the ideals of the Enlightenment.

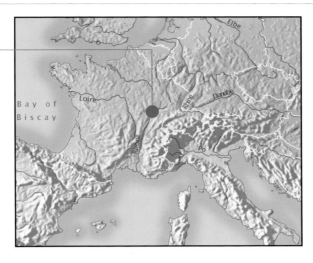

Designed in the style of a temple, the Director's House, flanked by the Saltworks, also contained a church and administrative offices.

*"Ledoux wanted the form of the Saltworks to be as pure as the course of the sun."*

—Institut Claude-Nicolas Ledoux

Salt was a valuable commodity in 18th-century France: The French economy benefited greatly from the industry (and also from the highly unpopular salt tax, called the *gabelle*.) In 1775, during the reign of Louis XVI, the French architect Claude-Nicholas Ledoux (1736–1806) was commissioned to design a grand new factory complex at Arc-et-Senans.

Ledoux's design promoted Enlightenment ideals of order and rationality. The buildings are laid out in a perfect semicircle, emphasizing industrial hierarchical order and organized systems of production. The management buildings are at the center of the complex, and all other buildings radiate outward, connected to the center by walkways and avenues. His most ambitious project, the Royal Saltworks, is considered Ledoux's masterpiece and an important early architectural achievement of the Enlightenment era.

Ledoux's original design was conceived as a circle. The second phase of the project, the other half of the circle, would have constituted an ideal city, complete with schools and hospitals. Only the first phase was completed (in 1779), however; further construction was put on hold by the French Revolution and during that time the saltworks ceased to operate.

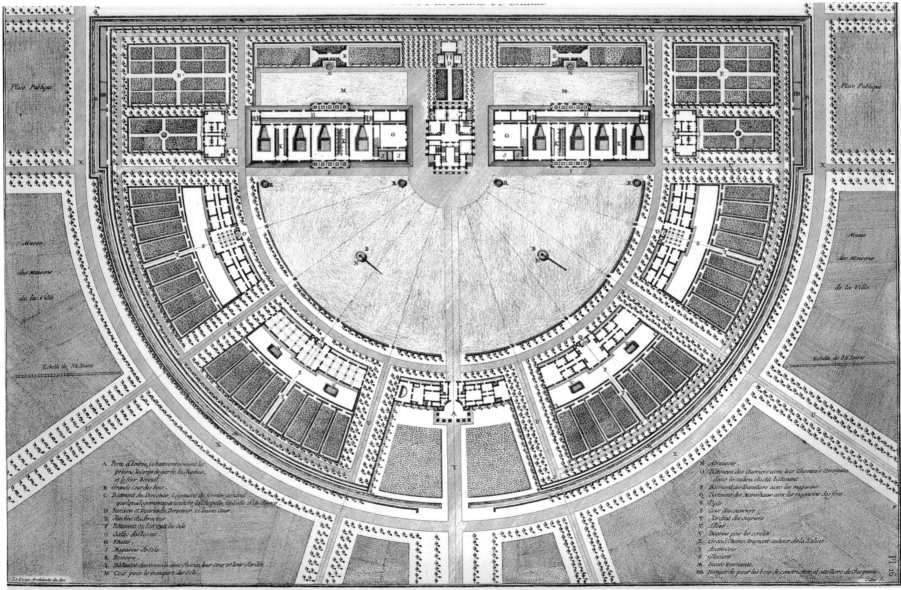

The complex of the Royal Saltworks included workshops and workers' homes laid out in a semicircle around the Director's House. The circle was to be completed by an unrealized ideal city.

# KIZHI POGOST

## Russia

**Period:**

1714, 1764

**Significance:**

These unique churches are prime examples of the Russian wooden architectural tradition.

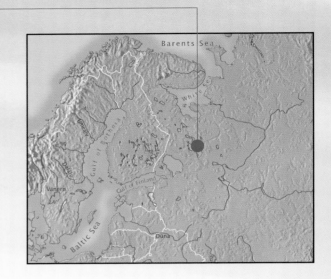

Two 18th-century churches in the lake region of Karelia in northern Russia exemplify an iconic Russian architectural tradition. The Church of the Intercession, built in 1764, is topped with 9 distinctive onion-shaped domes; the larger Church of the Transfiguration (1714) has 22 domes. The churches stand side by side on the tiny Kizhi Island on Lake Onega. Unlike most religious buildings, they have a centralized design and do not have a single frontal façade.

The craftsmanship evident in the Kizhi churches is of the highest order. No metal parts were used in their construction—they were assembled using interlocking wooden joints cut with axes.

*With its 22 domes, the Church of the Transfiguration is among the world's tallest log structures. It was the site of official functions until it was closed for services in 1937.*

Notches and dovetails were cut into logs and joined to build the structures of Kizhi Pogost. The pines were cut elsewhere and transported to the island, itself an impressive feat for the time.

*With its larger neighbor designated the "summer church," the nine-domed Intercession Church served as the "winter church."*

# BAUHAUS

*Emblematic of the style emblazoned on its façade, the Bauhaus building in Dessau was used by the school for only six years.*

## Germany

**Period:**

1919 to 1933

**Significance:**

The Bauhaus Movement revolutionized architectural and design practice, profoundly influencing 20th-century art and design.

*Exposed columns, unadorned exteriors and wide windows realized the Modernist rallying cries that "form follows function" and "ornament is a crime."*

The great modernist design movement, Bauhaus, was begun in Weimar Germany by the architect Walter Gropius (1883–1969). Gropius founded the Bauhaus School in 1919, where he promoted an aesthetic philosophy that embraced the world of modern, mass-produced materials while honoring the key principles of the Arts and Crafts movement. He encouraged his students to utilize modern and innovative materials to create elegant utilitarian designs.

Gropius sought to narrow the gap between art and craft and fostered a climate of interdisciplinary cooperation. The Bauhaus Movement revolutionized

contemporary architectural and design practice and had a lasting and wide-ranging influence across art and design of the 20th century.

The Bauhaus School moved to Dressau in 1925, and then to Berlin in 1932. The Nazi Party disapproved of the movement, likening it to Communism and labeling it anti-German. In 1933 the party closed down the school.

*"We want an architecture adapted to our world of machines, radios and fast cars."*

—Walter Gropius, founder of the Bauhaus School

*Designed by Ludwig Mies van der Rohe and Lilly Reich in 1929, the Barcelona chair, a classic of modern design, was first displayed in an exposition pavilion also designed by van der Rohe.*

*Poured concrete was a modern innovation in the region when the White City was built in the 1930s.*

## Israel

### Period:

From the 1930s to the 1950s

### Significance:

Tel Aviv's architecture typifies Modernist design principles. The city has the largest concentration of Bauhaus-style buildings in the world, with nearly 5,000 examples.

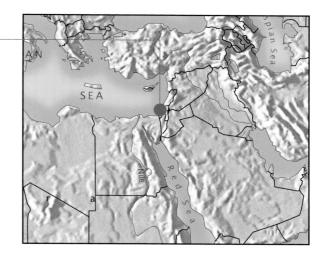

*A residential building on Ben Yehuda Street demonstrates how the Bauhaus style was adapted to Tel Aviv's climate and culture with smaller windows, flat roofs and balconies.*

Founded during the Ottoman Empire in 1909, Tel Aviv has changed hands many times in its 100-year history. Under the League of Nations Mandate after the First World War, Tel Aviv was reconfigured within the Modernist principles of "organic" urban planning under the auspices of Scottish Architect Sir Patrick Geddes (1854–1932). Nicknamed the "White City" because of its preponderance of light-colored buildings, Tel Aviv also has the largest concentration of Bauhaus-style buildings—some 5,000—in the world. Many of its modernist architects were trained in the Bauhaus style in Germany and immigrated to Israel in the 1930s after the Nazis' rise to power.

*A new appreciation of Tel Aviv's unique architectural heritage has recently led to the renovation of long-neglected buildings.*

# RIETVELD SCHRÖDER HOUSE

## Netherlands

**Period:**

1924

**Significance:**

This private home in Utrecht is the only existing building to fully exemplify the principles of the Dutch De Stijl Movement.

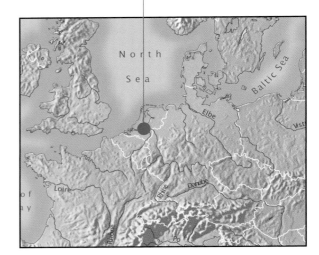

Built at the end of a residential block, the Rietveld Schröder House was designed without concern for blending into the surrounding neighborhood.

This small private house in Utrecht in the Netherlands is perhaps the only building to fully exemplify the principles of the Dutch De Stijl movement, which advocated pure abstraction and the radical reduction of form and color. The Rietveld Schröder House was built in 1924 for Mrs. Truus Schröder-Schräder and her three children; it was designed by the Dutch designer and architect Gerrit Rietveld (1888–1964) and is a pioneering example of Modernism in architecture.

The exterior of the house is a series of rectangular, strictly geometric forms in glass, concrete and steel, and utilizes only primary colors and black and white. The interior, which includes movable walls, was ingeniously designed to meet Mrs. Schröder-Schräder's particular specifications and the needs of her children. After her death, the iconic building became a museum. It has been open to the public since 1987.

Conceived as a "machine for living," the modular home featured movable walls so that the residents could create open spaces and rearrange rooms as they desired.

Exterior linear elements employ the primary colors red, yellow and blue, underscoring the simplicity of De Stijl.

*"The opposites that as living beings we are most interested in, perhaps, are tranquility and excitement, or repose and stir. Tranquility or repose by itself is boredom, uselessness. Excitement or stir by itself is uncertainty, fidgetiness, sloppiness, indecisiveness, the plague of unwilling motion. Tranquility and excitement are one in all art."*

—Dutch designer and architect Gerrit Rietveld (1888–1964)

# TUGENDHAT VILLA IN BRNO

Designed by the internationally acclaimed German architect Ludwig Mies van der Rohe (1886–1969) in the late 1920s, the Tugendhat Villa in Brno was constructed on the principles of architectural functionalism and exemplifies Mies van der Rohe's well-known dictum "less is more." The villa was built for Fritz and Greta Tugendhat, who lived there until 1938, when they fled to Switzerland to escape the Nazis.

It was constructed with reinforced concrete over a metal framework, a "skin and bone" system that eradicated the need for internal supporting walls. Mies Van der Rohe also custom-designed the furniture that was installed in the villa.

The villa was taken over by the Nazis during the Second World War and in the following decades was used for a number of purposes until its restoration in the early 1980s.

*Mies Van der Rohe designed the luxurious villa as living artwork that would require no further ornamentation than the furnishings, tropical woods and onyx wall specified in his design.*

## Czech Republic

**Period:**

1930

**Significance:**

The villa exemplifies the principles of architectural functionalism.

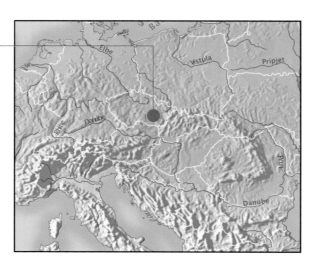

*View and landscape were incorporated into the design of the villa, the walls of which were partially transparent to allow changes in light throughout the day.*

# LOUIS BARRAGÁN HOUSE

## Mexico

**Period:**

1948

**Significance:**

The Louis Barragán house is a synthesis of architectural styles that brings together the influences of Modernism and the architecture of pre-Hispanic Mexico.

Louis Barragán's work is a synthesis of architectural styles and traditions that brings together the influences of Modernism and the architecture of pre-Hispanic Mexico. The undisputed foremost Mexican architect of the 20th century, he is known for his Modernist interpretations of the brightly colored traditional Mexican houses. The combination of austere reductive forms and solid areas of vibrant color created a sensuous and uniquely Mexican form of Modernism and won him the widespread admiration of fellow architects.

Barragán (1902–1988) built this extraordinary house in a suburb of Mexico City in 1948. A masterpiece that exemplified his distinctive style, it functioned as his home and his studio until his death.

*"My architecture is autobiographical … underlying all that I have achieved."*

—Mexican architect Luis Barragán (1902–1988)

*Barragán adapted the International style with local influences in his application of colors and surface textures.*

*Barragán's personality emerges in characteristic moments of humor and warmth—such as in these multicolored walls.*

Unlike most major capital cities, which generally grow slowly over time, Brasilia is a planned 20th-century city that was constructed in the center of Brazil in just 41 months.

The idea of moving the capital city from the coast to the underpopulated center of the country was not new; Brazilian statesman José Bonifácio presented the idea and even proposed the name for the new city in 1823. A foundation stone was laid in the proposed site in 1922, but no action was taken until the middle of the century, when President Juscelino Kubitschek resurrected the grand scheme. Construction of the new city began in 1956, and Brasilia was officially inaugurated in April 1960. Urban planner Lucio Costa worked with architect Oscar Niemeyer to build their vision of a stylistically coherent and harmonious metropolis.

The epic project drew workers to the construction site from all over the country. Today it has the largest concentration of modern architecture in the world.

## Brazil

**Period:**

1960

**Significance:**

Brasilia is the only purpose-built, 20th-century national capital.

*The National Congress Building was designed by Oscar Niemeyer, principal architect for the new capital.*

*Angels sculpted by Alredo Ceschiatti descend into Brasilia's Metropolitan Cathedral.*

*Bruno Giorgi's monumental sculpture honoring the laborers who built Brasília is installed at the Square of the Three Powers. The capital was planned with the plaza as its conceptual center.*

# SYDNEY OPERA HOUSE

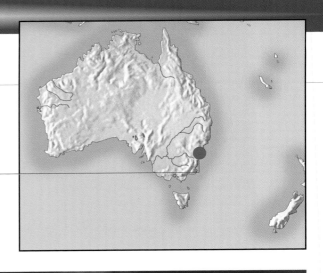

## Australia

### Period:

1973

### Significance:

The Sydney Opera House is one of the 20th century's most innovative architectural and engineering achievements.

National icon and world-famous landmark, the Sydney Opera House was named a World Heritage Site in 2007 and formally recognized as a masterpiece of 20th-century design and structural engineering.

Danish architect Jørn Utzon designed the innovative building and moved to Australia to oversee its construction. The Opera House was to be built on Sydney's urban waterfront overlooking the harbor; Utzon's design evoked the natural forms of seashells, a reference to Sydney's coastal identity. After prolonged interruptions and internal disputes over the costs and technical hurdles of building this unconventional structure, Utzon withdrew in 1966 from direct involvement in the project amid great controversy. Queen Elizabeth II formally inaugurated the Opera House in 1973 as millions attended the ceremony. In 2003, Utzon received the Pritzker Prize, the highest honor in the field of architecture.

*"To me it is a great joy to know how much the building is loved, by Australians in general and by Sydneysiders in particular."*

—Jørn Utzon, Danish architect and designer of the Sydney Opera House

*Over a million white and cream-colored tiles cover the Opera House's roofs. Seen from a distance, the tiles merge as a gleaming white.*

*Innovative in both their design and engineering, the shells of the Opera House's roofs were the result of years of intense collaboration. The solution was achieved with the aid of one of the first applications of computers in structural analysis.*

*Architect Jørn Utzon attributed the inspiration of his design to the peeling of an orange. A governmental change of administration resulted in Utzon's departure from the project that he had envisioned.*

# M A P S

# CANADA

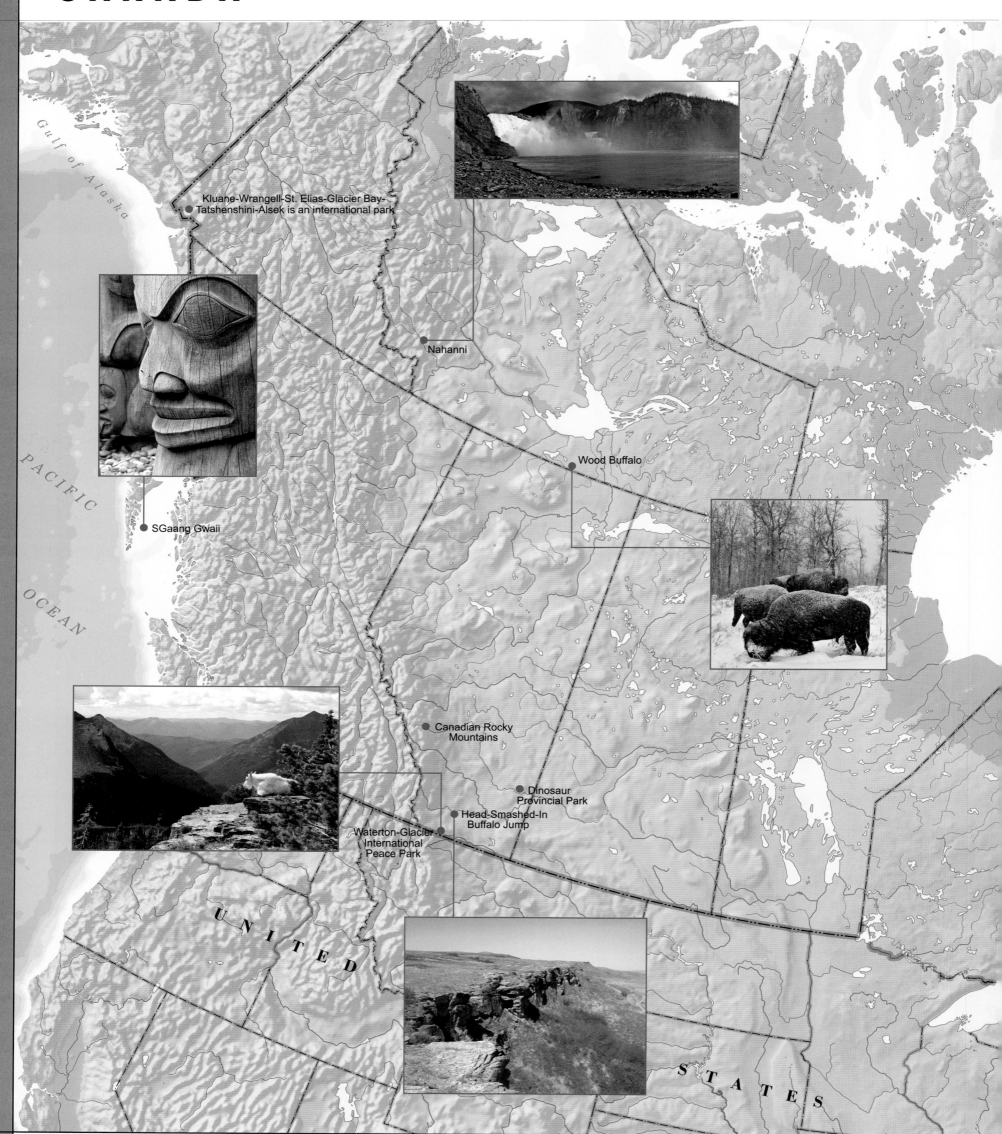

Kluane-Wrangell-St. Elias-Glacier Bay-Tatshenshini-Alsek is an international park

Nahanni

Wood Buffalo

SGaang Gwaii

Canadian Rocky Mountains

Dinosaur Provincial Park

Head-Smashed-In Buffalo Jump

Waterton-Glacier International Peace Park

Gulf of Alaska

PACIFIC OCEAN

UNITED STATES

GREENLAND
(KALAALLIT NUNAAT)

B a f f i n
Bay

A R C T I C

O C E A N

H u d s o n

B a y

L'Anse aux Meadows

Gros Morne

Miguasha

Québec

Lunenburg

Rideau Canal

A T L A N T I C

O C E A N

# UNITED STATES

PACIFIC

OCEAN

Olympic National Park

Waterton-Glacier International Peace Park

Yellowstone

Redwood

Yosemite

Mesa Verde

Grand Canyon

Pueblo de Taos

Chaco Culture

Carlsbad Caverns

H

A

W

A

I

I

ACIFIC OCEAN

PACIFIC OCEAN

Oahu

棚の中に
入らないで下さい
DANGER KEEP OUT

Hawaii Volcanoes

MEXICO

PACIFIC

OCEAN

SWEDEN

BALTIC SEA

Curonian Spit

LITHUANIA

Vilnius
Kernavé

RUSSIA

Castle of the
Teutonic Order
in Malbork

Toruń

Bialowieza Forest

BELARUS

Museumsinsel Berlin

Centennial Hall • Warsaw

POLAND

Muskauer Park

Wroclaw

Churches of Peace
in Jawor and Swidnica

Dresden

Zamość

Krakow
Auschwitz • Wieliczka Salt Mine

L'viv

Prague
Kutná Hora

CZECH

Kalwaria

Wooden Churches of
Southern Little Poland

Litomyšl Castle

REPUBLIC

Zelena Hora

Jewish Quarter
in Třebíč

Holy Trinity Column
in Olomouc

Kroměříz

Bardejov

Telč

Villa Tugendhat
in Brno

Vlkolinec

Spišský Hrad

Primeval beech forests
of the Carpathians

Hólašovice

SLOVAKIA

Český
Krumlov

Lednice - Valtice

Banská Štiavnica

Aggtelek

UKRAINE

AUSTRIA

HUNGARY

ROMANIA

# MEDITERRANEAN EUROPE

UNITED KINGDOM

NETHERLANDS

BELGIUM

LUXEMBOURG

GERMANY

CZECH REPUBLIC

Le Havre ● Amiens
Mont-Saint-Michel
Versailles ● Paris
Chartres ● ● Provins
Fontainebleau
Reims

GERMANY

Nancy ● Strasbourg

Wachau ● Vienna
Salzburg ● Schöbrunn
Neusiedlersee

F R A N C E

Loire Valley
Bourges
Saint-Savin
Fontenay
Vézelay

Saltworks of
Arc-et-Senans

Abbey of St. Gall
Bern
Lavaux
SWITZ.
Jungfrau
Bellinzone
Müstair

LIECHT.
Hallstatt
Semmering
A U S T R I A
Graz

SLOVENIA

Saint-Emilion
Bordeaux
Vézère Valley
Lyon

Monte San Giorgio
Santa Maria
delle Grazie
Sacri
Monti
Crespi d'Adda
Verona
Valcamonica
Vicenza
Venice
Aquileia
Poreč
Škocjan Caves

Santiago
de Compostela
Lugo
Oviedo
Altamira Cave
Las Médulas
Vizcaya Bridge

Savoy
Padua
Ferrara
CROATIA

Oporto ● Guimãraes
Alto Douro
Côa Valley
Atapuerca
Burgos Cathedral
San Millán
Orange
Avignon
Pont du Gard
Canal du Midi
Mont Perdu
Carcassonne
Arles

Genoa
Modena
Ravenna
Plitvice Lakes

MONACO
Cinque Terre

S P A I N
Vall de Boí
Madriu-Perafita-Claror
ANDORRA

Pisa
Florence
SAN MARINO
Urbino
Šibenik

Salamanca
Segovia
Avila
Escurial
Alcala
Toledo
Cáceres
Aranjuez
Guadalupe
Cuenca
Aragon
Poblet
Barcelona
Tárraco

San Gimignano
Siena
Val D'Orcia
Pienza
Assisi
Trogir
Split

I T A L Y

Batalha
Alcobaça
Tomar
Sintra
Lisbon
Evora
Mérida

PORTUGAL

Scandola
Peninsula

Adriatic Sea

Cerveteri
Vatican
Tivoli
Rome

Rock-Art of the
Iberian Peninsula
La Lonja
de la Seda

Caserta
Naples
Costiera Amalfitana

Pompei
Alberobello
Matera
Cilento

Castel del
Monte

Seville
Cordoba
Ubena and Beaza
Doñana
Ibiza
Palmeral of Elche
Granada

Su Nuraxi
di Barumini

T y r r h e n i a n
S e a

M E D I T E

Aeolian
Islands

A L G E R I A

Agrigento
Villa Romana del Casale
Syracuse
Val di Noto

Megalithic Temples
MALTA
Valetta
Hal Saflieni Hypogeum

R R A N E A N

TUNISIA

L I B Y A

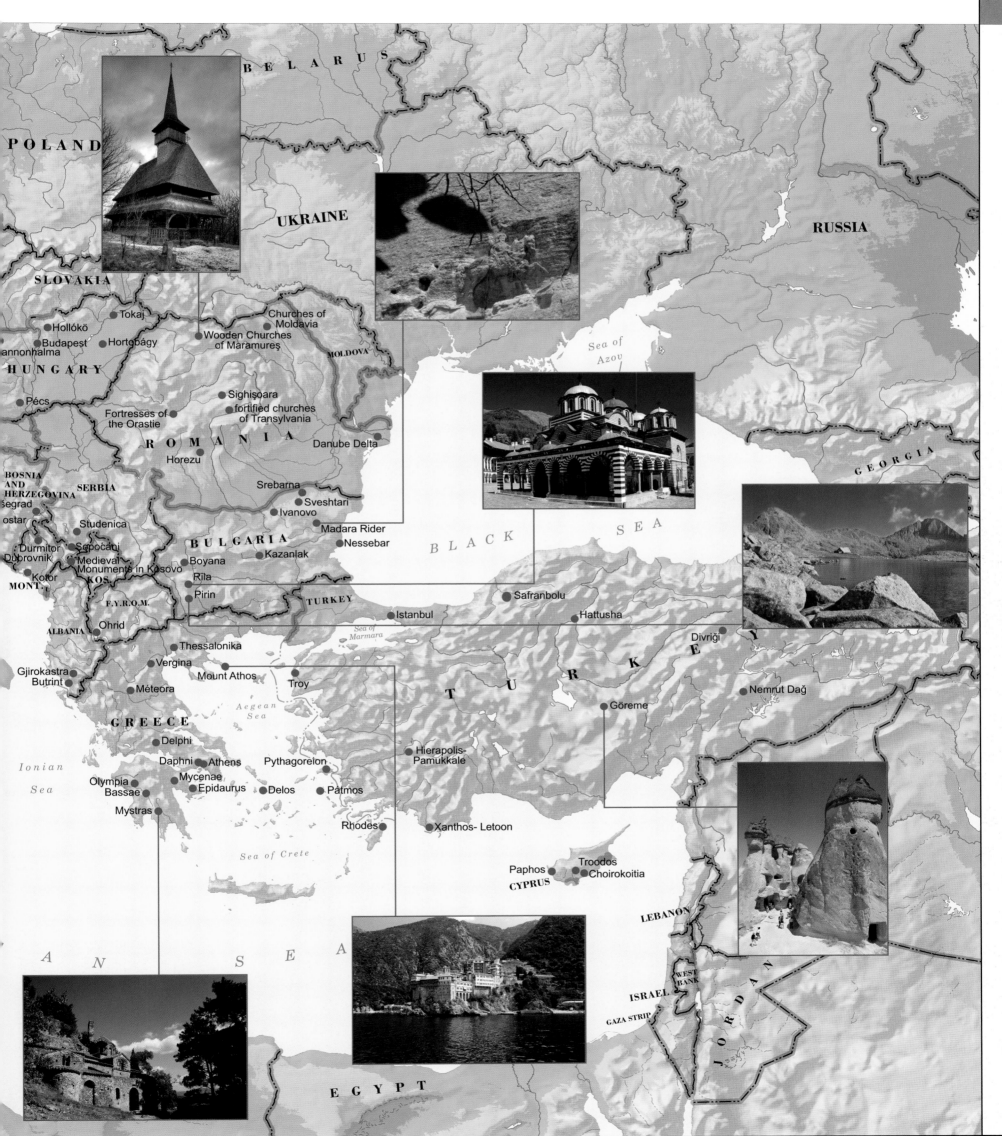

POLAND

BELARUS

UKRAINE

RUSSIA

SLOVAKIA

Tokaj

Hollókö

Hortobágy

Budapest

annonhalma

HUNGARY

Churches of Moldavia

Wooden Churches of Maramureş

MOLDOVA

Pécs

Sighişoara

Fortresses of the Orastie

fortified churches of Transylvania

ROMANIA

Danube Delta

Horezu

BOSNIA AND HERZEGOVINA

SERBIA

Srebarna

segrad

Sveshtari

ostar

Ivanovo

GEORGIA

Studenica

Madara Rider

Durmitor

Sopoćani

Nessebar

BLACK          SEA

Dubrovnik

BULGARIA

Kazanlak

Medieval Monuments in Kosovo

Boyana

Kotor

Rila

MONT.

KOS.

Pirin

F.Y.R.O.M.

TURKEY

Safranbolu

Ohrid

Istanbul

Hattusha

ALBANIA

Sea of Marmara

Thessalonika

Divriği

Vergina

Gjirokastra

Mount Athos

Troy

T    U    R    K    E    Y

Butrint

Méteora

Nemrut Dağ

Aegean Sea

GREECE

Göreme

Delphi

Daphni

Athens

Pythagorelon

Hierapolis-Pamukkale

Ionian Sea

Olympia

Mycenae

Bassae

Epidaurus

Delos

Pátmos

Mystras

Rhodes

Xanthos- Letoon

Sea of Crete

Troodos

Paphos

Choirokoitia

CYPRUS

LEBANON

A        N

S        E        A

WEST BANK

ISRAEL

JORDAN

GAZA STRIP

EGYPT

Sea of Azov

# RUSSIA AND NEIGHBORING COUNTRIES

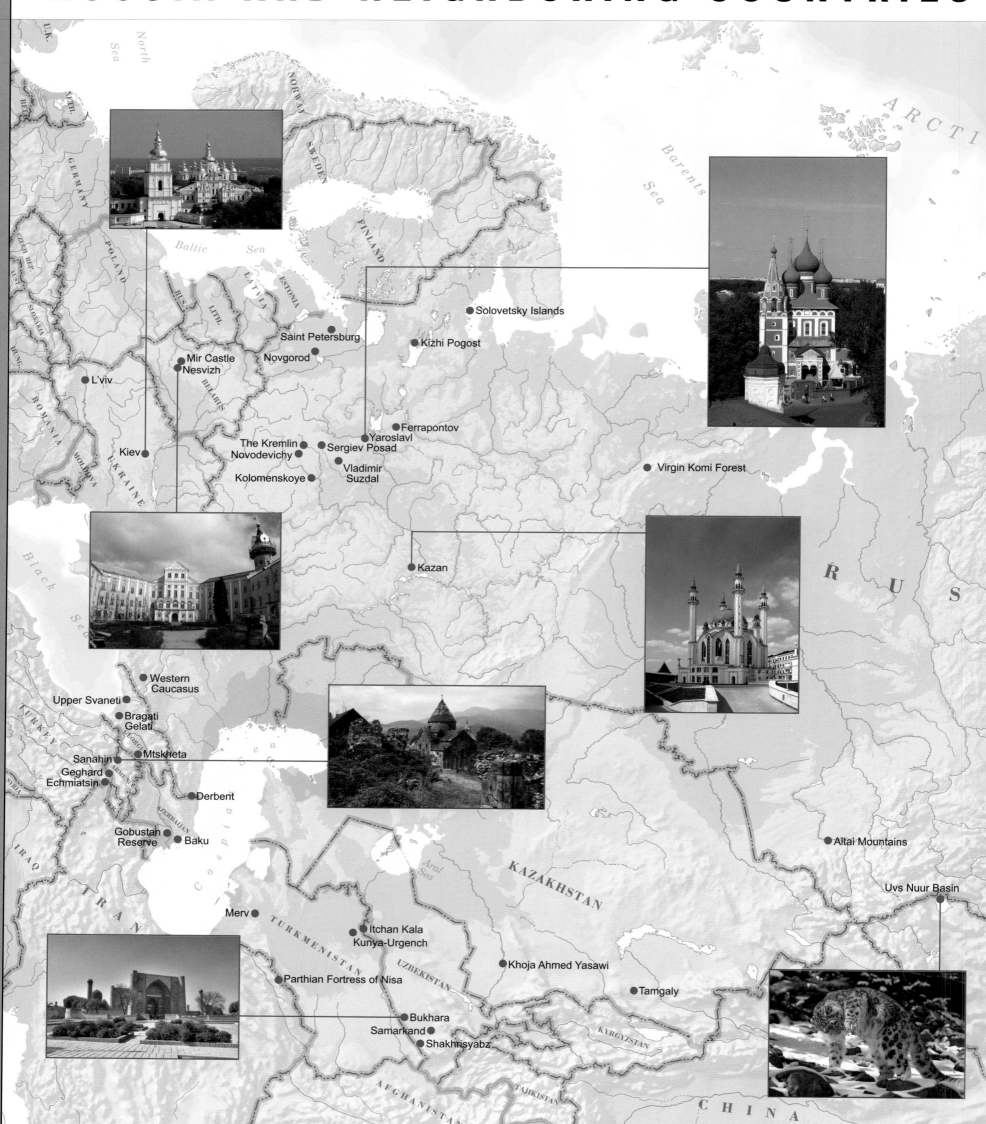

ARCTIC

North Sea

Barents Sea

U.K.
BEL.
NETH.
GERMANY
CZECH REP.
AUST.
SLOVAKIA
POLAND
ROMANIA
MOLDOVA
UKRAINE
BELARUS
LITH.
RUS.
LATVIA
ESTONIA
FINLAND
NORWAY
SWEDEN

Baltic Sea

Solovetsky Islands
Kizhi Pogost
Saint Petersburg
Novgorod
Mir Castle
Nesvizh
L'viv
Kiev
Ferrapontov
The Kremlin
Novodevichy
Sergiev Posad
Yaroslavl
Kolomenskoye
Vladimir
Suzdal
Virgin Komi Forest

Kazan

R U S S

Black Sea

Western
Caucasus
Upper Svaneti
Bragati
Gelati
Sanahin
Geghard
Echmiatsin
Mtskheta
Derbent
Gobustan
Reserve
Baku

TURKEY
SYRIA
IRAQ
IRAN
GEORGIA
ARMENIA
AZERBAIJAN

Caspian Sea

Aral Sea

KAZAKHSTAN

Altai Mountains

Uvs Nuur Basin

Merv
Itchan Kala
Kunya-Urgench
Parthian Fortress of Nisa
Khoja Ahmed Yasawi
Tamgaly
Bukhara
Samarkand
Shakhrisyabz

TURKMENISTAN
UZBEKISTAN
KYRGYZSTAN
TAJIKISTAN
AFGHANISTAN

CHINA

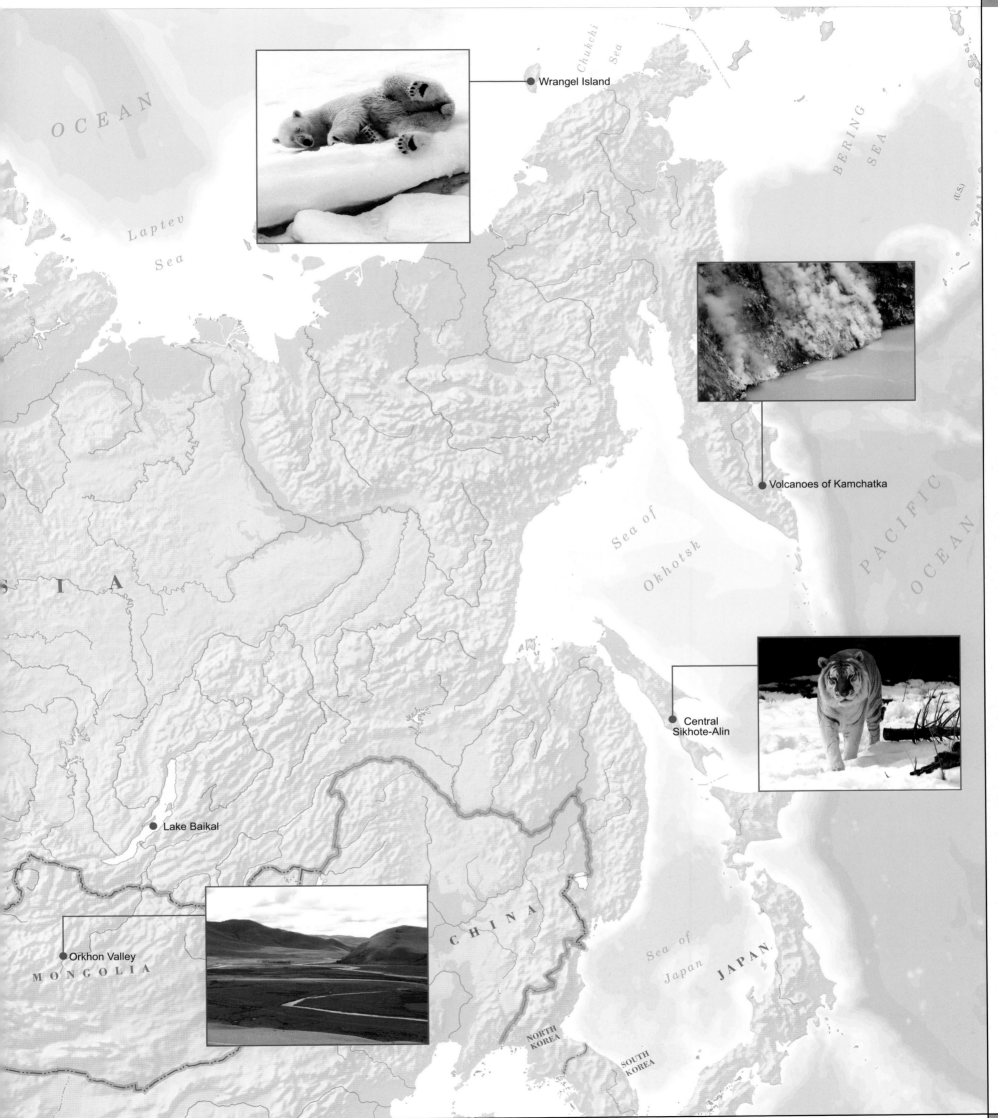

OCEAN

Laptev Sea

Chukchi Sea

BERING SEA

(U.S.)

Wrangel Island

Volcanoes of Kamchatka

PACIFIC OCEAN

Sea of Okhotsk

Central Sikhote-Alin

Lake Baikal

RUSSIA

CHINA

Orkhon Valley

MONGOLIA

Sea of Japan

JAPAN

NORTH KOREA

SOUTH KOREA

# SOUTHERN ASIA

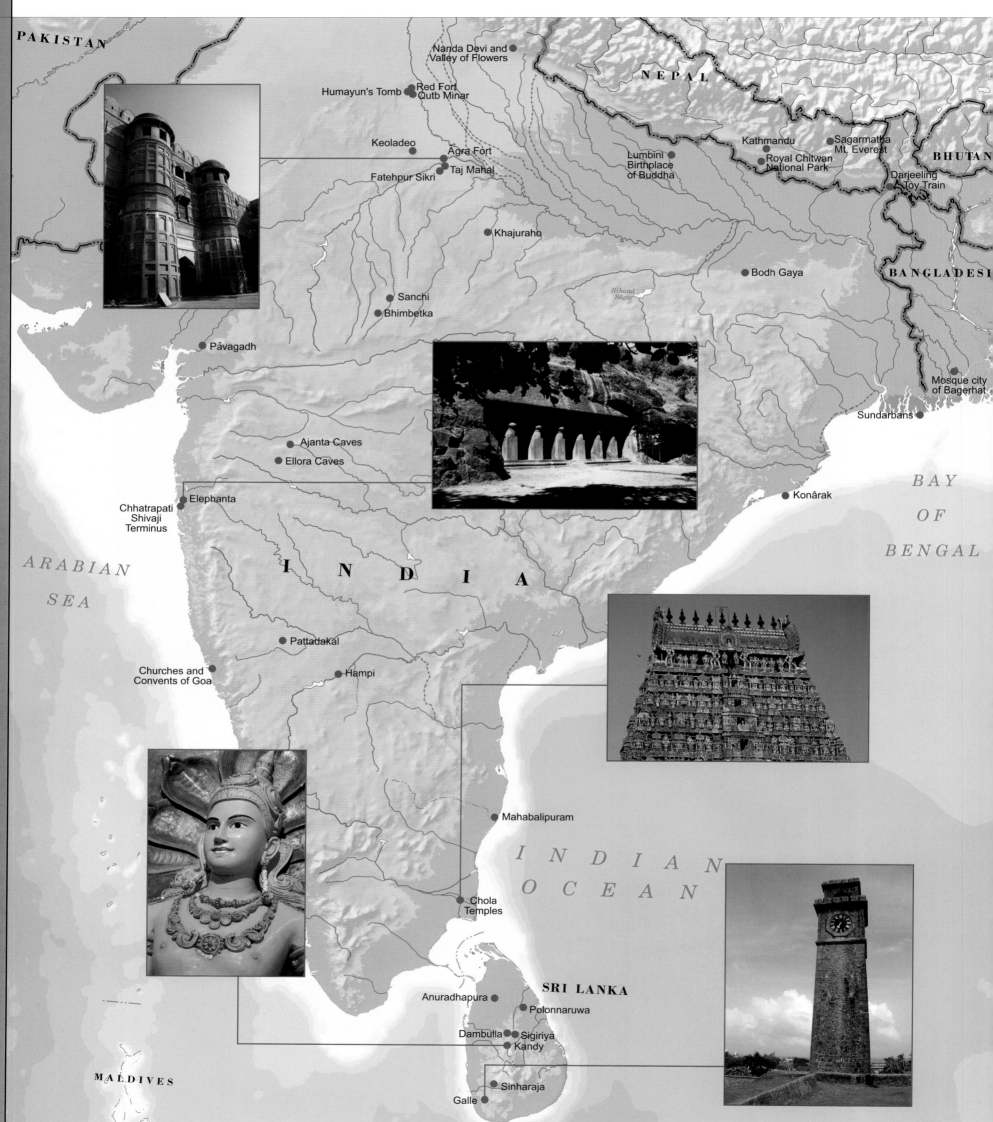

PAKISTAN

Nanda Devi and
Valley of Flowers

NEPAL

BHUTAN

Humayun's Tomb
Red Fort
Qutb Minar

Keoladeo
Agra Fort
Fatehpur Sikri
Taj Mahal

Kathmandu
Sagarmatha
Mt. Everest

Lumbini
Birthplace
of Buddha

Royal Chitwan
National Park

Darjeeling
Toy Train

BANGLADESH

Khajuraho

Bodh Gaya

Sanchi
Bhimbetka

Mosque city
of Bagerhat

Pāvagadh

Sundarbans

Ajanta Caves
Ellora Caves

Konârak

Elephanta

BAY

Chhatrapati
Shivaji
Terminus

OF

BENGAL

I  N  D  I  A

ARABIAN

SEA

Pattadakal

Churches and
Convents of Goa

Hampi

Mahabalipuram

INDIAN

OCEAN

Chola
Temples

Anuradhapura

SRI LANKA

Polonnaruwa

Dambulla
Sigiriya
Kandy

MALDIVES

Sinharaja

Galle

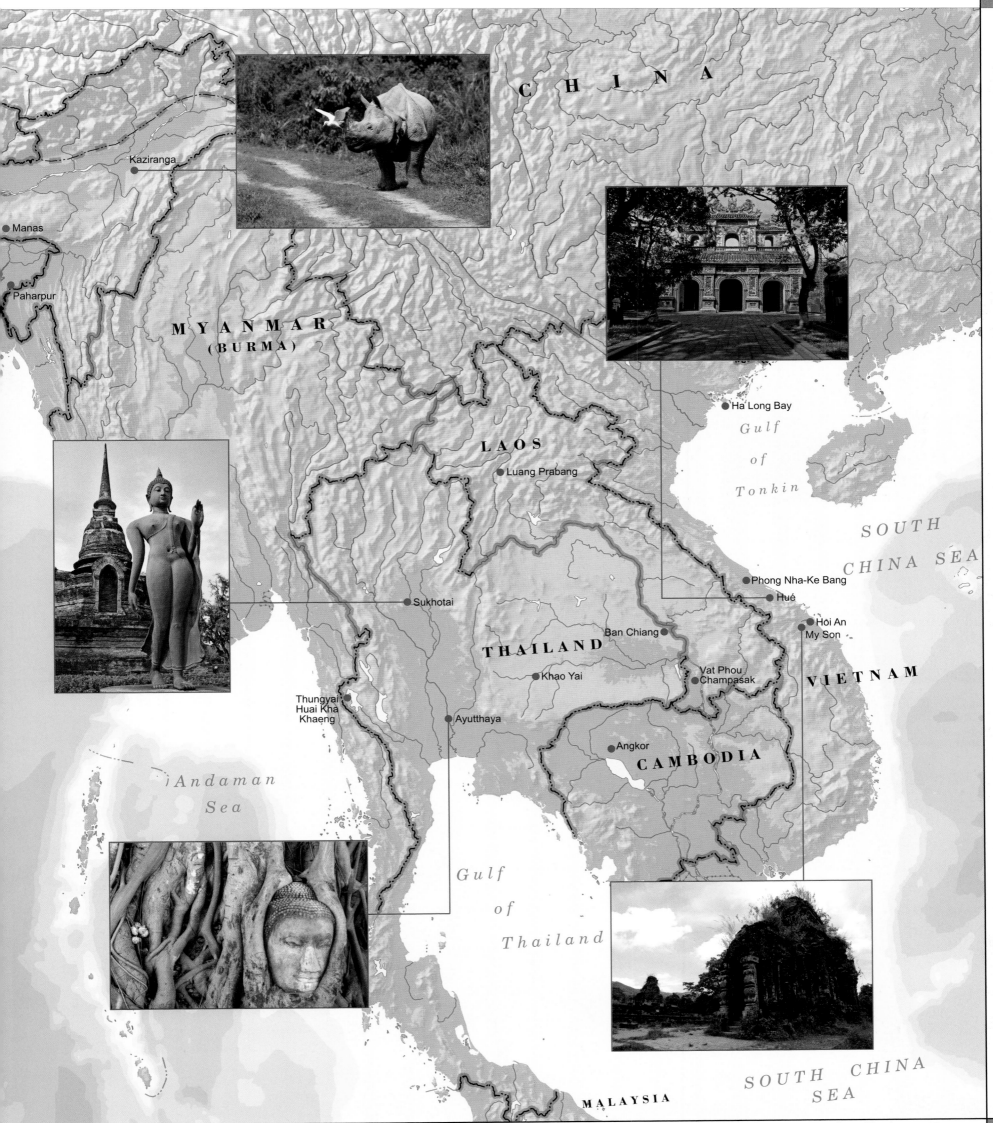

Kaziranga

Manas

Paharpur

MYANMAR
(BURMA)

CHINA

Ha Long Bay

Gulf
of
Tonkin

LAOS

Luang Prabang

SOUTH

CHINA SEA

Phong Nha-Ke Bang

Sukhotai

Hué

Ban Chiang

Hoi An
My Son

THAILAND

Khao Yai

VIETNAM

Vat Phou
Champasak

Thungyai
Huai Kha
Khaeng

Ayutthaya

Angkor

CAMBODIA

Andaman
Sea

Gulf

of

Thailand

SOUTH CHINA
SEA

MALAYSIA

# SOUTHWESTERN ASIA

Caspian
Sea

TURKEY

CYPRUS

Aleppo

SYRIA

Takht-e Soleyman

Dome of Soltaniyeh

MEDITERRANEAN
SEA

Crac des Chevaliers
Ouadi Qadisha
LEBANON Baalbek
Byblos
Anjar
Tyre        Damascus
Acre
Biblical Tels    Bosra
ISRAEL
Tel-Aviv
Jerusalem
Masada    Um er-Rasas
Quseir Amra

Palmyra

Hatra    Ashur

IRAQ

Samarra

Bisotun Inscription

Naqsh-e Jahan Square    Esfahan

Tchogha Zanbil

IRAN

Pasargadae
Persepolis

Negev    JORDAN
Petra

EGYPT

RED

SEA

SUDAN

SAUDI    ARABIA

Qal'at al-Bahrain    BAHRAIN

QATAR

UNITE

ERITREA

ETHIOPIA

Sana'a

Shibam

YEMEN

TURKMENISTAN

CHINA

AFGHANISTAN

PAKISTAN

Bamiyan Valley

Minaret of Jam

Takht-i-Bahi

Taxila

Rohtas Fort

Fort Lahore

Shalamar Gardens in Lahore

Bam

Moenjodaro

OMAN

ARAB EMIRATES

Bat

The Aflaj System

Bahla Fort

Thatta

O M A N

Arabian Oryx Sanctuary
Removed from the list in 2007

A R A B I A N    S E A

I N D I A

The Frankincense Trail

# EASTERN ASIA

KYRGYZSTAN

TAJIKISTAN

MONGOLIA

● Mogao Caves

PAKISTAN

CHINA

Jiuzhaigou Valley ●

● Huanglong

Sichuan Giant ● Dujiangyan
Panda Sanctuary

● Potala Palace

● Mount Emei    ● Dazu
Rock Carvin
Chongqing

● Three Parallel Rivers

BHUTAN

● Lijiang

BANGLA-
DESH

South China Karst ●

INDIA

Shiretoko

Imperial Tombs of the
Ming and Qing Dynasties

Koguryo
Kingdom

**N. KOREA**

Chengde

Shirakami-Sanchi

The Great Wall
Yungang         Forbidden City
Grottoes        Peking Man    Temple of Heaven
                              Summer Palace

Koguryo
Tombs

*Sea
of
Japan*

Ping Yao

Changdeokgung Palace   Jongmyo Shrine
Hwaseong Fortress                      Shirakawa-go     Nikko     **JAPAN**
                       **S. KOREA**    Gokayama

Mount Taishan                Gyeongju
Yin Xu                                  Seokguram Grotto           Kyoto
      Qufu          Haeinsa Temple      Bulguksa Temple    Iwami Ginzan   Nara
Longmen Grottoes                                                    Horyu-ji
                    Dolmen Sites                Hiroshima   Himeji-jo
Terracotta                                      Itsukushima           Kii Mountains
Warriors

                    Jeju Volcanic Island

Wudang Mountains        *Yellow
                         Sea*
    Suzhou
                                        Yakushima
    Huangshan Mountains
    Xidi and Hongcun
Lushan

Wulingyuan

Mount Wuyi

                        *Philippine
**TAIWAN**               Sea*
Kaiping    Macao
Diaolou

# OCEANIA AND NEIGHBORING COUNTRIES

INDIA

Arabian
Sea

Bay
of
Bengal

LAOS

THAILAND

VIETNAM

South
China
Sea

CAMBODIA

SRI
LANKA

Sulu
Sea

MALDIVES

BRUNEI
Gunung Mulu · Kinabalu

MALAYSIA

Celebes
Sea

SINGAPORE

INDONESIA

Tropical
Rainforest
Heritage

Java Sea

Vigan

Rice Terraces

PHILIPPINE
SEA

Ujung Kulon

Borobudur · Sangiran Early Man
Prambanan

Komodo
Dragon

SOUTH
CHINA
SEA

Baroque Churches

PHILIPPINES

INDIAN

Puerto-Princesas
Subterranean River

OCEAN

Shark Bay

Tubbataha Reef

Sulu
Sea

MALAYSIA

CELEBES SEA

INDONESIA

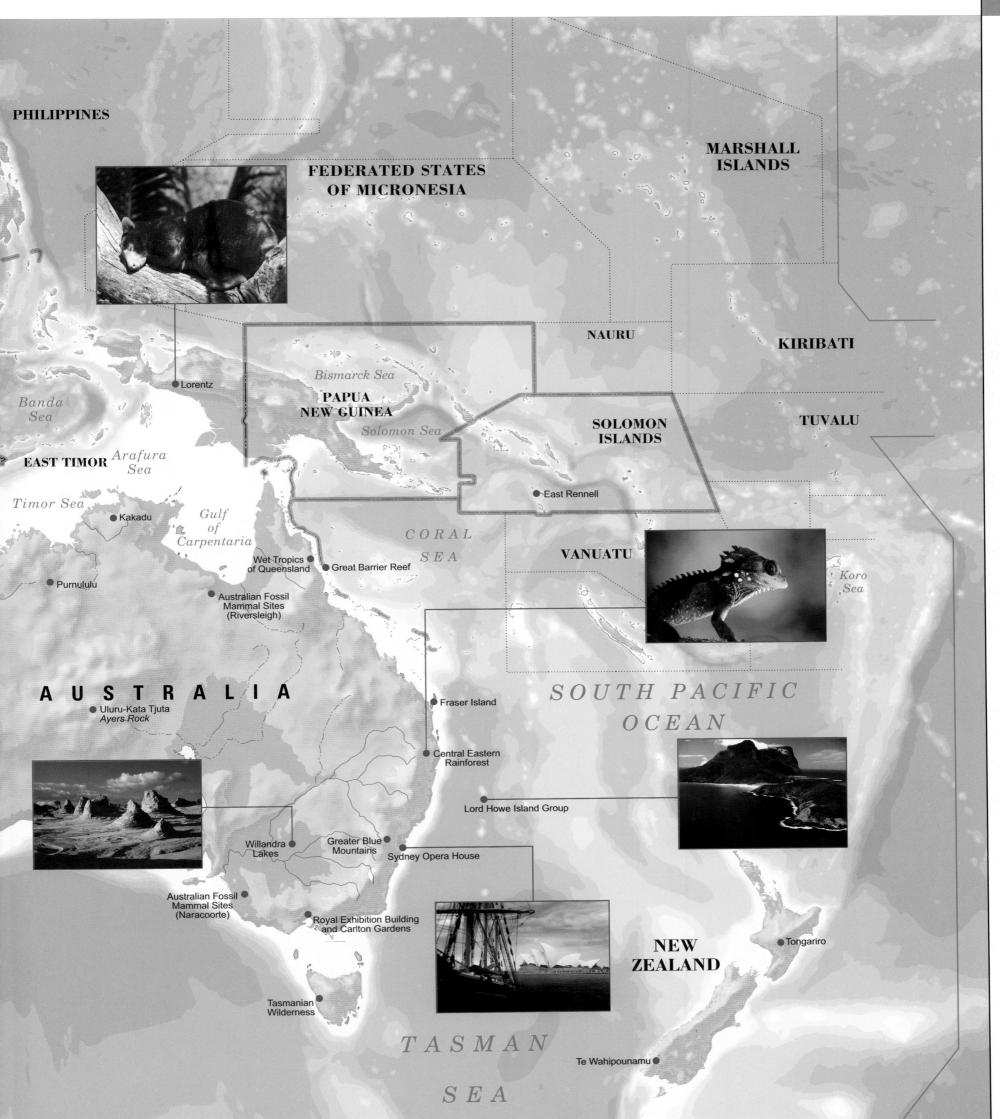

PHILIPPINES

FEDERATED STATES
OF MICRONESIA

MARSHALL
ISLANDS

*Bismarck Sea*

NAURU

KIRIBATI

*Banda
Sea*

● Lorentz

PAPUA
NEW GUINEA

*Solomon Sea*

SOLOMON
ISLANDS

TUVALU

EAST TIMOR   *Arafura
Sea*

*Timor Sea*

● Kakadu

*Gulf
of
Carpentaria*

East Rennell ●

*Koro
Sea*

CORAL

SEA

VANUATU

● Purnululu

Wet Tropics
of Queensland ●   ● Great Barrier Reef

● Australian Fossil
Mammal Sites
(Riversleigh)

AUSTRALIA

SOUTH PACIFIC

● Uluru-Kata Tjuta
*Ayers Rock*

● Fraser Island

OCEAN

● Central Eastern
Rainforest

Lord Howe Island Group

Willandra
Lakes

● Greater Blue
Mountains ●

Sydney Opera House

Australian Fossil
Mammal Sites
(Naracoorte)

● Royal Exhibition Building
and Carlton Gardens

NEW
ZEALAND

● Tongariro

Tasmanian
Wilderness

*TASMAN*

Te Wahipounamu ●

*SEA*

# INDEX

## A

Aachen Cathedral, 11, 216
Aapravasi Ghat, 344
Aborigines, 134–35
Abu Simbel, 158–59
Acropolis, 170–71
Adams, John, 126
Aesop, 172
Afghanistan, 265
Agave Tequila, 120–21
Aïr and Ténéré Natural Reserves, 109
Al Khazneh, 259
Alaska, 63
Al-Azhar University, 258
Albert Dock, 331
Aldabra Atoll, 22
Aleppo, 165
Aletsch Glacier, 88
Alexander the Great, 263–64
Alps, 88, 210
Alta, 148
Altamira Cave, 145
Alto Douro, 127
Amazon Basin, 16–17, 42, 98
Ampitheater of El Jem, 189
Andes, 98, 302
Angel Falls, 99
Angel, Jimmie, 99
Angkor, 282–83
Antiochus I, 178
Aoraki, 100
Appalachian Mountains, 116
Aquileia, 185
Arabian Oryx Sanctuary, 55
Arc de Triomphe, 204
Argentina, 68, 72–73, 142
Arles, 195
Astronomical Clock, 243
Aswan Dam, 10, 158–59
Atapuerca, 139
Atatürk, Mustafa Kemal, 347
Athens, 170–71
Auschwitz, 350
Australia, 51–52, 66–67, 71, 76–77, 85, 102, 118, 134–35, 367
Austria, 211–13, 346
Avila, 224
Aztecs, 298, 311

## B

Baalbek, 164
Badlands, 96

Baja California, 58
Bamberg, 218
Bamiyan Valley, 265
Bandarin, Francesco, 217
Banff National Park, 80–81
Banks, Joseph, 67
Barcelona, 354–55
Barragán, Louis, 364
Barsana Monastery, 248
Bartholdi, Frederic Auguste, 324
Basilica di Santa Maria del Fiore, 230
Bath, 192–93
Bauhaus, 360
Bay of the Descending Dragon, 112
Belém Tower, 226–27
Belgium, 202–3, 334
Belize, 13, 56–57
Belize Barrier Reef Reserve System, 56–57
Bellinzone, 210
Bemahara Reserve, 95
Berne, 208–9
Bhimbetka, 147
Big Ben, 199
Bingham, Hiram, 291
Black Sea, 62, 115
Blackfoot Confederacy, 97
Blue Mountains, 118
Bolivia, 42, 302
Bonaparte, Napoleon, 160, 228, 250, 252
Bonifácio, José, 365
Bordeaux, 128
Borobudur, 288
Bosnia, 340–41
Bosphorus Bridge, 347
Bosra, 187
Botswana, 146
Brasília, 365
Brazil, 16–17, 28, 68, 154, 318, 365
Brugge, 203
Buch, Julius, 337
Buda Castle, 246–47
Budapest, 246–47
Bulkily, Richard, 94
Bulwer-Lytton, Edward, 184
Bumbaru, Dinu, 12
Bungle Bungle Range, 102
Burden, William Douglas, 38
Burgess Shale, 80
Burgos, 225
Burle, Marie-Helene, 47
Bwindi Impenetrable National Park, 35
Byzantium, 347

## C

Cahokia Mounds, 293
Cairo, 258
Cambodia, 282–83
Cameron, Christina, 11–12
Camiño de Santiago, 222
Campeche, 313
Canada, 11, 63, 80–81, 96–97, 138, 292, 304–5, 335
Canadian Rockies, 80–81, 97
Canaima National Park, 99
Canal du Centre, 334
Canal Rideau, 335
Cape Floral Protected Area, 110
Cartagena, 317
Carthage, 189
Castillo de San Felipe de Morro, 321
Castle of San Felipe de Barajas, 317
Castro, Fidel, 314
Caucasus Mountains, 115
Central African Republic, 54
Central Amazon, 16–17
Central Suriname Nature Reserve, 29
Chambord, 196
Charlemagne, 216
Château Frontenac Hotel, 304–5
Chesil Beach, 89
Chile, 303, 318
China, 44–45, 86, 141, 256–57, 272–75, 308
Chinese Imperial Palace, 274
Christophe, Henri, 343
Church of the Intercession, 358–59
Church of the Transfiguration, 358
Churchill, Winston, 349
Circular Migration, 48
City of Quito, 11
Ciudad de Mexico, 311
Cliff Palace, 294
Clinton, Bill, 68
Cocteau, Jean, 202
Colelez Mountains, 114
Cologne, 217
Colombia, 301, 317
Colorado River, 78–79
Colossi of Memmon, 156
Colossus of Rhodes, 176
Constantinople, 347
Convention for the Protection of Cultural Property in the Event of Armed Conflict, 10
Cordilleras, 98
Corell, Robert, 65
Costa, Lucio, 365

# INDEX

## S

Saami, 124–25
Sagarmatha, 104–5
Sagrada Familia, 354
Sahara Desert, 109, 152–53
Saint Anne's Church, 240
Saint Basil's Cathedral, 241
Saint-Émilion, 128
Saint Jacob's Cathedral, 252
Saint James, 222
Saint Mark's Cathedral, 234–35
Saint Nicholas' Naval Cathedral, 348
Saint Paul's Basilica, 308
Saint Peter's Basilica, 180
Saint Petersburg, 348
Saladin Citadel, 258
Salinger, Pierre, 122
Salt, Titus, 333
Saltaire, 333
Salvador de Bahia, 318
Salween River, 86
Salzburg, 211
Samos, 172
Sana'a, 261
San Augustin, 301
San Diego Wild Animal Park, 79
San Francisco de Asis Church, 316
Sangay National Park, 98
San Gimignano, 232
Sangiran Early Man Site, 140
San Juan, 321
Sans Souci, 343
Santiago de Compostela, 222
Santo Domingo, 310
Schliemann, Heinrich, 179
Schönbrunn, 346
Schupp, Fritz, 336
Scotland, 94
Scott, Peter, 45
Selous Game Reserve, 21
Selous, Frederick Courteney, 21
Senegal, 11, 342
Serengeti National Park, 48
Serra da Capivara, 154
Seven Pagodas, 268
Seven Summits, 103
Seychelles, 22
SGaang Gwaii, 292
Shark Bay, 71
Shaw, George Bernard, 251
Sheppard, David, 13
Shibam, 260
Sian Ka'an, 26
Sibenik, 252

Siberia, 37
Sichuan Giant Panda Sanctuaries, 44–45
Sidmouth Lighthouse, 89
Sierra Club, 10
Sierra Nevada Mountains, 92
Sighisoara, 249
Sima de los Huesos, 139
Simien, 11
Sintra, 229
Skara Brae, 150
Skocjan Caves, 113
Slovenia, 113
Smith, Kes Hillman, 23
Solomon Islands, 74
South Africa, 110–11, 345
Southern Alps, 101
Spain, 139, 220–25, 354–55
Spanish Inquisition, 224
Sri Lanka, 284–85
Stalin, Joseph, 349
Stanley, Henry Morton, 108
Stari Most, 341
Statue of Liberty, 326–27
Stockholm Conference, 10–11
Stonehenge, 132–33, 151
Stones of Stenness, 150
Sub-Antarctic Islands, 53
Sudan, 161
Sultan Ahmed Mosque, 347
Sumatra, 39
Summer Palace, 275
Suriname, 29
Sweden, 124–25, 149, 238, 339
Switzerland, 88, 129, 137, 208–10
Sydney Opera House, 366–67
Syria, 165, 169, 187

## T

Tadrart Acacus, 152–53
Tagore, Rabindranath, 266
Taï National Park, 30
Taj Mahal, 266–67
Taliban, 265
Tamerlane, 271
Tanum, 149
Tanzania, 13, 21, 48, 103, 306
Tasman, Abel, 52
Tasmanian Wilderness, 52
Tattersall, Ian, 139
Te Heuheu Tukino, IV, 119
Te Wahipounamu, 100–101
Tel Aviv, 361
Temple of Apollo, 174
Temple of Jupiter, 164

Temple of the Sun, 296
Ténéré Natural Reserve, 109
Tenochtitlan, 311
Teotihuacan, 298
Tequila Volcano, 120
Teutonic Knights, 244
Thailand, 41
Thebes, 156–57
Thorsell, James, 29
Three Parallel Rivers of Yunnan
        Protected Areas, 86
Thungyai–Huai Kha Khaeng Wildlife
        Sanctuaries, 41
Tiananmen Square, 274
Tibet, 276–77
Tiemes, Bert, 251
Tikal, 300
Tivoli, 194
Tiwanaku, 302
Tokaj, 126
Toledo, 220–21
Tongariro National Park, 119
Toy Train, 338
Trail of Tears, 116
Trakai Castle, 240
Transylvania, 248
Trogir, 253
Tropical Rain Forest Heritage of Sumatra, 39
Troy, 178
Truman, Harry S., 24, 349
Tsingy de Bemahara, 95
Tsodilo, 146
Tubbataha Reef Marine Park, 75
Tugendhat Villa in Brno, 363
Tungurahua volcano, 98
Tunisia, 189
Turkey, 114, 178–79, 347
Twain, Mark, 338
Tyndall, John, 88
Tyre, 163
Tyrrell, Joseph, 96

## U

Uffizi Gallery, 231
Uganda, 35, 108
uKhahlamba–Drakensberg Park, 111
Ukraine, 62
Uluru-Kata Tjuta National Park, 85
UNESCO World Heritage Trust, 10
United Kingdom, 46–47, 89, 94, 132–33,
        150–51, 190–93, 198–200, 330–33
United Nations Educational, Scientific,
        and Cultural Organization
        (UNESCO), 10–11, 14

United States of America, 11, 24–25, 63, 78–79, 83, 90–93, 97, 116–17, 293–96, 321–25, 356
Utzon, Jørn, 366
Uxmal, 299
Uzbekistan, 270

# V

Val d'Orcia, 130
Valcamonica, 143
Valetta, 237
Valley of Kings, 157
Valparaiso, 319
van der Rohe, Ludwig Mies, 360, 363
Vancouver, George, 63
Varberg Radio Station, 339
Vega, Gaspar, 56
Venezuela, 99
Venice, 234–35
Venice Charter of 1964, 10
Versailles, 207
Vesuvius, 184
Vézère Valley, 144
Via Francinega, 130
Victoria Falls, 69
Vieira, Alfonso Lopes, 229
Vienna, 213
Vietnam, 112
Vigan, 309
Vijayanagar, 269
Vilnius, 240
Vinales Valley, 122
Virunga National Park, 32–33
Visby, 238
Vittala Temple, 269
Vlad the Impaler, 249
Volcanoes of Kamchatka, 82
Völklingen Ironworks, 337
Volubilis, 186

# W

W National Park of Niger, 31
Wade, Abdoulaye, 342
Wakankar, Vishnu Shridhar, 147
Walda, Hafed, 188
Warsaw, 351
Wartburg Castle, 219
Waterton Glacier, 97
Weatherill, Richard, 294
Welsh Castles of King Edward, 200
Wenzhong, Pei, 141
West Norwegian Fjords, 87

Western Caucasus, 115
Western Wall, 167
Wet Tropics of Queensland, 51
Whale Sanctuary of El Vizcaino, 58
White, Stewart Edward, 48
Wieliczka Salt Mine, 11
Willemstad, 320
Winter Palace, 348
Wooden Churches of Maramures, 248
World Conservation Union (IUCN), 10–11, 14
World Heritage Convention, 10–13
World Heritage in Danger, 19, 23, 32–34, 54, 109, 123, 265, 287
World War II, 10, 349–53
World Wide Fund for Nature (WWF), 10
Wouda, Dirk Frederik, 329
Wrangel Island Reserve, 36

# Y

Yangtze River, 86
Yasavi, Khoja Ahmed, 271
Yellowstone National Park, 11, 90–91
Yemen, 260–61
Yoho National Park, 80
Yosemite National Park, 92–93
Yucatan Peninsula, 26, 299
Yugoslavia, 250, 340
Yunnan Province, 86

# Z

Zambezi River, 69
Zambia, 69
Zanzibar, 306
Zealots, 168
Zedillo, Ernesto, 58
Zhi, Lu, 45
Zhoukoudian, 141
Zimbabwe, 69
Zollverein, 336
Zytglogge, 209

3 1489 00573 8537

DISCARDED BY
FREEPORT
MEMORIAL LIBRARY

FREEPORT MEMORIAL LIBRARY